BASEBALL MEMORIES & DREAMS

Other Titles from National Baseball Hall of Fame Books

Picturing America's Pastime:
Historic Photography from the Baseball Hall of Fame Archives
2021

Memories from the Microphone:
A Century of Baseball Broadcasting
2021

So You Think You Know Baseball:
The Baseball Hall of Fame Trivia Book
2021

BASEBALL MEMORIES & DREAMS

Reflections on the National Pastime
from the Baseball Hall of Fame

Foreword by Ozzie Smith

For permission requests, please contact the publisher at:
Mango Publishing Group
2850 S Douglas Road, 4th Floor
Coral Gables, FL 33134 USA
info@mango.bz

For special orders, quantity sales, course adoptions and corporate sales, please
email the publisher at sales@mango.bz. For trade and wholesale sales, please
contact Ingram Publisher Services at customer.service@ingramcontent.com or
+1.800.509.4887.

Baseball Memories & Dreams: Reflections on the National Pastime from the
Baseball Hall of Fame

Library of Congress Cataloging-in-Publication number: 2022931066
ISBN: (print) 978-1-64250-877-2, (ebook) 978-1-64250-878-9
BISAC category code SPO012000, SPORTS & RECREATION / Essays

Printed in the United States of America

This collection of essays is dedicated to those who support the Hall of Fame's mission to preserve baseball history, honor excellence in the game, and connect generations of fans.

Table of Contents

Foreword

By Ozzie Smith, National Baseball Hall of Fame Class of 2002

Ozzie Smith addresses the crowd gathered in Cooperstown for his Induction Ceremony on July 28, 2002. (Baseball Hall of Fame/ Milo Stewart)

Nineteen hundred and eighty-two was a special year for me and for the Cardinals organization.

Coming to St. Louis from San Diego, I knew I was going to get the opportunity to experience what winning was all about. And from the All-Star Game until the end of the season, I knew it was going to be one of those historic years.

Then, we get to Game 1 of the World Series and face a great Milwaukee Brewers club known as Harvey's Wallbangers—and we lose by an outrageous score of 10-0.

So it's after the game, and I'm on my way home with Willie McGee, who was living with me at the time. And I said to Willie, "This is probably our toughest challenge. This club is going to be very tough for us to beat."

Eight days later, when Bruce Sutter struck out Gorman Thomas to end Game 7, we had done it: World Champions. And yet, only with the passage of time did we realize what we were able to accomplish.

The National Baseball Hall of Fame and Museum sums up its mission in just six words: Preserving History, Honoring Excellence, and Connecting Generations. Those are the stories that appear in every issue of the Hall of Fame's official magazine, *Memories and Dreams*.

For every player whose hard work and sacrifice brought them to the big leagues, those stories will resonate. And for every fan who has loved baseball, those stories are treasures.

When you are in the middle of history, I don't know if you ever really know it. You know if you make a good play or if you get a key hit, but the next hit—the next play—can change things completely. You know that it's not over until the last out is recorded. So you have to be able to put everything aside except for the next pitch.

Even after we clinched the title in 1982, it took a few years before I understood what we had been able to accomplish. It just takes a while to absorb it all. And even now, looking back at it forty years later, it's sometimes tough to believe it happened.

You get to a period of time when you're able to reminisce. But when you're in it, when you're performing those actions, the appreciation isn't there. For us players, it's our job. You're going about your job every day, and you can't worry about a specific moment, even ones that down the road can seem so significant.

Even today, when I hear Jack Buck make that call in Game 7 and say: "That's a World Series winner!"—that's when I really know that we won it. Thankfully, with the passage of time, I'm able to see how special it was.

The thing I always worked for as a professional was consistency in what I did. Consistency separates average players from good players and good players from great players. That's what we had with the Cardinals team in 1982. Even when we lost that first game by such a lopsided score, we knew we could win it if we just got back to playing our game. And we did. We settled in and played.

Now, we have the privilege of being able to get together and remember what we did. It's almost like a collective memory, where when you're together certain things are brought up that maybe you forgot about. And you can do the same thing for others. That's the beauty of doing something like this as a team. It's what makes it so special.

Preserving History. As players, we had to live in the moment. But with our stories, we can sure work to preserve that history today.

Then—if you're lucky—you get to a moment like the one I had in Cooperstown twenty years after the World Series win. The connections that are made at the Hall of Fame, which range from meeting your own heroes to the players that come after you, are incredibly special.

I never played the game thinking that one day I would be considered a Hall of Famer. I wanted to be a ballplayer that people looked at and said that he was good every day. Earning election to the Hall of Fame comes as a byproduct of working hard to be consistent every day.

So when it came time to stand on the stage in Cooperstown on July 28, 2002, it was surreal because I looked behind me and saw the game's greats—the people that I looked up to and admired, the people who were considered the greatest at what they did.

To be able to say that I'm in the Hall of Fame with Hank Aaron, Willie Mays, Sandy Koufax, Tommy Lasorda…it's as unbelievable today as it was twenty years ago. To be considered in the same vein with those players is something that still touches my heart to this day.

And when I return to Cooperstown each year, it just gets better. Being a Hall of Famer creates another level of relationships with the players and managers who were in the opposing dugout. For me, it's relationships with Bob Gibson, Reggie Jackson, and Phil Niekro—all the people you competed with and against as professionals.

One of the things I really treasure today is the phone call I got from Phil right before he passed away in 2020. I still keep it on my phone, and I always will. It's those type of memories that make your heart flutter—a connection that you are able to develop with one of the game's legends.

And it's not just your old friends you see in Cooperstown. With the new electees every year, it's a chance to connect with players you saw playing after your career was over. Now, they come up to me and tell me how they used to watch me on television and how I inspired them.

It might make you feel a little old, but it's an incredible feeling—a blessing, really—to know that you had that kind of impact and that you touched people.

My mom always expressed the importance of giving back. It's one of the greatest talents you can have, being able to have people look up to you and admire you. And when you have had the chance to play professional baseball, that in and of itself makes it easy to try to help somebody else.

Giving back has always been a part of my being. And from those who have achieved much, much is expected—rightfully so. When you can use your name and likeness to help someone or some cause, it probably doesn't cost you anything more than time. And being retired, I have plenty of time.

Honoring Excellence. I think this is one of the great blessings of being a Hall of Famer—not just among your peers, but among those who make a difference in your community and your world.

This year, like virtually every year, we'll welcome new members into the Hall of Fame. The Cooperstown "veterans" will show our new brothers the lay of the land, sharing what they can expect with their new status. In turn, they'll help us look through their eyes as first-timers—bringing back those special feelings that come when you stand on the Induction Stage for the first time.

It makes you remember how you got here.

If you're fortunate enough to have been a success in anything, you've been fortunate enough to have people preaching the same message to you. It's nothing new or complicated: Work hard, and you'll get out what you put in. My mom, as well as my coaches in high school and in pro baseball—all of them told me the same thing.

No success comes without blood, sweat, and tears. If you're willing to spill blood, break a sweat, and get through the hard times, at the end of the journey, you'll be where you want to be.

For every one of us who has stood on that stage at the Clark Sports Center, the journey would have been impossible without the bonds we all forged along the way.

Connecting Generations. It's the relationships that matter most.

What follows are some of our favorite stories from more than a quarter century of *Memories and Dreams*. Every one of them embodies elements of history, excellence, and connection that make us appreciate the game even more.

See you soon in Cooperstown.

Preface

The essays in *Baseball Memories & Dreams* were selected by our staff from articles featured in the Hall of Fame's official magazine *Memories and Dreams*. The magazine began publication over two decades ago, offering readers new perspectives from some of baseball's best writers on the history of the game, its place in American culture, and the excellence embodied in the careers of our Hall of Famers.

The selection of the essays, more than 60 in total, was guided by a desire to present the full landscape of baseball's rich history. The organization of the book mirrors, in a way, a visitor's experience at the Hall of Fame itself. Readers will find essays that examine the intersection of baseball and America; tell the stories of baseball history found in the Hall's artifact collections; and offer insights by and about Hall of Famers. There are essays on African Americans, Latinos, and women in baseball, and even a chapter on the experiences of baseball players who served their country during wartime.

The book is meant to satisfy the well-informed fan as well as the more casual reader. Little known stories—such as the House of David barnstorming teams which toured the country from the 1920s through the 1950s and the Cuban-based Havana Sugar Kings, who ruled minor league baseball in 1959—will surprise many readers. And a closer look into more well-known topics—such as the lore surrounding "Who's On First" or "Casey at the Bat," and the hardships Hank Aaron faced when breaking Babe Ruth's home run record—will also be enlightening.

The roster of authors includes a wide range of those who have contributed to the magazine over the years. Mainstays of baseball writing such as Hal Bodley, Peter Gammons, and Tim Kurkjian are included alongside writers from outside the game like John Grisham, Paul Dickson, and Chief Justice Frank J. Williams and Hall of Famers themselves, like Johnny Bench, Nolan Ryan, and Joe Torre.

All essays are presented as they were originally published in *Memories and Dreams*, with an occasional change made only for consistency of punctuation and style. A brief summary of the author follows each piece, along with a note about the date of original publication, which will help readers understand the context in which the essay was written.

We've provided a detailed table of contents as well as an index to help link readers to the essays written by their favorite writers, or to topics they are most interested in. However, a casual browse may be the best way to enjoy the book, as you will find unique and engaging content throughout.

Chapter 1

Baseball and American Culture

Struck Out but Never Retired

Ernest Thayer's timeless ode to the Mighty Casey turns 125 this year

By Richard Pioreck

Mudville.

The word conjures visions of failure, disgrace, and joylessness, but also more importantly, the joy of baseball for the spectator and the player, together with the hope that springs from rejuvenation and immortality.

June 3, 2013, marks the 125th anniversary of the publication of Ernest L. Thayer's "Casey at the Bat" in the *San Francisco Examiner*. Over the years, much has been written about the poem's literary merit, about who is the model for Casey, and about which town is Thayer's Mudville. Nearly seven hundred books featuring "Casey at the Bat" have been published, almost half of these children's books. Dozens of recordings and films—including three of DeWolf Hopper's iconic dramatic recitations of "Casey"—have been produced.

What does all this mean? You might say while "Casey" sprung from baseball, today "Casey" is bigger than baseball, part of the cultural fabric known to just about every American—whether baseball fans or not. In trying to place "Casey" as a cultural icon, don't overlook the subtitle, "A Ballad of the Republic." What does that mean? That "Casey" is a folk tale, a romance for those drawn to "Casey" and even to those who have only a nodding acquaintance with the poem. So besides the questions often asked—who is Casey and where is Mudville—the larger question is, "What does 'Casey at the Bat' mean to Americans?"

Novelist Reed Farrel Coleman said, " 'Casey at the Bat' floods me with memories about the poem and about the age at which I first heard it. It evokes images of old-time baseball, of burly mustached men in dirty, loose-fitting uniforms and strange caps—men who chewed tobacco and spat juice and who used chipped and pitted bats the size of tree limbs. "Casey" captures the essential nature of baseball, of how it is a game of dashed hopes and failure. I first heard the poem in elementary school in Brooklyn in the mid '60s, when men like Willie Mays and Mickey Mantle and Hank Aaron and Roberto Clemente played the game. It seemed I lived in an age of Caseys."

After 125 years, the mind's eye easily sees the Mighty Casey's final swing, its torque and the force it generates in nothingness that propels Casey into an American icon. Life follows art with "Casey at the Bat":

> **"And now the pitcher holds the ball, and now he lets it go,**
> **And now the air is shattered by the force of Casey's blow."**

Another meaning people have found in "Casey" includes "pride goeth before a fall." Still other reviewers draw the lesson that cautions heroes to lead a life of humility and not make a show of false humility so to avoid being humbled as Casey is.

Why? America likes her heroes humble and grateful for their success. Heroes should not behave as if success and adulation are their due. On the other hand, many see Casey's message as overcoming adversity by picking yourself up and trying again:

> **"Clung to that hope which springs eternal in the**
> **human breast;"**

The poem's tone is hopeful for the future even in the face
of defeat:

> "Oh, somewhere in this favored land the sun is
> shining bright;
> The band is playing somewhere, and somewhere hearts
> are light"

This sentiment is part of the indomitable American spirit:

> "Then from 5,000 throats and more there rose a lusty yell;
> It rumbled through the valley, it rattled in the dell;
> It knocked upon the mountain and recoiled upon the flat,"

Lose a fortune today, make a new fortune tomorrow. In baseball
terms, anyone can go from last to first or move from the outhouse
to the penthouse.

In this vein, the poem was quite literally an overnight success.
DeWolf Hopper's dramatic recitation at Wallack's Theater on
Broadway on August 14, 1888—Thayer's birthday—came as a
surprise for members of the New York Giants and Chicago
White Sox who were in the box seats; they wildly cheered
Hopper's performance, demanding several encores. No less
than eight future Hall of Famers were in attendance—and
most were shocked at the inclusion of a baseball piece in the
evening's entertainment.

"When I dropped my voice to B flat, below low C, at 'the
audience was awed,' I remember seeing Buck Ewing's gallant
mustachios give a single nervous twitch," Hopper recalled later.
"And as the house, after a moment of silence, grasped the
anticlimactic denouement, it shouted its glee."

Forty-four years later, Christmas week in 1932, Radio City
Music Hall included Hopper on the inaugural bill because by
then Hopper, who had performed his dramatic recitation over

10,000 times by his count, was one of the most famous orators in the nation.

Many people said they came to know and love "Casey at the Bat" by first hearing it, not reading it. Most of these "Casey" fans sought to read the poem after first hearing it.

"My father gave dramatic readings of 'Casey' to us as kids," reminisced a long-time fan. "We were instantly transported to the stands in Mudville and shared deeply in the tension, the fear, the hope, the anticipation, and of course, the ultimate disappointment of the Mudville crowd. 'Casey' captures perfectly why I love baseball more than any other sport. The game unfolds slowly, play by play. Everything builds at a measurable pace until the big play occurs and the crowd leaps collectively from its seats. You have time to chat with your neighbor, second-guess the manager, predict the strategy, and then to explain why you were right and he was wrong when it doesn't work out."

Jackie Gleason's dramatic reading as Reginald Van Gleason II—a la Hopper—captivated many fans of that era. But many younger "Casey" fans, those under age forty-five, first encountered the poem in Disney's animated version, or in one of the nearly three hundred children's books featuring the poem in the last forty years.

No matter how people meet "Casey,' Ernest Thayer's poem still strikes a chord in the American heart. Those who understand baseball know what Thayer means—how failure, disgrace, and joylessness can jockey for position in the heart with the joy of baseball, the hope that springs from rejuvenation and immortality.

Richard Pioreck was a freelance writer from East Meadow, NY, and an English professor at Hofstra University. This essay originally appeared in Memories & Dreams, *Issue 3, 2013.*

Growing Up with the Game

By John Grisham

My first memory of throwing and catching a baseball goes back to the age of five, or maybe six—those years are not that clear. It was not a leisurely game of catch with my father, nor was it a pickup game in the neighborhood. It was beside an old barn at the edge of a cotton field in rural Arkansas, with a man I would never see again. But I would always remember him.

I was throwing with Juan, a migrant Mexican worker on our farm. I had a ball and glove that I'd found under the Christmas tree months earlier. Juan had neither. His hands were like leather, and he could throw a baseball from our house to our barn, which seemed like a mile. We worked on my fastball and my curve, and I have often suspected that Juan was the first of many to realize the severe limits of my talent. But he was patient, and after a long day of picking cotton, I could always coax him into another game of catch. We would throw until dark, then I would walk to the front porch and listen to a game on the radio. Juan would go to sleep.

We were Cardinals fans, and the highlight of every day was the sound of Harry Caray's voice coming to us all the way from St. Louis. My grandfather had followed Dizzy Dean and the Gashouse Gang. My father worshipped Stan Musial. My Cardinals were Bob Gibson and Lou Brock. Baseball links generations like no other sport and few other traditions. Our church and family were the most important institutions. Baseball was a very close third.

After we left the farm, we moved each summer to a different town around the Deep South. My brothers and I could instantly judge the quality of life in every new place by a quick inspection of the local ball fields. We usually arrived too late to register for the youth leagues, and so instead we spent hours each day playing pickup games with the neighborhood kids.

I was ten before I wore my first uniform. I wore it badly and played even worse, but when I dressed for a game, I felt like a Cardinal. The coach wisely kept me on the bench, but because he was a good coach, he taught me my first lesson from baseball. If you want to play more, then practice more.

The second lesson quickly followed the first; we lost every game but two. Winning is easy, but losing with grace takes guts. Our coach made us smile after each loss. Baseball is a game of failure, he said. Get three hits out of ten at bats, and they'll put you in the Hall of Fame.

My career peaked when I was twelve. I had some nice stats. I made the all-star team and realized that the major leagues would indeed be just a few years away. This brought about the third lesson. The game will humble you. Get cocky, believe it when others say you're good, and a slump will arrive overnight and last two weeks.

In the spring and summer, our lives revolved around the ballparks in those small towns. We would play all day on the fields, then run home, clean up, put on our uniforms, and hustle back, lay the chalk, rake around the bases, cut the grass, fill the water coolers, warm up, and get ready for the real games.

Since there was little else to do in town, everyone came to the ballpark. The fathers and the old men brought their lawn chairs and sat behind home plate, where they corrected the umpires and yelled instructions to those of us on the field. Between innings, they relived the days of their youth with tales of home runs hit over trees and sliders that would buckle knees. The mothers and grandmothers would gather near the bleachers, where they would watch the toddlers, and maybe the game, while planning church socials and weddings and talking about the urgent social matters of the town. The older teenagers would hang together behind the dugout. Some would hold hands and sneak away; others would actually hide in bushes and smoke.

There was always a crying baby or two because everybody came to the games.

I remember all sorts of activities taking place during our games. Peas were shelled, quilts knitted, checkers played, votes solicited and promised, fights started and settled, romances carried out in the shadows behind the bleachers. And through it all, you could hear Harry Caray somewhere in the background, with his colorful, scratchy voice, describing every play of our beloved Cardinals.

The languid and sporadic pace of baseball allows folks to visit, to engage, to catch up on important matters. No other sport is less rushed.

My fondest childhood memories are of those long, hot, summer nights at the ballparks with everyone I knew gathered close by, watching us boys play our games. I can still feel the heavy air, the dust from the infield, and the sweat of action, and I still hear the sound of the game—the chatter from the infield, the shouts of the coaches, the calls from the umpires, the idle laughter of the old men behind the backstop, the cheers from the mothers, the encouragements from the fathers, the babies, the Cardinals on the radio.

As children, we were not only allowed to play baseball every day, we were *expected* to. It made us laugh and cry, win and lose; it broke our hearts and it made us feel like champions. And it brought everyone together.

Baseball was life in those wonderful days.

John Grisham is one of America's bestselling authors and a lifelong baseball fan. He has written over thirty books including The Firm, The Pelican Brief, *and* The Rainmaker. *This essay originally appeared in* Baseball As America, *and was later reprinted in* Memories & Dreams, *Issue 4, 2004.*

The Rail Hitter?
Abraham Lincoln and baseball: Two symbols of American identity
By Chief Justice Frank J. Williams

Legend has it that Abraham Lincoln was playing baseball when a contingent from the Republican National Convention arrived at his home in Springfield, Illinois, in 1860, to notify him of his nomination for the Presidency. Lincoln supposedly told a messenger to "Tell the gentlemen that I am glad to know of their coming; but they'll have to wait a few minutes till I make another base hit."

Even more dramatic is the yarn weaving baseball into Lincoln's death narrative. According to this tale, as Lincoln lay dying from his gunshot wound, he summoned General Abner Doubleday to his bedside, expending his last breath of life to whisper the plea, "Abner, don't let baseball die."

If these stories seem too good to be true, it's probably because they are. Unfortunately for baseball enthusiasts, neither story is supported by reliable historical evidence. Lincoln never regained consciousness after being shot, and Doubleday, also the subject of baseball's greatest myth, was not even at Lincoln's bedside when he died. Further, it is questionable whether baseball was even played in Springfield, Illinois, in 1860; it certainly was not around during Lincoln's youth in Indiana and Illinois in the 1820s and 1830s. While there is some limited evidence that Lincoln was a casual spectator and occasional participant of the game, baseball was not so important to him that it would have taken precedence over news of his nomination or would have occupied his dying words, had he been able to speak.

Rather than truth, what these myths reveal is Lincoln's great symbolic power—even over a game with which he had little to do. Baseball was in its infancy during the middle of the nineteenth century, having evolved from earlier, largely British, stick and ball games. It was played primarily in Northeastern cities such as Boston, Philadelphia, and New York, and it was defined by a different set of rules in each place. It is therefore remarkable that by the end of the century, the various styles managed to coalesce into a single game reaching all corners of the country and engraining itself as the National Pastime. In light of this incredible feat, it is no surprise that baseball's story would intertwine with that of Abraham Lincoln, one of this country's greatest inspirations for unity and patriotism.

Currier & Ives lithograph print depicting Abraham Lincoln and his three opponents in the 1860 presidential election as baseball players.

This is not to say, however, that baseball wasn't already part of the American conscience during Lincoln's time. In fact, baseball was enough of a symbol that in November of 1860, Currier & Ives published a political cartoon using the game's imagery and terminology to represent Lincoln's presidential election victory. Entitled "The National Game. Three 'Outs' and One 'Run.' Abraham Winning The Ball[,]" the cartoon provided commentary on the historic 1860 election by depicting the four presidential candidates and their relative positions on the issue of slavery.

Representing the Constitutional Union party, John Bell is shown holding a baseball bat inscribed with the term "fusion"— signifying his party's opposition to disunion. Using the baseball vernacular of the time, Bell laments that the three election losers "should strike 'foul' and be 'put out' while old Abe made such a 'good lick.' "

Stephen A. Douglas, the Northern Democrat, is portrayed holding a bat engraved with the term "non-intervention," signifying his advocacy of popular sovereignty. He responds to Bell that Lincoln won because "he had that confounded rail to strike with. I thought our fusion would be a 'short stop' to his career."

True to the Southern Democrat platform of extending slavery into the western territories, John C. Breckenridge holds a bat labeled "slavery extension." He is depicted holding his nose, remarking as he turns away from the others, "I guess I'd better leave for Kentucky, for I smell something strong around here, and begin to think, that we are completely 'skunk'd.' "

Lincoln stands triumphant on home plate holding up the baseball. He also grips a bat proclaiming his vision of "equal rights and free territory." He counsels his fellow candidates that, "If any of you should ever take a hand in another match at this game, remember that you must have 'a good bat' and strike a 'fair ball' to make a 'clean score' & 'home run.' "

Baseball's connection to the Civil War is not limited to a mere cartoon. The US Sanitary Commission encouraged the game to be played in army camps as a means of exercise and diversion from the many stresses of war. Seeing an opportunity to cultivate a sense of camaraderie and loyalty in their commands, officers also supported baseball games between soldiers. It was not uncommon for teams from different regiments and brigades to compete against each other on the fields near encampments.

There also are accounts of baseball being played by prisoners of war in both Union and Confederate prison camps. Prison guards watched and even participated in some of the games—a further testament to baseball's unifying power. Also, because baseball was less common in the South when the War began, the War likely contributed to the spread of the game through its exposure in Southern camps.

On the home front, however, the Civil War initially had a disruptive effect on baseball as players headed off to war and baseball clubs disbanded. Nevertheless, men who did not enter military service and boys not old enough to serve continued to play the game. At times, baseball also served as a source of funding for the war effort. For example, in 1862, the Continental Base Ball Club of Brooklyn held a series of charity baseball games between the borough's two best ball clubs. The ten-cent admission charge paid by the 20,000 fans in attendance over the course of three days went to the Sanitary Commission of Brooklyn to help sick and wounded soldiers.

Even if Abraham Lincoln and baseball had a limited history together, they share a similar legacy as national icons. Each demonstrated an extraordinary unifying capacity during this country's greatest period of strife, and both continue to serve as landmarks of American identity.

Frank J. Williams is the former Chief Justice of the Rhode Island Supreme Court and the founding chairman of the Lincoln Forum. This essay originally appeared in Memories & Dreams, Issue 6, 2008.

Diamonds & Railroads
**The advent of regional rail service made baseball
as we know it possible**
By Steve Buckley

In 1969, during a year-long celebration of the hundredth anniversary of professional baseball, the Massachusetts-based Fleetwood Recording Co. produced an album that sought to tell the history of the game in two action-packed, anecdote-laden sides of vinyl.

Produced in concert with Major League Baseball and narrated by actor James Stewart and broadcaster Curt Gowdy, the album had everything ball fans would have expected, from Russ Hodges' heart-pounding call of Bobby Thomson's Shot Heard Round the World to Vin Scully's rhythmic, exquisitely paced description of Sandy Koufax striking out Harvey Kuenn to complete the Dodgers legend's perfect game.

It also had some surprises, including a scratchy recording of an aging ballplayer from the nineteenth century reminiscing about the days when teams depended on America's railways to get from city to city.

"I was playing in Des Moines, Iowa, and you'd get on a train and you'd carry your bats and your own bag and your own uniform rolled up," the player said. "You'd get on a train with the old wicker seats, and they were burning coal, and you'd get in the car in July and August and go from Des Moines to Wichita, Kansas, all night, part of the next day, and if you'd open up the window, you'd be eatin' soot and cinders all night, and if you closed the window, you'd roast to death."

Baseball. Trains.

Without one, we never would have had the other.

"They kind of came along at the same time, and it was huge," said author and historian Peter Morris, who has written extensively on nineteenth century baseball. "Any time something is new and popular, anything that's a trend is going to hitch itself to that metaphorically, and in this case, literally."

And baseball in the mid-nineteenth century was clearly trending upward.

"But the whole idea of trying to get nine people from one place to another was not at all easy at a time when the roads were still pretty primitive and most of the transportation was by water," Morris said. "Just getting over the Allegheny Mountains in the nineteenth century was an arduous task."

In 1848, when the California Gold Rush began, many fortune seekers from the east would travel by boat around Cape Horn in South America and then head north to San Francisco. The first Transcontinental Railroad, which opened in 1869, changed that. As Stephen Ambrose wrote in *Nothing Like It in the World*, his wonderful biography of the Transcontinental Railroad, "… less than a week after the pounding of the Golden Spike, a man or woman could go from New York to San Francisco in seven days…so fast, they used to say, 'that you don't even have time to take a bath.' "

That very year—1869—was when Harry Wright founded one of the first openly professional baseball teams, the Cincinnati Red Stockings. And just like that, teams from one city were traveling to play teams in another city, teams that had different uniforms, different nicknames, and, especially before the evolution of baseball, different rules.

"You really don't have standard rules until you get teams from one city playing teams in the next city," Morris said. "You had players in Cleveland playing by one set of rules, and you had players in Cincinnati playing by a different set. But the rules start to become standard in the late 1860s as the railroad is connecting the country and you see the professional game of baseball coming. It's really not a coincidence."

When the National League was formed in 1876, train travel made it possible for teams to be located in Boston, Chicago,

Cincinnati, Hartford, Louisville, New York, Philadelphia, and St. Louis. The league champion Chicago White Stockings took four road trips during their sixty-six-game season, the longest of those covering twelve games, twenty-six days, and four cities.

Chicago White Sox players gather for a photograph on the Royal Gorge Hanging Bridge in Fremont County, Colorado, on their way to Spring Training in San Francisco prior to the start of the 1910 season.

Baseball would never have blossomed as America's National Pastime had not the railroads become advanced to the degree that passengers could travel from one city to another in hotel-level comfort. Those wicker chairs and coal furnaces would over time be replaced by plush seating and steam engines; by the twentieth century, players were bedding down in sleeper cars and taking their meals in dining cars.

It was not always luxurious—certainly not by today's standards. As the late Boston Red Sox outfielder Dom DiMaggio wrote in *Real Grass, Real Heroes*:

"The rookies traveled in the third car, the last one—the one that whipped from side to side every time the train went around a bend."

But, wrote DiMaggio, "Ballplayers from the 1940s will tell you to a man that when baseball teams started flying, a certain bonding that held teams together went out of Major League Baseball. We got to know each other as you only can when you're on a train together for twenty-four hours, or thirty-six or more."

Jack McCormack, the current traveling secretary of the Red Sox, said the late Johnny Pesky, a teammate of DiMaggio's with the Red Sox, echoed those same feelings.

"He told me the players got very close," McCormack said; "A lot of card games, [a] lot of time to talk to each other."

But just as the train was vital for the evolution of baseball to a national phenomenon, air travel made possible the 1957 moves of the Brooklyn Dodgers and New York Giants to Los Angeles and San Francisco, respectively, thus opening up the West Coast for Major League Baseball.

But this isn't to say that the train, in all its glory, has been dismissed by big league ball clubs as a mode of transportation. To this very day, some East Coast teams still rely on trains from time to time, and for the same reasons the Cincinnati Red

Stockings were using them in 1869—because they're the easiest way to get from Point A to Point B.

McCormack will occasionally use the railways when his math tells him they're a better way to go than the airports.

"Let's see, I've done Boston to New York, Baltimore to Philly, and Baltimore to New York," he said. "We were going to go from Boston to New York on the day of the Boston Marathon this year, but we changed because of all the people trying to get out of the city after the race.

"We took a train last year from Baltimore to Philly, and it took fifty-eight minutes," he said. "And it was about two minutes to the hotel once we got there. We were in the hotel in an hour and five minutes. Says a lot when you're usually going out to the airport and dealing with all that."

McCormack, as part of his job, has become a student of how teams traveled in the days before airports came into everyday use.

"That's why Monday off-days came to be, because teams on the east were traveling to the west—Chicago and St. Louis," McCormack said. "So you'd have those Sunday doubleheaders before making those twelve-to-fifteen-hour trips.

"I think it would be fun," he added. "It does get a little nostalgic, to me and to some of the players as well. I was thinking about that a while back when we were at the train station and there was a guy shouting, 'Allllllll aboarddddd!' and then, bango, you're off in five seconds.

"It reminded me that we were doing something from days gone by. It was a good feeling."

Steve Buckley is a senior writer for The Athletic; *previously, he was a sports columnist with the* Boston Herald *for nearly twenty-four years. This essay originally appeared in* Memories & Dreams, *Issue 3, 2019.*

Diamonds to Dollars
A.G. Spalding revolutionized the game on and off the field
By Bill Francis

Spalding is a household name with a longstanding reputation as one of the top sporting goods manufacturers in the world. But few may realize the company's history dates back almost 150 years, or that its namesake was one of baseball's all-time great players and a Hall of Famer.

Albert Goodwill Spalding's one passion was baseball, and he was successful at numerous aspects of the game. Starting first as a famous pitcher, he also made a name for himself as a manager, front office executive, and business magnate—during his lifetime, his name was as well-known as anyone's in the country.

Although baseball first gained a foothold in the consciousness of Americans as an amateur game, the sport would soon develop not only top-notch players but also a fervent fan base. By the end of the nineteenth century, baseball was solidly entrenched as the National Pastime.

Born in 1850, Spalding made a prudent decision to give up a five-dollar-a-week job in a grocery store to try his hand at playing baseball. The right-handed hurler proved adept from the start during the budding sport's earliest foray into professionalism.

In seven years as a big league pitcher, first with the National Association's Boston Red Stockings from 1871 to 1875, and then as a player/manager with the National League's Chicago White Stockings in 1876 and 1877, the native of Byron, Illinois, finished with a 252-65 career record—and with his .795 winning percentage the best in big league history.

Spalding, who played his last game on August 31, 1878, two days shy of his twenty-eighth birthday, had other plans, though. His withdrawal from the ballfield was the result of increasing needs of a new business, a sporting goods shop that was rapidly growing in size.

A partnership agreement between Spalding and his brother, J. Walter Spalding, a former bank bookkeeper in Rockford, Illinois, was formed on February 3, 1876. The brothers' investment was four hundred dollars each, with their mother, Harriet, advancing them the entire starting capital.

The first A.G. Spalding & Brothers store, which measured about twenty feet by sixty feet, opened in Chicago at 118 Randolph Street in February, 1876. The instantly flourishing Windy City business made a reported $11,000 that first year. Taped to the lone desk was the company motto: "Everything is possible to him who dares."

A small A.G. Spalding & Bros. advertisement in the April 30, 1876, *Chicago Tribune* is headlined with "Western Base Ball Emporium" while also referring to the company as "Wholesale and Retail Dealers in Base Ball and Cricket Goods, Croquet, Archery, Fishing Tackle, Fine Cutlery, etc. etc."

That first year also saw A.G. Spalding & Bros. secure the rights to produce the official baseball of the National League, an early publicity coup as well as a distinction they would hold until 1976. The company also furnished, under the A.J. Reach Company name, the baseballs used by the American League beginning with the Junior Circuit's inception in 1901.

Before long, A.G. Spalding & Bros. were advertising themselves as the largest manufacturers of athletic supplies in the world. But baseball was a specialty, and they produced, among other items, balls, uniforms, caps, stockings, shoes, gloves and mitts, and catcher's equipment.

Having played in an era where gloves didn't exist, Spalding appreciated the availability of this new piece of baseball equipment.

"I had for a good while felt the need of some sort of hand protection for myself," said Spalding. "For several years, I had pitched in every game…and had developed severe bruises on the inside of my left hand. For every ball pitched, it had to be returned, [and] every swift one coming my way from infielders, outfielders, or hot from the bat must be caught or stopped, [so] some idea may be gained of the punishment received."

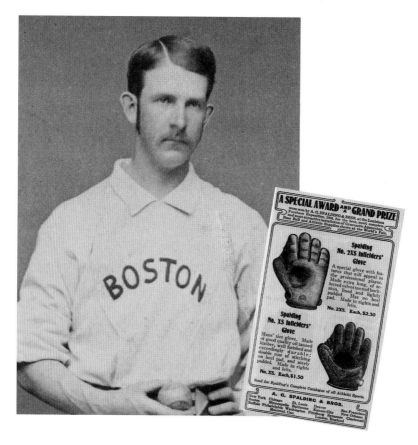

Albert Spalding, one of baseball's star players during his career with the Boston Red Stockings and Chicago White Stockings, would later go on to open a chain of sporting goods stores.

The Spalding trademark in those first years featured a baseball with the name Spalding printed between the seams, and each came with a promise: "Spalding's trademark on what you purchase is a guarantee that the goods are the best."

Soon A.G. Spalding & Bros. dominated the sporting goods industry. And it wasn't long before one of the most distinguished figures in the game's history—and one of the professional game's early pioneers—became its most prosperous former player. Though Spalding was elected president of the Chicago White Stockings in 1882, he left his position in 1891 to concentrate on his rapidly growing business. By 1887, with his company producing more than one million bats a year, reports pegged Spalding's worth at over $250,000. By the 1890s, he was heading a multimillion-dollar business whose namesake was a millionaire.

Hall of Famer Henry Chadwick wrote in 1896: "Mr. Spalding's whole career, from the beginning of his baseball success in 1867 to that of his leadership of a great business house in 1896, stands forth as a shining example of what high integrity of character, good business capacity, and true American pluck, energy, and enterprise can accomplish in our great Republic."

By 1885, A.G. Spalding & Bros. had expanded their national reach by opening a store in New York City, located at 241 Broadway. Spalding athletic and sporting goods were also available in Albany, Buffalo, Cincinnati, Cleveland, Denver, Dubuque, Grand Rapids, Indianapolis, Kansas City, Louisville, Minneapolis, Omaha, Philadelphia, Pittsburgh, Portland, Providence, Rochester, St. Louis, Syracuse, and Washington, DC.

In Spalding's seminal book on the game's early years, 1911's *Base Ball: America's National Game*, he reprints an interview in which he is asked if his baseball background had helped him in his business ventures.

"I never struck anything in business that did not seem a simple matter when compared to complications I have faced on the Base Ball field," replied Spalding. "A young man playing Base Ball gets into the habit of quick thinking in [the] most adverse circumstances and under the most merciless criticism in the world—the criticism from the bleachers. If that doesn't train him, nothing can. Base Ball in youth has the effect, in later years, of making him think and act a little quicker than the other fellow."

When Spalding passed away at the age of sixty-five on September 9, 1915, the nation took notice.

"That there should ever be another man who would stand in exactly the same relation to the people of the United States as the late A.G. Spalding is impossible," the *St. Louis Post-Dispatch* editorialized soon after Spalding passed. "As a famous pitcher, a manager, a magnate, a maker and vendor of the requisites of the game, and a publisher of the standard authority on baseball, he made his name as well-known as that of Presidents and better known than that of the most popular of other leaders."

The *Sporting News*, calling itself "The Baseball Paper of the World" at the time, put Spalding's life, both on and off the field, in perspective.

"Indeed, of such variety was Spalding's work in and for the game that it is difficult to determine in which particular part he was the greatest," read the editorial. "As a pitcher, his record will stand for all time. As a manager, few equal his achievements; as a club owner, he ranked among the real big and broadminded men in that circle. As a manufacturer of baseball paraphernalia, he had a grasp on the needs of the sport that was wonderful, and his purveying had much to do with the spread of the sport, for he made it possible for every youth in the land whose inclination turned toward it to fit himself with a 'big league' bat or ball or glove at nominal cost."

Spalding was elected to the National Baseball Hall of Fame in 1939, the year the Cooperstown institution held its first Induction Ceremony.

Bill Francis is the Senior Research and Writing Specialist at the National Baseball Hall of Fame and Museum. This essay originally appeared in Memories & Dreams, *Issue 6, 2017.*

Mail, Money, and the National Pastime
Baseball has long been a symbol of America on stamps and coins
By David Moriah

They are iconic pieces of the United States, parts of Americana as old as the country itself. Stamps and coins therefore have a natural and enduring connection to the National Pastime.

In 2014, the United States Mint—via the National Baseball Hall of Fame Commemorative Coin Act—will issue five-dollar, one-dollar, and half-dollar coins in celebration of the Museum's seventy-fifth anniversary. The coins will be among dozens of coins and stamps issued by the government to celebrate baseball.

It may be hard for young fans to imagine, but in the distant past—before the invention of the Internet, Facebook, Twitter, and Instagram—there was a primitive way people communicated called a "letter."

The letter was written on paper with implements such as pens and pencils using ink and lead. In order to pay the cost of transporting these letters, the sender purchased something called a "stamp"—which collectors and historians have long valued as one of the iconic symbols of our nation.

These stamps, typically about one-inch square, were—and are—emblazoned with colorful photos and artwork. Early stamps featured American heroes like George Washington and Benjamin Franklin, as well as American symbols such as the flag, the Grand Canyon, and the Golden Gate Bridge.

In 1939, a hundred years after the mythical birth of baseball in Cooperstown, NY, and more than 150 years after the American Revolution, the first stamp commemorating the grand American game of baseball was issued. Another thirty years passed before the second baseball-themed stamp was released in 1969, marking another centennial anniversary—this time baseball's debut as a professional sport when the 1869 Cincinnati Red Stockings took the field for the first time with salaried ballplayers.

Since then, the pace of baseball-themed stamps has accelerated. Stamps have been issued honoring individual players, classic ballparks, tributes to the Negro Leagues, and Olympic baseball.

Baseball-themed stamp collectors debate whether a 1969 stamp honoring American folk artist Grandma Moses should be included since artwork depicted on her stamp included a ball game in the background, or whether multi-sport athlete Jim Thorpe's 1984 stamp should qualify even though he's portrayed in a football uniform. The talented Thorpe also spent six years in Major League Baseball and appeared in the 1917 World Series.

In all, more than fifty stamps undeniably qualify as portraying baseball from many different angles.

"The Post Office began to realize that while many of their new releases drew little or no attention, there was always a strong interest in baseball stamps," explained Pete Henrici, owner of the Baseball Nostalgia shop, located in the shadow of Doubleday Field in Cooperstown. Henrici offers a large collection of "first day covers," a term referring to an envelope with a postmark issued on the first day of a stamp's release. For baseball stamps, the gold standard is to have a cover bearing the postmark of the Cooperstown, NY, post office.

It all began in 1939.

The release of the first stamp commemorating baseball on June 12, 1939, was meant to coincide with the opening of the National Baseball Hall of Fame and Museum, appropriately situated in the tiny, upstate New York village where General Abner Doubleday was thought to have invented the National Pastime. The 1939 stamp was the brainchild of Postmaster

General James A. Farley, a rabid baseball fan, and President Franklin D. Roosevelt, a fan and stamp collector himself.

In announcing the upcoming stamp's release, the President stated, "Every boy in America could get a first-day cover." As a result of this bold proclamation, the Cooperstown post office was flooded with requests from boys, and presumably some girls, many of whom sent requests without the required self-addressed envelope and three cents for the stamp, the going rate for first-class postage in 1939.

According to Post Office regulations, such requests should have been denied, but Cooperstown postmaster Melvin Bundy stepped in to save the day. Reaching deep into his own pockets, Bundy reportedly covered the cost of both stamps and return envelopes to satisfy the longings of thousands of American youth and fulfill President Roosevelt's promise.

President Roosevelt was an avid stamp collector who enjoyed autographing both covers and sheets of stamps that he gave as gifts to friends and admirers. At the 1939 opening of the Baseball Hall of Fame and Museum, Postmaster General Farley was in attendance and secured signatures of many of the players on hand on a sheet of the 1939 centennial stamps, which he later presented to the President.

Over eighty-one million stamps were produced, and the 1939 baseball centennial stamp remains a popular item for both philatelists (those who specialize in collecting stamps) and baseball memorabilia collectors.

An interesting footnote is the question of whether the centennial stamp should rightly be considered the first baseball stamp issued by the US government or whether that designation should be given to a 1934 Philippine stamp featuring a batter and catcher marking the Manila Far Eastern Championship Games. From 1898 until its independence in 1946, the Philippine islands were under the control of the United States, so a technical case could be made that the first baseball-themed stamp issued under government auspices was, in fact, the 1934 Philippines issue.

If there is an abundance of baseball stamps for philatelists and baseball memorabilia collectors to pursue, the catalog of baseball-related coins is much thinner. The US Mint releases a handful of commemorative coins each year, and although issued in specific denominations, these coins are not meant for public circulation but rather go straight to the collectors' marketplace.

The first baseball-themed commemorative was produced in 1992, baseball's first year as an Olympic event, in conjunction with that summer's Olympics in Barcelona, Spain. The coin, featuring a pitcher closely resembling Nolan Ryan, was part of a three-coin set.

Three years later, baseball reappeared as the subject of another commemorative, once again connected to the Olympics. This time it was in anticipation of the Olympic Games to be held in Atlanta, Georgia, in 1996. Similar to the 1992 issue, the baseball coin was flanked by coins featuring other Olympic sports.

All this was but a prelude to the big event in the baseball coin world. In 1997, on the fiftieth anniversary of Jackie Robinson's historic breakthrough into Major League Baseball, the US Mint marked the occasion by producing one-dollar silver and five-dollar gold coins, each portraying the fiery Robinson sliding in his classic steal of home in the 1955 World Series.

Only 5,174 of the most desirable "uncirculated" Robinson five-dollar gold coins were released, which makes it "the lowest mintage US commemorative produced since 1982," according to Jamie Hernandez, price guide editor of Professional Coin Grading Service. He added, "Because of its low mintage, it's also the most valuable of any modern gold commemorative coin."

David Moriah is a freelance writer and regular contributor to The Sports Collectors Digest. *This essay originally appeared in* Memories & Dreams, *Issue 5, 2013.*

Baseball's Greatest Skit
Abbott and Costello's classic routine has become film royalty
By Tim Wiles

"This is better than getting an Oscar," quipped Lou Costello in 1956, when he and his comedy partner Bud Abbott donated a gold record for "Who's On First?" to the Hall of Fame.

The presentation was made by Abbott and Costello to Hall of Fame Director Sid Keener and Vice President Paul Kerr, live on the Steve Allen Show, October 7, 1956. Abbott and Costello performed the classic routine on Allen's show that night, in what at least one source reports was their swan song–the final performance of the classic skit they claimed to have done 15,000 times. Other guests on the special "Salute to Baseball" included Mrs. Babe Ruth, Mickey Mantle, and Sal Maglie.

The following day, the Dodgers' Maglie would pitch well against the Yankees in the World Series, allowing two runs on five hits–one of them a Mantle homer–but history was on Don Larsen's side that day during his meeting with destiny.

The perfect game followed the perfect skit.

Abbott and Costello became a comedy team in 1936 and quickly had success with the "Who's On First?" routine, which they debuted on the Kate Smith radio show in 1938. At first, the show's producer was reluctant to let them do the baseball routine, but he gave in; and the routine went over so well that the duo ended up with their own radio show shortly thereafter–leading to a reported contract stipulation that the duo must perform the skit on the air at least once a month. Soon the comedians were cast in Hollywood films and debuted a shortened version of "Who's On First?" on the big screen in 1940's *One Night in the Tropics*. Another shortened version appears in 1942's *Who Done It?*

Soon after, they did what many consider the definitive filmed version of the skit in *The Naughty Nineties*. This is the familiar version where Sebastian Dinwiddie (Costello) strolls onstage selling popcorn and peanuts, interrupting the baseball talk being given by Abbott's Dexter Broadhurst in his "St. Louis Wolves" jersey. Aficionados will notice the painted banner behind the duo, which advertises the Paterson Silk Sox, a famed industrial league team from Costello's New Jersey hometown. Costello would always find a way to work a Paterson reference into his work. Abbott, on the other hand, hailed from Asbury Park, NJ, though he was really a child of the circus and carnival vaudeville circuit.

Both men were baseball fans, and Costello in particular developed a friendship with Joe DiMaggio, who some sources contend inspired and encouraged the young comedians to develop a baseball skit. DiMaggio even appeared in the skit with Abbott and Costello on the *Colgate Comedy Hour*.

The exact origins of the "Who's On First?" skit are hard to pin down, as similar wit, wisecracking, wordplay, and precision timing were hallmarks of the vaudeville stage. The routine is thought to have been partially inspired by an old routine having to do with directions to Watt Street. "What Street? Watt Street."

A similar British skit has to do with a student named "Howe" who came from "Ware," and who now lives in "Wye." These and other vaudeville routines are thought to have inspired the creation of "Who's On First," though others have staked their claims on having written the piece, notably songwriter Irving Gordon, who is best known for "Unforgettable."

Society for American Baseball Research (SABR) researcher Ray Zardetto gave a presentation on the skit at the organization's annual convention in Atlanta earlier this year, for which he interviewed Lou's daughter Chris Costello.

"So many people have tried to take credit for writing 'Who's On First,' but the fact of the matter is this: My dad wrote it with Bud (Abbott) and John Grant," Chris Costello said.

Grant was a longtime screenwriter for Abbott and Costello. "Dad and Bud and Grant put the routine together based on a series of old vaudeville sketches they knew and their own abilities to play around with words."

The immortal skit has been performed at the White House and was named the best comedy routine of the twentieth century by *Time Magazine* in 1999. In 2003, the Library of Congress chose the first radio version of the sketch from 1938 for inclusion in the National Recording Registry, an effort to digitize and preserve the recordings most central to American culture. DeWolf Hopper's 1915 recording of "Casey at the Bat" was the only other baseball or sports related piece included in the initial selection of fifty recordings. In 2005, the line "Who's on First?" was included on the American Film Institute's list of the one hundred most memorable movie quotes.

In addition to the aforementioned gold record, the Hall of Fame also holds a copy of the Abbott and Costello "Who's On First?" board game from the 1970s, a library clippings file on the routine and its famous performers, and numerous recordings of the skit. "Who's On First?" has been a fan favorite in the Museum for decades.

Perhaps as a result of the honored place the routine has had in the Hall for many years, a popular misconception exists about Abbott and Costello. Visitors and callers often pose the trivia question, "Who are the only two people in the Hall of Fame who had nothing to do with baseball?" The question is frequently repeated by radio disc jockeys as trivia, but the question is flawed in two ways.

Abbott and Costello are not "in the Hall of Fame," as inductees, but rather their work is featured in the Museum and Library. And it is far from the truth that they "had nothing to do with baseball," as this comedy routine is among the most popular and beloved found in American popular culture.

"Who's On First?" has made many appearances in pop culture, from *The Simpsons* to *Seinfeld* to the movie *Rain Man*, where Dustin Hoffman's autistic character Raymond Babbitt recites the routine to himself when he feels that he is under great stress. A classic movie clip appears in *Pete 'n' Tillie*, a 1972 film starring Walter Matthau and Carol Burnett. In the film, Burnett catches Matthau teaching the routine to his son and asks him why he would spend time on such silliness.

"Abbott and Costello are not silly," he responds; "This is art!"

Sometimes life imitates art, as it did in 2007 when the Dodgers promoted Chin-Lung Hu to the big club. His first big league hit was a home run, and it took until his sixth game for him to stop at first base after a single.

By then, fans were familiar with legendary Dodgers broadcaster Vin Scully rooting on the young player: "Let's hope Hu gets a base hit, folks. I can't wait to say Hu's on first."

Tim Wiles was the director of research for the National Baseball Hall of Fame and Museum. He is now the director of the Guilderland Public Library in Guilderland, NY. This essay originally appeared in Memories & Dreams, *Issue 6, 2010.*

75 Years on the Small Screen
How television transformed baseball into a national obsession
By Curt Smith

However clear Bill Stern's rhetoric was, his subjects were opaque in baseball's first televised game three-quarters of a century ago. Princeton edged Columbia, 2-1, on May 17, 1939, at Baker Field—a contest broadcast to a handful of TV sets in the New York area.

The crowd attending the game had the advantage that day, as the person with the worst seat at Baker Field had a better view than anyone watching at home.

W2XBS used a single camera fifty feet from home plate—"woefully lacking," said the *New York Times*. One camera at one site "does not see the complete field. Baseball by television calls for three or four cameras." At least the viewer didn't suffer long. The ten-inning game took two hours and fifteen minutes.

The problem was the picture, which was delivered through NBC's $150,000 van and relayed to a transmitter atop the Empire State Building, then picked up at local outposts. Action on the nine-by-twelve-inch screen "…was blurred, with reproduced faces dark," said the *Times*. The ball was rarely seen. Players resembled "flies."

On August 26, 1939, NBC telecast its first professional game when the Cincinnati Reds came to Brooklyn to face the Dodgers. The reviews weren't much better. "No monitor, only two cameras at Ebbets Field," said Dodgers announcer Red Barber. "I had to watch to see which one's red light was on, then guess its direction."

It was an inauspicious start for televised baseball games—but the relatively new technology would eventually change the game in ways no one could imagine.

Radio seemed immovable. In 1946, Americans owned fifty-six million radios compared to only 17,000 televisions. Slowly, though, TV became irresistible: By the mid-1950s, 10,000 sets were being sold every day.

Springtime for TV baseball was really the autumn of 1951. The Dodgers and Giants had tied for the National League pennant, and CBS and NBC aired the best-of-three playoff between the teams, making it the first national network sports telecast. Next, NBC broadcast TV's first national World Series as the Yankees beat the Giants in six games. Baseball's postseason had a Southern sound: Florida's Barber; Georgia's Ernie Harwell and Kentucky's Russ Hodges of the Giants; and Alabama's Voice of the Yankees, Mel Allen.

"People ask why so many voices came from the South," said Harwell. "We grew up in a storytelling place."

Allen and Barber were baseball's first two larger-than-life TV voices, and each of them went on to receive the National Baseball Hall of Fame and Museum's first Ford C. Frick Award for broadcast excellence in 1978. A distant cousin of poet Sidney Lanier, Barber made the mound a "pulpit." Allen was even more identified with American TV at mid-century—he called twenty World Series—and was so famed that, hailing a cab in Omaha one night, he said simply, "Sheraton, please." The cabbie nearly drove off the road upon hearing Allen's voice.

Improvements in coverage came quickly. New York's WPIX and WOR put baserunner and close-up cameras near each dugout and at first and third base. In 1951, WGN in Chicago invented today's center field camera. Color TV commenced on August 11 of that year when the Dodgers played against Boston. In 1952, the Fall Classic debuted the novel split screen.

"The whole country followed it—farmers, factory workers, kids smuggling radios into class. Life stopped for the Series," said Brooklyn Bridge TV creator Gary David Goldberg.

What they saw lingers. In Game One of the 1954 Series, the Indians' Vic Wertz tested New York's young center fielder.

"There's a long drive way back in center field—way back, back," cried Jack Brickhouse. "It is—oh, what a catch by Mays!"

The game's greatest moments seemed to be made for the nation's newest craze.

In 1953, ABC launched sport's first network TV series: Dizzy Dean's mega-popular *Game of the Week*. In 1955, joining CBS, *Game* lured 80 percent of the sets in use. Dean sang "The Wabash Cannonball," referred to nearly everyone in the universe as "pod-nuh," and interpreted English as no one has or is likely to. A batter "swang." A hitter stood "confidentially at the plate."

Two years later, CBS added a Sunday to its Saturday *Game*, few knowing what Ol' Diz would say next. By 1960, three networks covered 123 games, the precursor to baseball's current alignment with FOX, ESPN, and TBS. But in 1966, NBC bought exclusivity, making it baseball's only network and Curt Gowdy its only voice.

Gowdy had been the Red Sox's lead announcer from 1951 until 1965. Ninth in 1966, the Sox won the 1967 AL pennant on the season's final day. Two years later, the even more once-awful Mets won the Series. "Waiting is [Cleon] Jones. The Mets are the world champions!" Gowdy said of Baltimore's Dave Johnson's ninth-inning fly. Ultimately, Gowdy called thirteen World Series, sixteen All-Star Games, and multiple Emmy Award-winning episodes of *The American Sportsman*.

In the 1971 World Series, the Pirates' Roberto Clemente showed what Commissioner Bowie Kuhn called a "touch of royalty," winning Series MVP honors after hitting safely in all seven games. Some sixty-one million fans saw him bang out three hits in Game Four in Pittsburgh when NBC televised the first Series night game ever played.

Starting in 1976, ABC was back in the baseball business, sharing the postseason and All-Star Game with NBC. Its *Monday Night Baseball* starred, among others, Bob Uecker teaming with Howard Cosell in the broadcast booth.

For a long time, TV interest rode a magic carpet woven by the 1975 Red Sox-Reds World Series classic, watched in all or in part by more than 124 million fans. Carlton Fisk's drive off Fenway's left-field pole for a Game Six-winning home run was immortalized by replay—something invented as early as 1959 during a game when Yankees starting pitcher Ralph Terry yielded his first hit in the ninth inning. On a whim, Allen asked director Jack Murphy about reshowing the hit—the first-ever replay.

At its core, instant replay fits football like a glove. "It's an analyst's sport," explained NBC's Bob Costas. "(but) conversation fills baseball's core. Talk about the guy sitting at the end of the dugout. 'Is he a character? Does he give guys the hot foot?' In baseball, technology should aid personality, as Fisk's shot showed while he was willing his ball to the fair side of the foul pole."

The next logical step was cable. Soon after television mogul Ted Turner bought the Braves in 1976, he rebranded his WTCG as "Atlanta SuperStation WTBS" and began beaming his team's games across the country. In 1982, Atlanta's modern big-league record 13-0 start was, said mikeman Ernie Johnson, "the 'two-by-four' hitting America between the eyes."

Superstations and the voices behind them rose: WOR's Tim McCarver, WTBS's Johnson and Skip Caray, and WGN's legendary Harry Caray. "There's a long drive!" Harry bellowed. "It might be! It could be! It is!"—whereupon Middle America went nuts.

Cable's birth eroded the networks' grip on the game, but national broadcasters still captured America's attention, perhaps none more so than Vin Scully. Scully has twenty-five Series, sixty-five years of Dodgers play-by-play, a lifetime achievement Emmy Award, and the 1982 Frick Award on his résumé. His history parallels the game's biggest moments:

October 4, 1955—"Ladies and gentlemen, the Brooklyn Dodgers are the champions of the world!"

April 8, 1974—Hank Aaron crossed a Ruthian line. "To the fence! It is gone!" Scully said, hushing. "A Black man is getting a standing ovation in the Deep South for breaking a record of an all-time baseball idol."

October 26, 1986—"So the winning run is at second base," he said in World Series Game Six. "Little roller up along first… behind the bag. It gets through Buckner! Here comes Knight! And the Mets win it!"

That Saturday night drama in the 1986 Series set up a Game Seven that routed *Monday Night Football* in audience share (55 to 14 percent) and rating (38.9 to 8.8) by drawing eighty-one million viewers—the most-watched-baseball game in history.

Two years later, Scully had another golden moment behind the microphone. Injured, the Dodgers' Kirk Gibson seemed sure to miss Game One of the 1988 Series—until pinch-hitting in the ninth. Oakland led, 4-3, as Gibbie limped to a 3-2 count. "The game right now is at the plate. High fly ball into right field! She iiiis gone!" said Scully, stunned. Sixty-seven seconds later: "In a year that has been so improbable, the impossible has happened!"

Change, however, was inevitable. CBS paid $1.04 billion for 1990 to 1993 network exclusivity. After MLB's short-lived Baseball Network experiment in 1994 to 1995, FOX bought regular season coverage, sharing Octobers with NBC. Cable giant ESPN came aboard in 1990 with five games a week, brought us the "K Zone," and launched a *Sunday Night Baseball* flagship.

The changes keep coming. But the fans' passion for the game on the screen remains the same.

"It's just got everything," former President George H.W. Bush said when asked why he loved the game.

For seventy-five years, televised baseball has shown us everything: Tony Gwynn's joy of hitting; manager Earl Weaver, for whom angst was a daily ode; a Cubs fan's confessions of the heart.

George Will said: "I write about politics, mostly to support my baseball habit."

Due largely to TV, it is a habit hard to break.

Curt Smith is Senior Lecturer of English at the University of Rochester and has authored eighteen books including his recent work Memories from the Microphone: A Century of Baseball Broadcasting. *This essay originally appeared in* Memories & Dreams, *Issue 5, 2014.*

Capping Things Off
Baseball has added a staple to modern culture and fashion
By George Vecsey

When Babe Ruth played for the Yankees, ball players wore caps with wide, clunky visors that kept the sun out of their eyes. (They played only day games back then, kids—a wonderful custom.)

The Babe never saw headgear he would not place on his head while barnstorming or visiting orphanages or dude ranches or golf courses: a rancher's sombrero, soldier's hat, or football helmet. A born performer, Ruth wanted to please and amuse.

However, when living the life of a burgher on Manhattan's West Side, The Babe often wore a soft, fluffy cap with a tiny peak, a type favored by drivers of newfangled automobiles. In the '20s and '30s, ball caps were strictly for ball fields.

And ball fans? Check out photos of World Series crowds at mid-twentieth century, a mostly annual occurrence in New York. Fans were wearing hats, fedoras, homburgs—plus jackets and ties. It was, you might say, a different time.

Nowadays, ball caps are the universal headgear of a good swath of the globe—not only slimmer and trimmer with longer peaks, but featuring ornaments and logos and colors to make parrots jealous. In 1996, Spike Lee craved a red Yankees cap, and George Steinbrenner—traditional, born-on-the-Fourth-of-July George—saw the business possibilities in many hues of Yankee-ness. (Spike is from Brooklyn, but that's another story.)

Ball caps are even part of the fashion pages. On July 19, 2017, no less an authority than Vanessa Friedman, fashion director and chief fashion critic of *The New York Times*, turned her attention and wit to an article, "How to Dress Down Like a Power Player," coining the absolutely perfect phrase "calculated schlubbiness."

Friedman defined it so: "Who can give the impression they care less about what they wear than the next guy?" adding, "Apparently, when you've reached the top of the mountain, literal and professional, it's really about the smarts, people, not the suits."

Recently, I asked Friedman whether there was a Mendoza Line for wearing ball caps—you know, the Mendoza Line: the minimal .200 batting average that often eluded Mario Mendoza, a good-fielding shortstop from Mexico. (He wound up with a .215 major league average and is in the Mexican Baseball Hall of Fame.)

Are ball caps acceptable at outdoor weddings, funerals, graduations, even presidential inaugurations?

"There are very few hard and fast rules for any garment these days, and most men I know, including my husband, do wear baseball caps as basic head covering pretty much all the time," Friedman replied in an email. "My feeling is: No hats at the dinner table. And I wouldn't advise it for a formal occasion or a serious meeting."

Friedman noted that major fashion houses now produce caps, T-shirts, and jeans, based upon streetwear "now seen on the runway."

How did the utilitarian ball cap become fashion apparel? The line seems to start with the New York Knickerbocker Base Ball Club, which introduced the uniform in 1849, including a hat "simply because it was the 1800s, and they were respectable men in a public space," wrote Troy Patterson in the *New York Times Magazine* on April 1, 2015. He added that around 1858, the Brooklyn Excelsiors "introduced the progenitor of the modern baseball cap, with its round crown and brief brim indebted to the jockey's headgear."

In 1954, the New Era Company of Buffalo, NY, introduced the forerunner of today's caps, but now everybody has discovered branding—multiple team uniforms and caps every season to keep affluent fans happy and consuming. In the past generation, stylistas have come to emulate the inner beauty of athletes sweating into their uniforms.

The ball cap is also a medical necessity. As somebody who sees a dermatologist regularly to monitor damage from long-ago summer days at Jones Beach, I rotate a dozen caps with various logos (American Pharoah, Casey Stengel Baseball Center, NYPD—all gifts from friends). I live in fear of outdoor ceremonies where it might be inappropriate to wear a ball cap on my balding head.

"I think that if you're going to a formal occasion outdoors, why not wear a straw fedora?" Friedman said in a phone conversation. "It's actually kind of 'hot.' Men look good in them and white linen pants and a striped jacket. But the issue is the hat. Most clothing items have been denatured. The trend is toward wearing something."

A search of the web does not yield a single photo of a ball cap on the sleek coiffure of *Vogue's* renowned editor, Anna Wintour, but that magazine has surely discovered the glory of the ball cap. The July 10, 2017, issue of *Vogue* includes a slideshow of celebrities wearing exotic headwear and other sporty garb: "Never one to keep things simple, Rihanna brings a touch of royal regalia to proceedings by fastening a silk headscarf over her Supreme hat. It's Queen Elizabeth-meets-streetwear."

The May 30, 2017, issue of *Harper's Bazaar* had an article by Ella Alexander entitled, "Should you, could you, wear a baseball cap?" After displaying ultra-cool women in designer caps, the article's conclusion was:

"Well, if nothing else, it's an alternative to summer frizz."

Now that the fashion world has jumped the shark, are there places where ball caps just should not go?

The proliferation of ball caps—bright, gaudy, plus utilitarian? My guess is The Babe would love it.

George Vecsey is an author and longtime New York Times *columnist who has covered baseball for nearly sixty years. His works include* Baseball: A History of America's Favorite Game. *This essay originally appeared in* Memories & Dreams, *Issue 5, 2018.*

Chapter 2

Artifact Spotlight

A Paper Trail to History
Scorecard from Game Three of 1951 NL playoff echoes Russ Hodges' legendary call
By Tim Wiles

"The Giants win the pennant! The Giants win the pennant! The Giants win the pennant!"

Russ Hodges' iconic broadcast of Bobby Thomson's monumental home run is perhaps the most famous sports call in American history. And though Hodges and his broadcast partner that day, Ernie Harwell, are now gone, the written history remains forever at the National Baseball Hall of Fame and Museum in Cooperstown.

The scorecard, signed by Hodges and Harwell following the Giants' 5-4 victory over the Dodgers in Game Three of the 1951 National League playoff, was donated to the Museum in 1970 by John V. Halk, a New York City police detective on Polo Grounds duty that day.

The scorecard not only serves as a primary source concerning the game itself, but also evokes the images and sounds of the day that Thomson hit "The Shot Heard 'Round the World." It remains a portal into the events of October 3, 1951, when the Giants completed the herculean task of erasing a thirteen game Dodgers lead to advance to the World Series.

Actually, it was the Dodgers who tied the Giants, as the Giants had pulled ahead on the final day of the season, beating the Braves 3-2 in Boston, thereby putting themselves in first place and ensuring at least a tie for the pennant. The Dodgers were locked in a dramatic fourteen-inning contest in Philadelphia, finally winning, 9-8, thanks in part to Jackie Robinson, who made a rally-killing diving catch in the 12th and then homered in the 14th.

The next day at Ebbets Field, the three-game playoff series began, and the Giants beat the presumably tired Dodgers and Ralph Branca, 3-1, on the strength of a two-run homer by Thomson, who belted eight of his thirty-two home runs that season against Brooklyn.

When the series moved to the Polo Grounds, the Dodgers came roaring back, blanking the Giants, 10-0, to send this battle between these great rivals to a final, winner-take-all game.

Hodges and Harwell, the Giants broadcast team who would eventually win Ford C. Frick Awards in 1980 and 1981 respectively, were ready for the big game, each in their different ways. Hodges, for his part, was feeling terrible, as he remembered in his 1963 book *My Giants*.

As the Giants—following the final scheduled regular-season game—rode the train home from Boston, where the weather had been cold and chilly, he got on the train's newfangled phone and called the office, where they were monitoring the Dodgers' extra-inning affair in Philadelphia. It was hard to hear over the train wheels, and Hodges was shouting a narration of the game to all the Giants players.

The weather, the shouting, and the excitement of the first two games, combined with lack of sleep, had given him "a wicked cold." The broadcaster, who would shortly issue the most famous call in history, wrote: "I was up gargling most of the night, and just to make sure I hadn't lost my voice, I kept talking into an imaginary microphone at home, which only made my throat worse. I had trouble breathing, my nose was running, and I was sure I had a fever."

Harwell was thinking philosophically as he drove in from
his home in Larchmont: "I felt a little sorry for my Giants
broadcasting partner that day. [I was thinking that] Ole' Russ is
going to be stuck on the radio, there were five radio broadcasts
and I was gonna be on coast-to-coast TV, and [so] I thought that
I had the plum assignment." The two men alternated days in
the first coast-to-coast televised sports broadcast—Harwell had
games one and three.

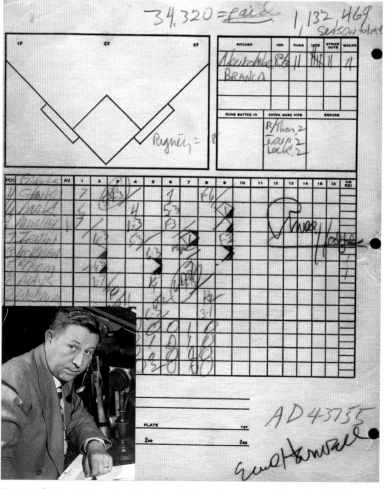

New York Giants broadcaster Russ Hodges' scorecard from the 1951
playoff game between the Giants and Brooklyn Dodgers.

"Well, as you remember, it turned out quite differently," Harwell remembered in his 1981 Frick Award acceptance speech. "Russ Hodges' record became the most famous sports broadcast of all time; television, no instant replay, no recordings in those days, and only Mrs. Harwell knows that I did the telecast of Bobby Thomson's home run."

Harwell's TV description of the home run was as spare as Hodges' radio call was pandemonium: " 'Thomson swings… it's gone.' The words were out of my mouth and I couldn't take them back. Now I saw Andy Pafko leaning back against the wall, and I had this horrible thought that I had reacted too soon," he remembered in the book *Voices of Sport*.

Ironically, in our video age, Hodges' manic radio description is often played over the television footage of the home run. Harwell, meanwhile, didn't speak for several minutes. "I let the picture tell the story," he remembered.

Harwell is correct that no one was recording television broadcasts at the time. He recalled that a kinescope recording would have been around three hundred dollars, and that was deemed too expensive. But a similar ethos prevailed on radio. Though there were five broadcasts emanating from the Polo Grounds that afternoon, none were taped. We know the greatest broadcasting call in sports history because of Giants fan Lawrence Goldberg and his mother, Sylvia.

Goldberg was listening to the game, but as the tension mounted, he had to leave home and get to work, so he asked his mother to hit 'record' on his reel-to-reel tape recorder when the game entered the bottom of the ninth. On the fiftieth anniversary of the game, he told the *New York Times'* Richard Sandomir about his fateful decision: "I knew I wouldn't be able to listen to the broadcast, and I knew something was going to happen. It was the third game of the playoffs. That kind of game had to be climactic."

The taping incident is a lesson for historians in the use and interpretation of primary sources. Hodges would often recall that Goldberg was a Dodgers fan who wanted to have a recording of the game's end in order to gloat over his Giants-fan friends. Goldberg, however, himself the more primary source when speaking of his own urge to tape, told Sandomir that he was a lifelong Giants fan.

Goldberg wrote to Hodges and asked him if he had a tape of the call, offering to lend his copy if needed. Hodges borrowed the tape and made records of it as a Christmas gift for friends.

Later, Chesterfield Cigarettes, mentioned in the half inning and one of the broadcast's sponsors, asked to make copies for marketing purposes. Goldberg was paid a hundred dollars and given access to Chesterfield's box at the Polo Grounds for the 1952 season. Hodges himself sent Goldberg a nice thank-you gift—a reel of blank tape—a thing that was probably not inexpensive or easy to come by in those days.

A half inning before Hodges' call, the moment did not seem ripe for history. The Giants came to bat in the bottom of the ninth trailing 4-1 against Don Newcombe, whom Hodges recalled "seemed to be getting stronger instead of weaker."

Alvin Dark led off and beat out an infield hit, going to third on Don Mueller's single to right. Monte Irvin popped up for the first out. Whitey Lockman doubled to the left field corner, scoring Dark and sending Mueller to third—he injured his ankle sliding and was replaced by Clint Hartung. At that point, Ralph Branca came in for Newcombe. With future Hall of Famer Willie Mays on deck and first base open, the Dodgers pitched to Thomson and Branca began with strike one. On an 0-1 count, Thomson swung and Hodges took over:

> Branca throws...there's a long fly...it's gonna be, I believe... the Giants win the pennant! The Giants win the pennant! The Giants win the pennant! The Giants win the pennant! Bobby hit it into the lower deck of the left-field stands...

> The Giants win the pennant, and they're going crazy...I
> don't believe it...I don't believe it...I will not believe it...
> Bobby Thomson hit a line drive into the lower deck of the
> left-field stands, and the place is going crazy! Oh, oh!...and
> they're picking up Bobby Thomson and carrying him off
> the field...

Take a close look at Thomson's square on Hodges' scorecard.
There's a pencil mark where he began to record the home run,
but it was never completed, probably due to the emotion of
the moment.

*Tim Wiles was the Director of Research at the National Baseball
Hall of Fame and Museum. He is currently the director of the
Guilderland Public Library in Guilderland, NY. This essay
originally appeared in* Memories & Dreams, *Issue 2, 2011.*

To Australia...and Beyond
125 years ago, baseball went global during the Spalding tour
By Tom Shieber

Some 125 years ago, in late October, 1888, two baseball clubs and an entourage of business managers, sportswriters, wives, and other enthusiasts of our National Pastime embarked on an extended off-season ball-playing tour.

The brains and money behind the expedition were provided by none other than Albert Spalding, a former big league pitcher (and future Hall of Famer) who parlayed his successful playing career into even greater success as a sporting goods mogul and baseball executive.

The effects from the goodwill achieved during the tour continued to be felt around the globe more than a century later.

As initially conceived, the American tourists were to leave Chicago, barnstorm through the western United States, sail across the Pacific to Hawaii (then known as the Sandwich Islands), continue on to Australia, where they would stay for a few months, and then return to the United States, all the while playing baseball. Indeed, the words "Spalding's Australian Base Ball Tour" appear atop the exhibition's official full-color poster, the only known copy of which resides in the collection of the National Baseball Hall of Fame and Museum. However, just a month into the journey, Spalding, ever the showman, abandoned his original plan in favor of one that would grab more headlines and provide greater exposure to himself and his sporting goods company: a trip around the world.

Well over a century later, in 1997, the Museum received an astonishing donation: a diary that detailed each day of the journey, penned by nineteenth-century ballplayer and Spalding World Tourist Jimmy Ryan. Written boldly atop the first page are the words "Tour of the Spalding BBC Around the World." Ryan's first entry, dated Saturday, October 20, 1888, reads as follows:

In order to further promote the interests of Base Ball, a few gentlemen from Chicago undertook to establish the National Game of America upon foreign soil. Accordingly, on the 20th of October 1888, they, in company with a number of ball players, reporters, and tourists, left Union depot on an expedition, known as the Spalding Australian Base Ball Tour.

A crowd of people collected to see our departure and also to view the newly decorated and handsome sleeping car Galesburg and dining car, Cosmopolitan, which were consigned to the party until our arrival in Denver, Colorado. The signal for starting was now heard, and with many farewells and good wishes, the train drew out of the Union station, amid the prolonged cheers of the multitude. The myriads of lights were fast receding in the distance, but on we plunged into the dark hours of the night, taking our first step toward that far away goal.

Everybody is in the best of health and spirits, and sounds of revelry were heard into the 'wee' small hours of the morning.

The diary, with its amazing firsthand account of the tour, is just one of dozens of artifacts related to this extraordinary voyage, each preserved in the Hall of Fame's unparalleled collection. For example, as mentioned by Ryan, the ballplayers spent much of their journey from Chicago to Denver in special railroad cars on the Burlington Route. The Hall of Fame has a small, specially-made booklet that served as a menu for meals aboard the Cosmopolitan dining car. Among the choices for the pampered diners were oysters, boiled salmon in a Hollandaise sauce, prairie chicken, and English plum pudding with brandy sauce.

The ballplayers on the journey formed two teams: The National League Chicago White Stockings (today known as the Cubs) and a team comprised of other professional stars (and lesser players) dubbed the All-Americas. Playing their way westward, the teams faced one another in exhibitions in Minnesota (Minneapolis and St. Paul), Iowa (Cedar Rapids and Des Moines), Nebraska (Omaha and Hastings), Colorado (Denver and Colorado Springs) and Salt Lake City in the Utah Territory. (It would be another eight years before Utah earned statehood.)

The tourists reached California in early November and spent nearly two weeks playing games up and down the coast. Finally, on November 18, the group boarded the Oceanic Steam Ship Company's *Alameda*, bound for Hawaii, New Zealand, and, ultimately, Australia.

The ship's passenger list, also a part of the Hall of Fame's collection of tour-related ephemera, not only bears the names of the ballplayers and other members of the touring party, but also the names of other passengers aboard the ship. One gentleman listed as bound for Auckland, New Zealand, was "O.D. Romney." Today, few people have heard of Orson Douglas Romney, a twenty-eight-year-old from Salt Lake City on a mission for the Mormon Church to the South Pacific. Better known is the name of his first cousin twice removed, Willard Mitt Romney, the Republican Party's 2012 nominee for President of the United States.

Poster promoting Albert Spalding's 1888-89 tour, initially planned for the Western US, Hawaii, and Australia. However, a month into the tour, Spalding abandoned his original plan for a tour around the world with stops in Egypt, Italy, France, and England.

After stopping in Honolulu and New Zealand, the ship finally reached Australia on December 14, nearly a month after leaving San Francisco. That evening, the tourists attended what was dubbed the "Grand American Gala Night" at Sydney's Theater Royal, where they saw the husband-and-wife duo of J.C. Williamson and Maggie Moore in their very successful play titled *Struck Oil*, as well as a light comedy called *The Chinese Question*. In between the two shows, Spalding and the ballplayers were brought on stage amidst thunderous applause. The program from the theater that evening is also part of the Hall of Fame's extensive holdings.

The Spalding party spent the next three weeks traveling the country, playing baseball—and even some cricket—in three southeastern states: New South Wales (Sydney), South Australia (Adelaide), and Victoria (Melbourne and Ballarat). Then, instead of returning to the States as originally billed, the group set sail for Egypt aboard the steamship *Salier*, a cabinet card of which can be found in the Hall of Fame's archives. Less than a decade later (in December 1896), this same ship wrecked off the coast of Spain, with some three hundred lives lost.

After a month's journey, the tourists arrived in Cairo, and on February 9, 1889, mounted camels and donkeys for a pilgrimage to the Sphinx and the pyramids. There, the Chicago and All-America teams played what was assuredly the first game of baseball on the sands of the Giza Plateau. A baseball from that historic contest, kept by tour umpire and future Hall of Famer George Wright, was donated to the Hall of Fame in 1942. Additionally, a photograph of the American party posing upon and in front of the Sphinx is part of the Hall of Fame's extensive photographic collection and has been featured in the Museum's exhibit "Picturing America's Pastime."

By mid-February, Spalding's party had reached Rome, where a large crowd, including the Queen of Italy, witnessed their game played at the famed Villa Borghese. After travelling west along the Mediterranean coast, making stops in Pisa, Genoa, Monte Carlo, Nice, and Marseille, the baseball tourists headed inland to Paris, where they spent a week enjoying the capital of France.

After significant effort, Spalding finally managed to stage a game of baseball in the "City of Light" at Parc Aérostatique, just across the Seine from the still incomplete Eiffel Tower. On the next day, March 9, the baseball entourage boarded the steamship *Normandy* for the voyage across the English Channel. Ryan described the harrowing journey in his diary:

> The night was pitch-dark and a severe storm was brewing; inside the harbor, the sea was very rough and the ship tugged away at her anchor chains, as if eager to get under weigh [sic].
>
> We soon started, however, and in a short space of time our miseries began. The ship plunged and pitched, tossed and shivered, while the wind whistled through the rigging, threatening to carry the ropes and spars with it. The storm now burst upon us with all its fury, and the little vessel laboured heavily under the tons upon tons of water which she was continually shipping. The scene below deck was undiscribable [sic], and as all the hatches were batten[ed] down tight, the smell was horrible. Men, women, and children were huddled together in the first cabin, some singing, some joking, but the greater majority, praying. Then, aside from these, was another party, who were so awfully seasick that they couldn't do either, if they wanted to. Of course, I was one of that class…

Once they reached land, the world tourists embarked upon an ambitious schedule of sightseeing and ball playing. The Chicago and All-America teams played nearly every day for over two weeks, facing one another in London, Bristol, Birmingham,

Sheffield, Bradford, Manchester, and Liverpool. Visits to Scotland (Glasgow) and Ireland (Belfast and Dublin) were also made, along with an obligatory stop to kiss the famed stone at the Blarney Castle.

The ballplayers met distinguished politicians, famed actors, renowned athletes, and numerous other celebrities. The future King Edward VII witnessed one contest and noted his opinion in royal third person: "The Prince of Wales has witnessed the game of Base Ball with great interest, and though he considers it an excellent game, he considers Cricket as superior." All the while, members of the baseball party collected valued keepsakes, ornate menus, and special programs, many of which now reside in Cooperstown.

On March 28, the Spalding entourage boarded the steamship *Adriatic* of the White Star Line for their final ocean voyage back to the States. After nine days, the ship reached New York harbor and received a hero's welcome. The clubs spent the final two weeks of the adventure attending celebratory banquets, being honored by local dignitaries, and, of course, playing ball. The globetrotting ball players took to the field in Brooklyn, Baltimore, Philadelphia, Boston, Washington, Pittsburgh, Cleveland, Indianapolis, and Chicago.

The tourists' final celebratory banquet took place at Chicago's famed Palmer House. The Hall's collection features one of the beautiful silk-covered menu cards that were presented to each dinner guest that evening, April 19, 1889. The following day, exactly half a year after the tour had begun, the ballplayers ended their adventure in appropriate fashion, with a baseball game at Chicago's West Side Grounds. With the All-Americas trouncing Chicago, 22-9, the final results of this "World Series" were complete: All-Americas 29 wins; Chicago 23 wins; and four ties.

Jimmy Ryan concluded his diary with one final entry, dated Saturday, April 20:

To day we have completed the circumference of the globe, for six months ago today we bid good bye to Chicago and entered upon our tour Around the World. We have given exhibitions of our National Game in every continent on the face of the globe and also thirteen foreign countries and travelled upward of a distance of thirty thousand miles. This afternoon as tourists we played our last game, and a great crowd greeted us as we appeared upon our native diamond. The game concluded, and so also did the greatest trip in the annals of sport, namely a Baseball Tour 'Around the World.'

Tom Shieber is the Senior Curator at the National Baseball Hall of Fame and Museum. This essay originally appeared in Memories & Dreams, *Issue 1, 2014.*

Clip and Save
**Bound volumes of the *New York Clipper* provide
a look at baseball's earliest days**
By Craig Muder

Paging through the Hall of Fame's nondescript black bound volumes of the *New York Clipper*, a reader finds column after column of theater reviews, rudimentary baseball box scores, and advertisements.

And then comes the April 22, 1865, issue. On the front page is a woodcut image of John Wilkes Booth, a once-famous actor who just eight days earlier had assassinated President Abraham Lincoln.

"When you see something like that, that's when you realize what an incredible resource this is," said Tom Shieber, the senior curator at the National Baseball Hall of Fame and Museum. "It's one thing to look at stories like this digitally or on microfilm. It's another to have the paper in front of you and know that someone 148 years ago was looking at this very page.

"It's like a time machine."

Eighteen bound volumes of the *New York Clipper*—nearly each one filled with fifty-two editions of the weekly paper dedicated to sports and theater—were donated to the Museum in its earliest years by Margery Cary of nearby Richfield Springs, NY. Her grandfather, Edgar Cary, and father, John D. Cary, both subscribed to the *Clipper* and were huge baseball fans who used the paper to track their favorite teams.

The issues cover the 1860s through the 1880s and are beautifully preserved, thanks to paper that featured a high-cotton, low-acid mix.

The papers serve as direct evidence of the popularity of baseball as it became the National Pastime.

"In the 1850s, baseball made the transition from a children's game to a game that was an acceptable activity for adults,"

Shieber said. "So into the 1860s, you see basic box scores in the *New York Clipper*, some featuring write-ups of [local games] and some from around the country, sent in by team secretaries. Next to those results, you'd have coverage of boxing, cricket, and other sports, then theater reviews and news.

"By the 1860s, baseball was viewed just like the theater and the racetrack: You went there for entertainment."

The *Clipper* devoted dozens of column inches to baseball in each issue. By the late 1870s, box scores from the new National League were on the same pages with amateur games.

"The results there are the same ones on the Internet today, with players like (Hall of Famers) George Wright and Jim O'Rourke in the box scores," Shieber said. "But for researchers, the real gold mine of information is in the write-ups, especially from the 1860s. There, you can see how the nuances of the game evolved and learn about how the game was played."

With the typeface about one-third the size of today's newspapers–"Everyone back then either had better eyesight or owned a magnifying glass," Shieber quipped–the *Clipper* crammed in the serialization of novels, answers to readers' questions (but not the questions themselves) and even sample chess boards in play-and-solve columns written by future Hall of Famer Henry Chadwick.

Ted Spencer, the Hall of Fame's former chief curator, found the *Clipper* packed with history involving both baseball and American culture.

"About fifteen years ago, I was asked to do a talk on baseball and the Civil War and found the *Clipper* to be a really valuable resource," Spencer said. "There are reports in there from soldiers playing ball at the front, and even a reference by a soldier talking about how they would play their next game if 'General Grant didn't send us to play General Lee'–a reference to a possible upcoming battle."

Historical tie-ins with baseball and entertainment are found throughout the *Clipper*, just like the reference to President Lincoln's assassin. The woodcut of Booth was likely done in advance of his assassination of Lincoln in preparation for a feature on the actor. The April 22, 1865, issue was published while Booth was still at large, and for the next month, the *Clipper* had extra wide black "bands" separating each column in a memorial to the slain president.

By the 1880s, the woodcuts on the front page featured images of the top ballplayers of the day.

"The combination of the information preserved in these volumes and the fact that the paper itself is still intact brings the history of baseball of that era to life," Shieber said. "That's what a museum and a library are supposed to do."

Craig Muder is the Director of Communications for the National Baseball Hall of Fame and Museum. This essay originally appeared in Memories & Dreams, *Issue 3, 2013.*

Wagnerian Triumph
Celebrating 100 years of baseball's most revered card
By Tim Wiles

Beautiful, sublime, mysterious, rare, and valuable—all of these adjectives have been used to describe the 1909 Honus Wagner T206 baseball card, and yet none can fully capture the essence of this iconic piece of cardboard.

The Wagner card has been described as "the Mona Lisa of baseball cards," and "the Holy Grail of card collecting." It is the subject of three books, one for adults and two for children. It was even the inspiration for a movie about Wagner, *The Winning Season*, released in 2004.

This year, the Wagner card turned one hundred years old. To mark the anniversary, the National Baseball Hall of Fame and Museum celebrated by displaying its two versions of the card—drawing card collectors to Cooperstown for the chance just to see The Card.

The passion for the T206 remains one of sport's greatest stories.

Fact and Fiction

As with all great stories, there are some myths and misconceptions. The Wagner card is not the rarest baseball card in history. And Honus Wagner was not opposed to the use of tobacco, as legend has described. But first, the historical facts.

In 1909, the American Tobacco Company, a consortium of smaller companies like Sweet Caporal, Sovereign, Drum, and Piedmont, decided that a set of baseball cards inserted into packs of cigarettes would give it a marketing edge over other brands. So they went to work creating a large and beautiful set of cards—one of the first colored sets, and one of the largest sets up to that time, at over five hundred cards. The lithographic artwork process proved especially beautiful, and the allure of the cards has held up over time, perhaps strengthened by their age and rarity.

Just as the cards were released, Wagner, star shortstop of the Pittsburgh Pirates, objected to his inclusion and his card was pulled from the set. No one knows how many Wagners made it into circulation, and in fact, no one knows how many exist today. Estimates range from twenty-five all the way up to two hundred.

The familiar story is that Wagner objected to the cards because he disliked being associated with tobacco. This is simply not true, as Wagner enjoyed smoking cigars and chewing tobacco—in fact, two companies issued cigar brands named after him. He lent his name to several tobacco advertisements throughout his career, and his 1948 Leaf baseball card shows him with a cheek-full of chaw and a pouch in his hand.

Others think that he objected to being uncompensated for the use of his image—but this also rings untrue. The tobacco company signed players up for inclusion in the set by hiring local sportswriters to get the players to sign contracts, earning ten dollars per player. Wagner returned his contract unsigned to sportswriter John Gruber along with a check, writing, "I don't want my picture in cigarettes, but I don't want you to lose ten dollars, so I'm enclosing [a] check for that sum."

If it wasn't about the money for Wagner, perhaps he made a distinction between his endorsement and use of cigars and chewing tobacco and cigarettes themselves. Historians Dennis and Jeanne DeValeria, in their biography of Wagner, contend that cigarettes were held in low esteem compared to other forms of tobacco, and that Pirates owner Barney Dreyfuss and player/manager Fred Clarke both despised cigarettes. Furthermore, a 1910 Pennsylvania law prohibiting the sale of cigarettes to minors was in the discussion stages. However, Wagner did permit the Murad cigarette company to run newspaper ads bearing his name and likeness during the 1909 World Series.

In 1916, nearing the end of his playing career, Wagner said, "Tobacco may shorten a man's life and interfere with his baseball career, but I guess it hasn't shortened mine a great deal. I have noticed that where a player starts to quit hitting, it will shorten his career a good deal quicker than tobacco."

WAGNER, PITTSBURG

The T206 Honus Wagner baseball card, produced by the American Tobacco Company between 1909 and 1911, is considered by many collectors to be the "Holy Grail" of baseball cards.

For the Kids

The welfare of children was almost certainly on Wagner's mind—
and others have suggested that his dispute was not even with
cigarettes, but with the decision to market them to minors that
was made plain by the cards' inclusion in cigarettes. A 1909
article in the *Charlotte (NC) Observer* noted the "remarkable"
interest of small boys in the "pictures of baseball men" which
came in every pack of Piedmont Cigarettes. The boys would
stand outside storefronts and beg the men coming outside for
their cards.

Even then, it was unclear whether the baseball cards were
the commodity being marketed. A couple of weeks later, in an
editorial entitled "Tempting the Children," the *Winston (NC)
Sentinel* stated: "The advertising man who conceived the idea
of putting baseball pictures in cigarette packages did a good
thing for his employers, but a mighty bad thing for the small
boy. There ought to be some way to prohibit this kind of thing. It
will do more to start young boys to smoking cigarettes than any
other agency of which we can conceive."

"He just didn't want children to have to buy tobacco
at a young age in order to get his cards," said Wagner's
granddaughter Leslie Blair in a 1992 interview.

Supply and Demand

What of the notion of the Wagner T206's rarity? Living in a culture
steeped in the economic law of supply and demand, we are
taught that as the supply of anything diminishes, the demand
is likely to go up, and so many people assume that the Wagner
T206 is the rarest of baseball cards. In fact, there are hundreds,
some say even thousands of baseball cards that are rarer than
the Wagner T206. There are many cards of which only one

known copy exists, making one presume they would be more valuable than the Wagner, since by definition, only one collector can own them. But they are not, and the Wagner remains king despite the odds.

The mystique began with a man named Jefferson Burdick, a solitary, reclusive man who collected tobacco cards and came up with the checklist system which gave the Wagner the T206 designation when he published his *American Card Catalog* in 1937. As a small boy, Burdick had been just like his peers, begging for "baseball men" from his father and other men who smoked. But Burdick didn't stop, collecting all sorts of paper ephemera, and eventually publishing the catalog, founding the hobby and donating his extensive card collection to the Metropolitan Museum of Art.

In the catalog, Burdick assigned values to all the T206 cards, usually less than a quarter apiece. But he valued the T206 Wagner at fifty dollars—it was apparently that rare and difficult to find, and thus the mystique began. By the 1970s, Wagners changed hands for hundreds of dollars, and a print ad in a collectors' publication promised that it could be worth as much as $1,500. By then, the die was cast, and the price of the card kept going up, driven by the desire of collectors to hunt—and find—the holy grail.

Despite the eventual realization that there were other cards that were rarer, the Wagner led the way to the baseball card industry growing up in the second half of the twentieth century.

"The card is valuable because it is famous; it is famous because it is valuable," noted Paul M. Green and Kit Kiefer in a baseball card book.

But what of the old laws of supply and demand? Seems they do apply—the card is quite rare, after all, just not the rarest.

"You are trying to apply logic to something that is about desire," noted Michael O'Keeffe, coauthor with Teri Thompson of the book *The Card*, all about the Wagner T206. O'Keeffe and Thompson spoke at the Hall of Fame on "Honus Wagner Day" in early August, the Hall's celebration of the centennial of baseball's most alluring card.

"It's a mixture of folklore, history, tradition, public relations, and marketing at its best," notes baseball historian Andy Strasberg, who went on to state, "The hobby and the sport are richer for all of these reasons."

At the Museum

The Hall owns two Wagner T206s, both of which came from New Jersey. Famed collector Barry Halper donated the first Wagner card to the Museum in 1984. Then-Hall President Ed Stack said at the time that the card "adds immeasurably to the Hall of Fame's prestige and satisfies the curiosity of countless visitors who constantly ask about the card." The second Wagner also came from Halper's collection—it was purchased by Major League Baseball and donated to the Hall in 2000, in time for the "Baseball As America" tour.

Today, one card is displayed in the Hall's baseball card exhibit and the other is "resting," the term museums use for items which need to spend time away from visitor's flashbulbs and other perils of being on display. The Hall displayed both Wagners together for the first time briefly on "Honus Wagner Day." Even more stars were aligned at the "Wagner Reunion," when ten Wagners were displayed together at the 2004 National Sports Collectors Convention in Cleveland.

Ironically, the T206 Honus Wagner is so celebrated that fans today know more about the card than about Wagner himself, one of the original five 1936 inductees to the Hall of Fame. Wagner is still a serious contender not just for the laurels as the best shortstop ever, but also as the best all-around player ever.

"There ain't much to bein' a ballplayer," he famously said, "if you're a ballplayer…" a quote which was celebrated in *The Baseball Experience*, once presented in the Hall's Grandstand Theater.

As his card enters its second century, Wagner still ranks in the top ten of all time in hits, singles, doubles, triples, and stolen bases. He led the National League in batting average eight times, RBI four times and on-base percentage four times. An outstanding fielder and baserunner, the speedy Wagner hit for a career batting average of .328 and was named to the All-Century team in 1999.

And yet, his legacy might be best summed up by a small piece of cardboard—the power of which continues to enthrall generations of fans.

Tim Wiles was the Director of Research at the National Baseball Hall of Fame and Museum. He is currently the director of the Guilderland Public Library in Guilderland, NY. This essay originally appeared in Memories & Dreams, *Issue 6, 2009.*

King of the One Game Wonders

Larry Yount is as much a major leaguer as his more famous brother, even though he never played in a game

By John Odell

Among the treasures of the Hall of Fame's Library archives are the biographical clippings files, which include every player who ever appeared in a major league game (a group now numbering more than 22,000).

The Museum adds to that archive throughout the year, creating a new file each time a player makes his debut. The data most treasured isn't how he did at the plate or on the mound—that can be found in other places.

Instead, the Library focuses on gathering the personal information that doesn't show up in the box score. The result is an astounding collection of the common and unusual, the typical and odd, and the tragic and triumphant that fleshes out the world of baseball beyond the ballfield.

Alphabetically, these files run from 2008 to 2009 Mariners closer David Aardsma all the way to Alex Zych, former equipment manager of the Kansas City Royals. In terms of volume, Babe Ruth's eight thick files top the list, while the careers of untold hundreds (or thousands) of others are summarized with a handful of clippings or less. Of course, there are the eight players who appeared in more than three thousand games, but the archive also has the 971 players whose entire career, as of the start of the 2012 season, is comprised of a single game in the "bigs."

While most of these one-game wonders are pinch hitters, pinch runners, and September call-ups, you may have heard of a few of them. Perhaps the most famous is three-foot-seven-inch Eddie Gaedel, famously sent up to bat by Bill Veeck in 1951 and destined to become the shortest player ever to appear in a big league game.

Fans of 1989's *Field of Dreams* may remember Burt Lancaster as Archie "Moonlight" Graham, but few know that Graham was a real major league ballplayer. The movie took surprisingly few liberties with his life. As portrayed in the film, Graham was a member of the single-game club. He had only a defensive appearance in the outfield, never made it to bat, and never played in the majors again. And he really did go on to become a beloved doctor in Chisholm, Minn.

Pitcher Bert Shepard's name might sound familiar to a few baseball fans who are also World War II buffs. Shepard's minor league career ended when he entered the service, and his chances to make the majors seemed to end when he lost his right leg after being shot down while flying over Germany. Following the war, fitted with a prosthetic leg, he made his only big league appearance when he pitched five-plus innings (and gave up only one earned run) on August 4, 1945, for the Washington Senators. All these stories and more can be found in the files.

There are also a few that are more unique. "Unique" is a word used carefully at the Hall because baseball's history is so long, has been so well recorded, and can be fact-checked so thoroughly.

For instance, Gaedel might have walked in his only career plate appearance, but that is not unique. With a few keystrokes, we can learn that a half-dozen other players had careers that exactly matched Gaedel's, though with more height and with much less hype.

So it is no small thing to say that no one—*no one*—had a more unusual major league career than Houston Astros pitcher Larry Yount.

Of course, plenty of non-major league players are in the files, including numerous Hall of Fame managers and executives. And yet, because of the strange circumstances of Yount's not playing, he is counted as a major leaguer.

Yount made his big league debut in a game during which he never threw a pitch or faced a batter. Then he never played in the majors again.

Drafted out of high school by Houston in 1968, Yount worked his way up the minor league ladder and received his call up to the parent club in September, 1971, toward the end of his fourth season in pro ball. During that year, he had fanned 121 batters in 137 innings in Triple-A Oklahoma City, and the Astros wanted to see what he could do at the major league level.

Uncle Sam, however, had first dibs and called on him to complete a week of military service, a common occurrence during the Vietnam War era. So after a week of no baseball at all, Yount finally ended up in the Houston bullpen. Maybe the layoff had an effect, and maybe not. It certainly did not help.

On September 15, Yount's opportunity came. With the host Astros trailing the Atlanta Braves, 4-1, in the top of the ninth, Houston manager Harry "The Hat" Walker called Yount's number. It was the perfect low-pressure situation to get a rookie's feet wet. With two weeks left in the season, the Astros were hovering around .500, some ten games out of the NL West race. Atlanta was also playing out the string. There was no save to blow, no pennant on the line. Only 6,513 fans attended the Wednesday night contest, and goodness knows how few were still at the Astrodome when Yount got the nod.

As Yount warmed up in the bullpen, his elbow began to stiffen, but he buckled down and reported to the game, where he was announced as the next pitcher. He hoped the elbow would loosen up with a few more pitches.

"You figure you'll run out to the mound, that the adrenaline will be pumping and that you'll figure out what's wrong," he later recalled. "I went to the mound and took a couple of tosses."

The pain, however, got worse as he made the last of his warm-up pitches. Yount was smart and did not want to risk his career in his debut, so he called in the trainer, who took him out. Both surely expected that Yount's turn would come again soon.

It never did.

The 1971 season ended without Yount getting in a game, not unusual given the forty-man rosters at the end of the year. He played in a fall instructional league without any trouble, then came to Spring Training in 1972, where he was the last player cut. The other pitchers he was competing against were out of options. Since Yount was not, the club could—and did—send him back down. He returned to the minors.

His elbow was not permanently injured. "It was a non-event, a glitch that had no factor in what followed," Yount explained. "I just never quite got the job done."

Over the remainder of his pro career, he pitched fine, just not well enough to be called up. He continued to work hard. He was traded to the Milwaukee Brewers, who had recently signed a phenom from California. Larry knew him well. It was Robin Yount, his younger brother. The younger Yount jumped from short-season A-ball to the majors in one year. Larry persevered, but eventually accepted the writing on the wall and retired from the game after 1975.

For his efforts on that September evening, Larry Yount earned the distinction of being the only pitcher in major league history who never appeared in the only game he ever played in. He never threw a pitch, never faced a batter, and never played again. However, because he was officially announced as the pitcher, he is in baseball's record book and has a file in the Hall of Fame.

Incidentally, Larry Yount's player file is not the only place in the Hall of Fame where he is referenced. In 1999, his younger brother, after a twenty-year career with the Brewers, was elected to the Hall of Fame. That July, Robin walked onto the Induction stage in front of an estimated 50,000 people in Cooperstown. Larry was there, too, and heard Robin's thoughtful Induction speech. With a crowd some eight times larger than the one in

Houston that saw Larry warm up but never throw an official pitch, the elder Yount found out what his little brother had learned from his experience.

"My brother Larry—he taught me how hard work and dedication to the game was the only way to make it."

Robin Yount's speech is also in the collection. You can look it up in the Hall of Fame Library.

John Odell is the Curator of History and Research at the National Baseball Hall of Fame and Museum. This essay originally appeared in Memories & Dreams, *Issue 3, 201*

Giving the House a Home
Donation by former House of David player adds important piece to Museum collection
By Jim Gates

"Locally, people know of them, older people who remembered seeing them play. But there is a whole generation or two that really know nothing about them," said House of David baseball historian Terry Bertolino in the Elkhart (IN) Truth.

Founded in 1903 as a religious community, the Israelite House of David was established for the purpose of reuniting the twelve lost tribes of Israel to await the Millennium.

But for many baseball historians and fans, the name House of David has become synonymous with baseball's barnstorming heyday. And today, thanks to a recent donation to the National Baseball Hall of Fame and Museum, the House of David legacy is alive and well in Cooperstown.

Headquartered out of the small town of Benton Harbor, Michigan, the House of David ran a number of successful business operations and also sponsored a variety of athletic programs. House of David founder Benjamin Purnell was an active sports enthusiast and encouraged his members to participate; in a reflection of the nation as a whole, baseball was their preferred pastime.

The House of David began playing organized baseball by 1913 as a weekend activity drawing impressive crowds at their home field in Benton Harbor, and by 1920, they were a regular feature on the American barnstorming circuit. The baseball team served several functions, the two primary purposes being to raise money for the community and as a means of recruiting new members to the faith. The basic tenets of the House of David included physical labor, celibacy, refraining from haircuts and shaving, and a strict vegetarian diet. The athletic teams were seen as a way to develop both the physical and spiritual discipline required by the religion.

In addition to their primary men's barnstorming team, the colony also sponsored a girls' squad and a junior boys' program.

Donning a variety of House of David uniforms and playing with flowing locks of hair and unshaven faces, the team stood out among the many barnstorming operations, and their reputation as an excellent baseball team was known throughout North America. Their unique physical appearance and a famed sleight-of-hand "pepper game" also helped to ensure large crowds wherever they traveled.

By the late 1920s the House of David began hiring professional players to further enhance their program; they included such luminaries as Grover Cleveland Alexander, Charles Bender, and Satchel Paige. While not required to convert to the full faith, these contract players were asked to grow facial hair, or to at least wear a false beard.

There may have been one exemption to the beard requirement, as the team signed nineteen-year-old Virne Beatrice Mitchell to a contract in 1933. Known as Jackie, and having earned some fame for striking out Babe Ruth and Lou Gehrig in an earlier exhibition contest, Mitchell became one of the first women to sign a professional baseball contract. Her salary was set at a thousand dollars per month, a significant sum in those days. This pay scale also serves to indicate the financial value the team held for the colony.

The quality of play was excellent, and the House of David's schedule included major league, minor league, and Negro League games. The program would expand to include as many as three different teams. However, by the early 1930s, legal troubles and internal religious differences began to take their toll, and the colony split into several factions, each of which continued to sponsor baseball teams. Although mainly consisting of contract players not associated with the religious colonies, the House of David teams continued to barnstorm throughout North America until the mid-1950s. Then, like so many other baseball programs, they faded from national memory.

To a certain degree, this loss is also represented within the collections of the Hall of Fame. While the Library and Archives now contains a nice file of articles, a selection of photographs, and a copy of several books about the House of David, the Museum once had very little in the way of artifacts from this famous team.

The Palladino family from the Philadelphia area recently changed this when they decided to make a family visit to Cooperstown. As they had called the Library in advance, the staff was able to provide them with access to its archival collection on the House of David. On the day of their tour, three generations arrived for their visit, including Joe Palladino Jr., his son Joe III, and two grandsons, Joe IV and Michael Aquilino. They dropped by the Library that morning and began a nice discussion about the history of the House of David team. It was at that point that Joe Jr. revealed that he had played with the team during the 1948 season, touring through upstate New York and several provinces of Canada. But the real surprise came when Joe Jr.

held up a small shopping bag and asked, "Would you like to see my uniform?"

The House of David is a tremendous part of America's twentieth century baseball story, and the family generously agreed to donate the uniform. To add some icing to this cake, Joe Jr. also included a signed baseball from his year with the team, along with several team and individual photos and a small journal where he had kept track of the game results.

Joe Palladino Jr. grew up in Philadelphia, playing high school ball and eventually participating in the South Philadelphia League, a local semipro operation. In 1948, when Joe was seventeen, his local coach recruited him to join a traveling House of David team that operated as a franchise and was run by a businessman named Sam Besinoff. Three South Philly players signed up to play, and they immediately departed for Albany, New York, where they would join the team, which was already engaged in the barnstorming schedule. It was in Albany that Joe Jr. received the uniform which is now part of the Hall of Fame collection.

The team, in a bus emblazoned with the House of David name, played all summer, traveling through upstate New York and then heading north, crossing the border at Niagara Falls to play through several Canadian provinces. The team was constantly on the move, playing as many games as possible. It was not unusual for them to play three games in one day. In addition to having their travel and hotel expenses covered, they were paid a percentage of the gate, with each player usually picking up thirty-five to forty-five dollars per game, and they also received two dollars per day as meal money. But if a game was rained out, they received no pay.

The team also played night games on a routine basis. The team bus was usually followed by a truck towing a portable lighting system. Harry Huff of Pottsville, Pennsylvania, had developed this portable system and worked with the House of

David to set up the lights, thereby allowing the team to get in an extra game on many occasions.

Spending so much time on the road would be a chance to experience North America, but Joe Jr. reports that he saw "ball fields, hotel rooms, and the inside of the team bus." There was very little time to be a tourist. Still, he felt it was a great way for a young man to spend a summer, getting paid to play baseball. It was an exciting time for the young ball player from Philadelphia, but Joe Jr. had only one regret: "I didn't get to see Canada."

Thanks to his generous donation, however, Joe Jr.'s legacy—along with that of the House of David barnstorming team—will be seen by countless visitors to the Baseball Hall of Fame.

Jim Gates is Librarian Emeritus at the National Baseball Hall of Fame and Museum. This essay originally appeared in Memories & Dreams, *Issue 2, 2010.*

Chapter 3

Hall of Famers

Winning Record
**Derek Jeter's talent, tenacity brought
the Yankees back to the top**
By Tyler Kepner

Under owner George Steinbrenner, the New York Yankees had made a habit of trading prospects for immediate needs.

A high school shortstop changed all that—a high school shortstop who seemed to have destiny waiting for him at Yankee Stadium.

"Gene Michael would tell everybody when (Derek) Jeter was coming through the system: 'He's not getting traded,' " said Brian Cashman, the Yankees' longtime general manager, referring to their early-'90s architect and protector of the sixth overall pick in the 1992 MLB Draft. "People would hit on Stick about Jeter when he was in the South Atlantic League and the Florida State League, and Gene was always like, 'We're not trading him, we're not trading him, we're not trading him!' "

Derek Jeter would justify the Yankees' faith. He became the cornerstone of the revival of the big leagues' glamour franchise and served as a fresh hero for a battered industry. He was exactly who the team and the sport needed, at exactly the right time, collecting five championships and 3,465 hits—sixth on MLB's career list—while serving as a role model fans could trust.

It all added up to a spellbinding résumé, one that landed Jeter in the Hall of Fame in January on his first try. He received 99.7 percent of the votes from the Baseball Writers' Association of America, the highest percentage ever for a position player.

"This is something that was not a part of the dream when you're playing," Jeter said at a news conference in the afterglow of the announcement. "When you're playing, you're just trying to keep your job."

Indeed, Jeter never took his success for granted. Lots of players say that, but Jeter demonstrated it before the 1996 season, when he won the AL Rookie of the Year Award by hitting .314 with 104 runs scored. The Yankees had installed Jeter as their shortstop that spring, wisely resisting a trade that would have sent Mariano Rivera to the Seattle Mariners for shortstop Félix Fermín. But Jeter never assumed he had the job.

Manager Joe Torre happened to catch a television interview with Jeter during that Spring Training. Asked about taking over as the Yankees' starting shortstop, Jeter said, "I'm going to have an opportunity to win the job."

Torre repeats the story often as a way to illustrate Jeter's uncommon humility and maturity.

"He was all about accountability and respect," Torre said, "without any sense of entitlement."

Jeter had watched the 1995 postseason from the bench as a non-roster player after batting .250 with no home runs in a fifteen-game cameo that season. He announced his presence on Opening Day in Cleveland on April 2, 1996, blasting a home run off Dennis Martínez while hitting ninth in the Yankees lineup. The Indians were the reigning AL champions—having fallen to the Braves in the World Series—but with that home run, a shift in the majors' power structure was under way.

That season, the Yankees returned to the Fall Classic for the first time since 1981—when Jeter had been seven years old—and roared back from an 0-2 hole to beat the Braves in six games in the World Series. They triumphed again in 1998, 1999, and 2000, when Jeter hit .409 with two homers to thwart the Mets in New York's first Subway Series since 1956.

Jeter was the Most Valuable Player, of course, which is how it had to be. He was the prince of the city, Superman in spikes. That's how he seemed in October, 2001, at least, dashing across the Oakland infield to rescue an errant throw, then flipping the ball to catcher Jorge Posada at the plate to preserve a slim lead in a must-win postseason game.

Derek Jeter connects with a pitch during the 2001 World Series against the Arizona Diamondbacks. Jeter appeared in seven World Series with the New York Yankees, winning five titles. (Ron Vesely)

The Yankees would lose the 2001 World Series and another in 2003, a year best known for their rousing comeback to beat Boston in Game 7 of the ALCS. The Yankees trailed by two runs in the eighth inning that night, five outs from elimination with Sox ace Pedro Martínez on the mound. Jeter's double started their famous game-tying rally, setting up current Yankees manager Aaron Boone's pennant-winning homer in the 11th inning.

"He is the greatest competitor that I ever had the chance to play with," Boone said following Jeter's Hall of Fame announcement. "If anyone out there epitomizes what a Hall of Famer is, it's Derek Jeter."

It was during the 2003 season that owner George Steinbrenner named Jeter captain, following in the tradition of Lou Gehrig, Thurman Munson, Don Mattingly, and others. The role suited Jeter, a natural leader who shared Steinbrenner's competitive ethos.

The Yankees' next championship came in 2009, in their first season at the new Yankee Stadium. In a six-game victory over the Philadelphia Phillies, Jeter batted .407 with 11 hits, a career high for his 33 Postseason series. His career .838 on-base plus slugging percentage in the postseason was even better than his .817 mark in the regular season, and in 158 postseason games, he had an even 200 hits.

In other words, while facing the strongest competition and under the most pressure, Jeter found a way to be the best version of himself.

"Everything about him evoked winning," said his first major league manager, Buck Showalter. "With Derek, it was all about the team."

Jeter proudly notes that he played only one game in New York in his entire career with the Yankees eliminated from the postseason[1]—and it was his very last home game, on September 25, 2014. Jeter came to bat in the bottom of the ninth with the score tied and a runner at second. He lashed the first pitch from the Orioles' Evan Meek through the right side for a single, a quintessential Jeter hit that scored the winning run.

It was the final fairy tale for a player who lived his dream, and when it was over, Jeter made one last visit to shortstop, savoring the stage alone as the cheers washed over him. He played 2,905

---

1   Unfortunately, this is inaccurate. The Yankees played several games in New York near the end of the 2013 and 2014 seasons in which they were eliminated from the postseason.

games, including the postseason, and never played another defensive position.

In retirement, however, Jeter has made a significant move—in both location and job. At the end of the 2017 season, he became the chief executive officer and part-owner of the Miami Marlins, who have not reached the postseason since beating the Yankees in the 2003 World Series.

"I want to win as much as anyone," Jeter said. "I didn't get into this to lose."

He has already done it once, with a playing career that helped restore the Yankees brand and draw fans back to the game. That journey ends now in Cooperstown, but the baseball legacy of Derek Jeter continues.

Tyler Kepner is the national baseball writer for the New York Times. *He covered Derek Jeter's Yankees from 2002 through 2009 and is the author of the bestselling book* K: A History of Baseball in Ten Pitches. *This essay originally appeared in* Memories & Dreams, *Issue 1, 2020.*

Tale of a Tiger
Alan Trammell's passion for the game paved the way to greatness
By Tom Gage

Alan Trammell's great career was ending. He knew he would be sad when retirement day arrived on September 29, 1996—and he was.

After missing much of the second half of the season because of degenerative issues in his left ankle, he had decided two weeks before the end of his twentieth season with the Detroit Tigers that their final game would also be his last as an active player.

When the game ended—after he had singled in his last at-bat but before he came out to say farewell to the fans—"I lost it," Trammell said. "I was an emotional wreck in the clubhouse tunnel."

Loving the game, however, was no longer enough for him to stay in the game. Hoping—but not certain—he'd be able to remain in baseball as a coach or instructor, he was on the brink of saying goodbye.

In his final at-bat, Trammell had singled off Milwaukee's Mike Fetters, the same kind of hit with which he'd begun his big league career in 1977.

"I went out the way I came in," Trammell said of the single to center. "It wasn't as solid as my first one, but I've not been hitting much of anything solid. That's why I made the decision to retire when I did."

In a brief critique of himself as Trammell spoke to the Tiger Stadium crowd that day, he said that as a player, "I don't know that I was great in any one area, but I was good in a lot of them."

Candid to the end, Trammell also said what everyone else already knew—and had for many years. Even now, it's what he says about his career.

"I knew I could play."

In the other dugout, Brewers manager Phil Garner told his team to watch the proceedings, because, "You just don't get the privilege to watch many moments like this. I wanted my players to see what class is all about.

"There's a place waiting for players like Alan Trammell. It's called the Hall of Fame."

Garner was right. It was waiting for him.

"Nobody played the game with more respect," Garner said after learning of Trammell's election. "In turn, I know of no one who the game respected more than 'Tram'—not just as a player, but as an individual. He deserves this honor. I'm so happy for him."

Known throughout baseball for "playing the game the right way," Trammell was voted into the Hall of Fame by the Modern Baseball Era Committee on December 10. But even as he learned of his election, Trammell had to maintain the classic self-discipline with which he played.

He received the good news while waiting to deplane from nearly the last row of a flight from San Diego to Orlando, where he would attend the Winter Meetings.

"I couldn't make a bunch of noise and start jumping around at the back of a plane," Trammell said. "That might have bothered some people."

But without a doubt, he got off that plane with a big beaming grin on his face. Never mind his gray hair or that by the time he's inducted, he will be sixty years old. There's an eternally impish look to Alan Trammell, as if sixty is the new twenty.

As much as being efficient and reliable, Trammell was known for the quiet constraint with which he played. He was not a showman, but as with Al Kaline—another Hall of Fame Tiger known for his class—Trammell always seemed to do everything instinctively well.

The numbers bear that out. He was a .285 lifetime hitter, slugged 412 doubles, stole 236 bases, and had nearly as many walks (850) as he did strikeouts (874). He also was the MVP of the 1984 World Series, batting .450 with two home runs and six RBI in the Tigers' five-game victory over the San Diego Padres.

Some of his skills came to him naturally. He was a talented student athlete who would have attended UCLA had he not signed with the Tigers as a second-round draft choice in 1976. Other skills were honed through dedication and the physical development that eventually allowed him to become a productive hitter "instead of looking," Trammell remembered, "like someone trying to hit with a wet newspaper, as Sparky used to say."

Sparky, of course, was Hall of Fame manager Sparky Anderson, whom so many Tigers held in high regard.

"Plain and simple, he was my mentor," Trammell said. "He wouldn't coddle us. He would teach us. You never made the same mistake twice when you played for Sparky—not if you listened to him. But what he said was always with the intent to make you better. This great honor (election to the Hall of Fame) doesn't ever happen if I hadn't played for him."

Even with that, Trammell wasn't convinced it was going to happen.

"I was kind of thinking I'd always be among those who would come close," he said, "and, sincerely, I was going to be OK with that. I still would have been happy and smiling. That's just me.

"But we can turn that page now. My gosh, what a thrill this is."

The biggest concern about Trammell as a ballplayer was the possibility that he might not have the strength to complement his fielding ability with enough offense at the big league level. He'd been downright scrawny in his early years with the Tigers. But while growing up in San Diego—where he'd often walk a mile or two to see the Padres playing in their MLB infancy—Trammell used his slender build to his advantage.

"We'd sneak in to watch the Padres play," he admitted. "My buddies and I knew three different ways of doing it. We never got caught. Being skinny came in handy. I could get through a lot of gates that weren't completely closed.

"If anyone had told me then that I'd spend some time in the big leagues being a cleanup hitter, I would have called them crazy."

As the years went on, though, it wasn't crazy to think that Trammell might someday be elected to the Hall of Fame. The path would lead him through thickets of vote totals that didn't always signify progress.

But Trammell never wavered in playing the game with joy—while treating it with respect.

Then one day, his phone rang—and he learned just how much he meant to the game that meant so much to him.

Cooperstown was calling.

Tom Gage is a former Tigers beat writer for the Detroit News *and the winner of the 2015 BBWAA Career Excellence Award. This essay originally appeared in* Memories & Dreams, *Issue 1, 2018.*

Boston Beckoned, Cooperstown Called

Pedro Martínez's journey to greatness featured tenacity, tough times, and a terrific arm

By Dan Shaughnessy

Pedro Martínez's path to Cooperstown began in a small house with a tin roof and a dirt floor about ten miles from the Dominican Republic's capital city. Along the way, Martínez threw rocks instead of baseballs and taught himself the language of his adoptive country.

Now, his eighteen-year journey in the big leagues, which featured some of the most dominant seasons ever recorded, has brought him to the sport's most revered destination.

"It's a great honor to be part of history," Martínez said upon his election to the Baseball Hall of Fame. "I've never forgotten that I lived in a shack…that I came from a poor community, a poor family. It's one single celebration right now."

The fifth of six children, Martínez grew up in Manoguayabo, on the outskirts of Santo Domingo. He signed with the Dodgers in 1988, when he was still sixteen, and studied English while in the Dodgers system. He made his big league debut with Los Angeles in 1992 and, five years later, won his first Cy Young Award with the Expos.

Martínez pitched for the Dodgers, Expos, Red Sox, Mets, and Phillies during his career, but it was his seven-year stint in Boston that put him in Cooperstown. Pitching for the Sox from 1998 to 2004, Martinez went 117-37 with a 2.52 ERA and 1,683 strikeouts over 1,383.2 innings. It was a stretch of dominance not seen since Sandy Koufax ruled the National League in the first half of the 1960s.

Martínez's 1999 Cy Young season saw him finish 23-4 with a 2.07 ERA, 313 strikeouts, and only 37 walks. A year later, he reduced his ERA to 1.74 to claim his third Cy Young Award in four seasons.

"Most pitchers had one or two dominant pitches," said Terry Francona, who was manager of the Phillies when Martínez won his Cy Young Award with the Expos and Boston's skipper in Martínez's final season with the Red Sox. "Pedro had four. You couple that with his ability to compete, his photographic memory, and his killer instinct, and you have one great pitcher. You have Pedro. He was just electric."

When Martínez was traded to Boston prior to the 1998 season, the player and the city became a match made in hardball heaven. "The atmosphere completely told me that something special was going to happen," Martínez remembered.

Three games in 1999 cemented Martínez's legacy in Boston. That July, the All-Star Game returned to Fenway Park for the first time since 1961. Martínez, as the starter in his home ballpark, became the first pitcher in history to begin the Midsummer Classic by striking out the side. He fanned two more in the second inning and was named game MVP after the American League's 4-1 victory.

Two months later, Martínez pitched one of the greatest games in the history of Yankee Stadium, fanning 17 batters and walking none in a 3-1 Red Sox win. He surrendered a solo homer to Chili Davis in the second inning, but that was it. Martínez faced only 28 batters and struck out eight of the final nine Yankees.

The other defining moment for Martínez that season came in October, when—while battling a sore shoulder—he came out of the bullpen to pitch six hitless innings in a 12-8 victory at Cleveland in the deciding game of the American League Division Series.

"Nobody really knew whether he was going to pitch that day or not," said Sox catcher Jason Varitek. "Once he got out there, there was no stopping him. He gave us everything he had."

The Red Sox and Martínez eventually suffered heartbreak in 1999 (and then again in 2003) at the hands of the Yankees, but

2004 proved to be Boston's year. The 2004 Red Sox staged the greatest comeback in baseball history, beating the Yankees in a seven-game ALCS after trailing three-games-to-none. The Sox then swept the Cardinals in the World Series, giving Boston its first championship in eighty-six years. Those Sox won three of Martínez's four postseason starts, including Game 3 of the World Series, when he pitched seven shutout innings. It was his final appearance in a Red Sox uniform.

"I hope everybody enjoyed it as much as I did," Martínez recalled. "Even with all the struggles up and down during the season, I enjoyed every moment of the season. I enjoyed my career in Boston."

Dan Shaughnessy has covered the Red Sox for the Boston Globe *since 1981 and was the 2016 recipient of the BBWAA Career Excellence Award. This essay originally appeared in* Memories & Dreams, *Issue 1, 2015.*

The Wiz Kid
Ozzie Smith followed his dreams to become one of baseball's best players and ambassadors
By Hal Bodley

Dreaming.

Ozzie Smith shut his eyes one day when he was twelve years old and could see a yellow brick road winding from his home in the tough Watts section of Los Angeles through hills and valleys to the fields of Major League Baseball. And somewhere over the rainbow, after thousands of bouncing balls, backflips, and base hits, he followed that road to become one of the game's greatest players, a true Hall of Famer.

Osborne Earl Smith, i.e., The Wizard: Yes, Ozzie's road to Cooperstown is the stuff of dreams.

There were thirteen consecutive Gold Gloves built around his acrobatic fielding, fifteen All-Star Games, a long list of fielding records, even 2,460 hits and 580 stolen bases, and, ultimately, the 2002 election to the Hall of Fame in his first year of eligibility.

"I never played the game to make the Hall of Fame," Smith said. "I played the game because I enjoyed it. But I wanted to play well enough to be considered for the Hall of Fame. The rest is icing on the cake."

No one in Cooperstown on that mostly cloudy July afternoon in 2002 will forget his moving, emotional, acceptance homily, one that left the large gathering spellbound. He compared his incredible career, his unbelievable journey, to the movie classic *The Wizard of Oz*. The roadmap of his trip was like "Dorothy's journey down the yellow brick road, with three delightful companions—the scarecrow, the tin man, and the cowardly lion."

Swallowing hard, he offered: "The core of my journey to the Hall of Fame was a dream that took shape in my heart one day while sitting as a child on the front steps of our home. That was the day I started dreaming about becoming a professional baseball player."

His first glove was a paper bag. He used to lie on the floor of his house, close his eyes, and toss a baseball and then catch it without looking at it—over and over.

"I remember I was exhausted from playing yet another game… I instead let the dream come into the playground of my mind," Smith recalled of his childhood wish to play big league baseball. "I embraced it. I embellished it to the point that I would select the position I would play."

Softly, beneath his waning words that day in Cooperstown when he said his route to the game's pinnacle was so like Dorothy's, Judy Garland's recording of "Over the Rainbow" began playing as tears turned to applause.

Ozzie Smith is sixty-three now. His hair is cropped short, and there are hints of gray around the edges, but there's no mistaking the contagious smile and the warmth he has always conveyed with his words. His numbers and achievements will withstand the test of time, and though they may define him, there's much more to this unique human being. "Giving back is the ultimate talent in life," Smith professed. "That is the greatest trophy on my mantel. I want to be proud of the place where I live. You hear so much negative about communities and so forth. I tell people if you want your community to be better, you have to get your hands dirty. You have to get involved. I'm not going to change the world, change every life that's bad, but if I can touch one or two people and make a difference in their lives, it's all worth it."

He reached deep inside as he added, "Ozzie Smith was a boy who decided to look within, a boy who discovered that absolutely nothing is good enough if it can be made better, a boy who discovered an old-fashioned formula that would take him beyond that rainbow—beyond even his wildest dreams."

Not so coincidentally, several years ago he played the role of the Wizard in the St. Louis Municipal Opera's production of *The Wizard of Oz*.

Smith is on the Hall of Fame's board of directors and serves as the Museum's Education Ambassador. Each year since 2002, he's been hosting PLAY Ball with Ozzie Smith on the Friday of Induction Weekend. The event has helped raise more than $250,000 (including nearly $40,000 this year) for the Museum's educational outreach programs and the Ozzie Smith Diversity Scholarships, presented annually to members of the Frank and Peggy Steele Internship Program for Youth Leadership Development.

"What we try to do is keep fans engaged and give them the opportunity to spend time with their favorite players and raise money for the education fund," Smith said.

No sooner had Smith returned to St. Louis after this year's Induction Weekend than he was knee-deep in helping promote the hundredth anniversary of the PGA Championship, held in early August at Bellerive Country Club.

Smith is president of the Gateway PGA Foundation and was instrumental in bringing the PGA Championship back to the storied club for the first time since 1992. He couldn't have been more pleased with how the weekend played out. Brooks Koepka held off a sizzling charge by Tiger Woods to become just the fifth player to win the US Open and PGA Championship in the same year. Every corner of the prestigious Bellerive course vibrated with roars as Woods, who couldn't even swing a club eleven months ago, shot a 64 that Sunday, his lowest final round ever in a major tournament.

Smith, who has let golf replace his competitive juices since baseball, is also president of the Gateway PGA Outreach Program.

"It is wonderful to see the city of St. Louis, which has been a major part of my heart for so long, connect with golf in such a significant way to bring hope to many who would otherwise not have that opportunity," he said. "We use golf as the hook, introducing kids to the game and the business of golf. But the most important thing is getting kids a good education. We feel the longer we can keep them in the classroom, hopefully the better citizens we will be able to produce."

Ozzie explains the hours he spends giving back now are an extension of the commitment it took to succeed on the field.

> As professional athletes, we talk about having the courage, the perseverance, the dedication it takes to be the very best at what we do. For me, it is and was a natural thing. What I did, I did every day. Anyone can make a great play every now and then. But what I did, I did every day. I might not have driven in a hundred runs each year, but I prevented a hundred runs from scoring against us.

Smith's magical glove redefined the position of shortstop. But despite his gifted hands, people kept telling the five-foot-eleven, 150 pounder that he was too small. He struggled to get noticed.

Eddie Murray, a classmate at Locke High School in Los Angeles, was signed by the Orioles and was soon on his way to a Hall of Fame career. Smith was overlooked, and so he enrolled at Cal Poly San Luis Obispo on a partial academic scholarship. He was then taken in the seventh round of the 1976 MLB Draft by the Tigers but opted to return to school.

After graduating in 1977, he was drafted by the Padres in the fourth round and received a five-thousand-dollar bonus. He spent four seasons in San Diego from 1978 to 1981 before being traded to the Cardinals in a deal that centered around Ozzie in exchange for Garry Templeton. In St. Louis, he blossomed and helped the Cards reach the World Series three times.

Whitey Herzog, himself a Hall of Famer, was the St. Louis manager and general manager at the time, and he coveted Smith.

"In December [after the 1981 season], Whitey actually got on a plane and came to San Diego to more or less recruit me," Smith said. "That was a breath of fresh air for me because the Padres weren't interested in resigning me. They were looking for a much better offensive shortstop, which they got in Templeton. When Whitey talked to me, it meant there was somebody who believed in me. He gave me the vote of confidence I needed."

Herzog's take: "It was the 26th of December, and I met with [Ozzie] and his agent out there. Before I took the red-eye back, I told him I'd love to have him come to St. Louis. I said, 'If you do decide to come, I'll sign you to a one-year contract. If you don't like me or St. Louis at the end of the year, I'll give you your release. If you do like St. Louis and you do like the Cardinals, and you want to play for me, I'll sign you to a long-term contract.' "

Herzog said Smith promised "to let me know in a couple of weeks. On January 10, he and his wife came to St. Louis. It was about 17 below zero. They were wearing long fur coats, and I thought, 'He's never coming to St. Louis and leaving San Diego, where it's 72 degrees every night when they play the national anthem.' "

Soon after, however, Smith called Herzog and said he was coming.

"That was probably the greatest thing that happened to the Cardinals during my time there," Herzog said recently. "He was the guy I needed."

Smith lived up to expectations, winning his third straight Gold Glove Award in his first year in St. Louis.

"We were much better at throwing and catching the ball and running the bases than a lot of the teams," Smith said. "Knowing that, we just did our thing."

The Cardinals opened 1982 with a 14-3 victory over Houston. They then lost three in a row, including an 11-7 thrashing by Pittsburgh.

"I remember the ride home after that game," Smith said. "We just decided as a team we would play the way we were capable of playing. And that's what we did."

The next day, the Cards edged the Pirates 7-6, the beginning of a twelve-game winning streak. The team's remarkable consistency became apparent: St. Louis wouldn't lose more than four straight games the rest of the season. The Cardinals won their first National League pennant in fourteen years—with the switch-hitting Smith batting .556 in a sweep of Atlanta in the NLCS—and then beat Milwaukee for their first World Series crown in fifteen seasons.

"He made more diving plays than I've ever seen," Herzog said. "I don't see how it was possible to play shortstop any better than Ozzie played it. He was the glue of our team. How important was it? We wouldn't have won any of it if we hadn't gotten him."

While his glove was never an issue—he took the defensive aspect of shortstop to another level—his hitting steadily improved in St. Louis. In 1985, Smith increased his batting average to .276 while helping the Cardinals to their second NL pennant in four years.

His bat was never bigger than in that year's NLCS against the Dodgers. With the series tied at two games apiece and Game Five tied, 2-2, in the bottom of the ninth inning, Smith faced righty Tom Niedenfuer at old Busch Stadium. He launched his first career homer batting left-handed in 3,009 at-bats to win the game.

"That was the crowning moment for me offensively," Smith said. "It wasn't until that ball actually cleared the right field fence that people started looking at me for more than defense."

Smith would hit .435—smashing a double and a triple among his 10 hits—in the Cardinals' six-game victory to earn the MVP Award. However, they were beaten in a dramatic seven-game World Series by the Kansas City Royals.

His third and final World Series appearance came in 1987 against the Minnesota Twins (the Cards lost in seven games) after what was arguably his best offensive season. Smith finished second to the Chicago Cubs' Andre Dawson in the NL MVP voting. Smith finished with 43 stolen bases and boasted career bests in batting average (.303), hits (182) and runs scored (104). He also drove in 75 runs, numbers that earned him a runner-up finish to the Cubs' Andre Dawson in NL MVP voting.

"If you couldn't play for Whitey, you probably shouldn't be playing," Smith said. "He only had two rules—be on time and give 100 percent. I loved playing for him because he allowed me to do my job. That's all I wanted."

Smith announced his retirement on June 19, 1996, effective at season's end. In July of that summer, he was chosen for his fifteenth All-Star Game, where he received a standing ovation from the 62,000-plus in the stands at Philadelphia's Veterans Stadium. The Cardinals retired Ozzie's uniform No. 1 on September 28, and he chose that occasion to perform his trademark backflip for one of the last times.

Philosophy?

"When you're playing, you want to be considered the best at what you do. I went about doing that, setting myself apart from the rest of the crowd. I didn't want to be one of many, which you certainly are if you're in the norm. But the guys who make the Hall of Fame are one of a few."

Now it's golf—and more golf.

"I try to play every day that ends in a 'y,'" he joked. "For all of us (retired baseball players), once we get away from the game, we still have that competitive nature. That void you have is something you're in search of filling. Golf fills that for most of us, and that's why we gravitate to it. Golf utilizes the skills we had when we played baseball—hand and eye coordination, timing. They're all incorporated in the game of golf. For me, it's one of the most fascinating endeavors I've taken up. Just when you think you've got it figured out, it jumps up and bites you. I can be in a good groove, and all of a sudden, it's as if I've never played before. When I see a guy win a tournament, I have a lot of respect for him because I know he's played well four straight days."

Smith, who carries a six-handicap, plays much of his golf at The Country Club of St. Albans, a suburb of St. Louis where he has a home.

"I also am a frequent player at Boone Valley Golf Club, which is in nearby Augusta," he said. "One of the perks of being the PGA president, I get to play all over. And, luckily, I'm invited to play in many charity events around the country."

He's the father of three children: sons Nikko and Dustin, and daughter Taryn.

And it was Smith who applauded Nikko, a popular singer and songwriter, when he cracked the top ten finalists of the 2005 edition of *American Idol*.

Now the road is a lush green fairway, dogleg to the left, bunker by a velvety green. And you can hear it: Fore up there! Here comes Ozzie Smith!

Hal Bodley, dean of American baseball writers, is correspondent emeritus for MLB.com. He has been covering Major League Baseball since 1958 and was USA Today *baseball editor/ columnist for twenty-five years before retiring in 2007. This essay originally appeared in* Memories & Dreams, *Issue 5, 2018.*

Born Into Baseball, Halled Into History

Ken Griffey Jr.'s date with Cooperstown always seemed a foregone conclusion

By Larry Stone

In a game with virtually no guarantees, Ken Griffey Jr. came as close as anyone could to being an active Hall of Fame player.

"If you could build a perfect player, it would be Ken Griffey Jr." said Rusty Kuntz, a Mariners coach in Griffey's rookie year of 1989.

Kuntz now jokes: "I could have said that the first time I saw him play in a Spring Training game."

On January 6, Griffey's accomplishments became immortalized with election to the National Baseball Hall of Fame as the leading vote-getter in history. Griffey received a stunning 99.3 percent of the votes, getting named on all but three of the 440 ballots submitted by members of the Baseball Writers' Association of America.

He'll join Mike Piazza as the Class of 2016, inducted July 24 in Cooperstown. It's a fitting coronation for a player who stands sixth on the all-time home run list with 630, was the youngest member of the All-Century Team named in 1999, won ten Gold Glove Awards and seven Silver Slugger Awards, and was voted as an All-Star starter thirteen times (five times as the majors' leading vote-getter).

Ken Griffey Jr., elected to the Hall of Fame in 2016, grew up in the game as the son of Cincinnati Reds outfielder Ken Griffey.

Describing himself as "humbled and honored" by this honor, Griffey became the first No. 1 overall draft pick to gain election—fulfilling the promise that everyone saw.

If ever a person was born to play baseball, it was George Kenneth Griffey Jr. Indeed, his very birthdate (November 21) and birthplace (Donora, Pennsylvania), both of which he shares with Hall of Famer Stan Musial, presaged his eminence.

His dad, Ken Griffey Sr., was a member of one of the most celebrated teams in history, Cincinnati's "Big Red Machine." Young Ken and his younger brother, Craig, would roam the clubhouse with Petey Rose, Eduardo Perez, Pedro Borbon Jr., and other sons, mentored by some of the greatest players in history and lovingly cared for by the white-haired manager, Hall of Famer Sparky Anderson.

"Baseball raised him," Ken Griffey Sr. said. "All Sparky said was, 'If we win, the kids could come in the clubhouse.' And we won a lot."

It's no wonder that Griffey was imbued with a ballplayer's sensibilities to go along with his natural talent. At the outset of his career, when a reporter noted that he was in his first Spring Training, Griffey corrected him: "This is my eleventh—ten with my dad, and one with the Mariners."

The promise began to become reality at Moeller High School in Cincinnati when Mariners area scout Tom Mooney, who recalls Griffey as "a man among boys," recommended him for the top overall draft spot. It could be seen in Griffey's first batting practice session at the Seattle Kingdome after the draft, where he wowed Mariners veterans like Alvin Davis.

"A few of us were questioning how good a seventeen-year-old kid could really be," Davis recalled. "He shows up, and he's the real deal. The legend kind of built from there."

Griffey doubled off Dave Stewart in his first major-league at-bat in Oakland in 1989 and homered off Eric King on the first pitch he saw at the Kingdome. He hit a two-run homer

to win a game in his first pinch-hitting appearance in May. All
of these feats were interspersed with a series of breathtaking
catches that drew the national spotlight to Seattle, a place it had
rarely landed.

The Griffey legend grew exponentially in 1990, when on
August 31, he and his father became the first father-son duo to
play together in MLB history. They hit back-to-back singles in
their first joint game, then upped the ante two weeks later with
back-to-back first-inning homers off the Angels' Kirk McCaskill.
Griffey still calls that the greatest thrill of his career.

But from early on, virtually everyone who assessed Griffey's
talent cited his five-tool ability, which was undeniable.

"There is nothing he couldn't do on the baseball field," added
Griffey's long-time Mariners' manager, Lou Piniella.

But it was his sixth tool—maybe call it charisma, or electricity,
or joie de vivre—that truly made Griffey stand out. The filmmaker
Ken Burns called it "joyous abandon," and it drew fans to him
like a magnet. The Griffey signature, of course, was his backward
hat. Early on, some baseball hardliners complained that Griffey
was disrespecting the game, but the real story is much more
endearing. As a youngster, young Ken would borrow his dad's
Reds cap, which was so big it would fall over his eyes. In order to
be able to see when he'd shag balls or play catch on the field, he
turned the hat around.

Griffey requested a trade to Cincinnati in 1999 in order to be
closer to his family, but not before helping to make baseball so
popular in Seattle that the team's threat of moving out of town
in the mid-1990s instead resulted in funding for Safeco Field.
Former team president Chuck Armstrong always referred to the
facility, which ensured the Mariners stayed in Seattle, as "The
House That Griffey Built."

After a two-month stint with the White Sox in 2008, Griffey
returned to Seattle in 2009 before retiring in June of 2010. Many
believe the toll of playing on the unforgiving artificial turf at the

Kingdome for more than a decade contributed to the injuries that marred the second half of Griffey's career. But by then, Griffey had already earned his Hall of Fame plaque.

"His mind worked at a different level," said Griffey's longtime Mariners teammate and close friend, Jay Buhner. "The rest of us, every now and then, we'd get locked in. He seemed to play his whole career at that level."

Larry Stone has been a sportswriter for more than thirty years and is currently a columnist for the Seattle Times. *This essay originally appeared in* Memories & Dreams, *Issue 1, 2016.*

The First Face of Baseball
Christy Mathewson changed the way the public perceived ballplayers
By Larry Brunt

In the early spring of 2015, after Derek Jeter retired, MLB.com ran a social media campaign to anoint the new "Face of Baseball." It's a relatively new concept that has been applied to players from Nomar Garciaparra to Mike Trout, one that was assigned retroactively to Jackie Robinson and Babe Ruth, among others.

But if there ever was a first "Face of Baseball," it was Christy Mathewson.

At the start of the twentieth century, baseball was considered an undignified game played by ruffians for the pleasure of gamblers. In fact, many players did come from tough backgrounds, swinging out of coal mines and pitching out of farmlands to eke out a living on the diamond. Few had college educations. Even fewer were seen as virtuous. Mothers– Mathewson's included–did not want their sons to grow up to be baseball players.

Christy Mathewson changed all that.

The son of a farmer, Mathewson attended Bucknell University on scholarship for three years—where he was an 'A' student, class president, a member of literary societies, and a star on the football and baseball teams.

When "Matty" began his major league career with the New York Giants in 1900, he had it worked into his contract that he wouldn't pitch on Sundays (a promise he'd made to his mother, and one he always kept), and he carried a Bible on the road. He was known for his honesty and integrity (with one umpire saying he knew he got a call right if Mathewson confirmed it). And he was bright, excelling at bridge and checkers. He was known to play multiple games at a time, sometimes blindfolded, and once beat a national champion.

Then there was his physical presence. At six-foot-one and 195 pounds, with a strong jaw, slightly dimpled chin, and kind blue eyes, he made an immediate impression.

"The sight of him was something," teammate Larry Doyle recalled. "My heart stopped for a moment. Just looking at him, he affected you that way. He looked so big and sure and, well, sort of good—like he meant well toward the whole world."

Fellow teammate John Meyers added, "He had the sweetest, most gentle nature. Gentle in every way."

For a game needing a role model, Mathewson was manna from heaven. And for as wholesome as he may have been in real life, newspapers further embellished his reputation. They said he never swore, drank, or bet (even though he fleeced many teammates at cards). Sportswriter Grantland Rice said he "handed the game a certain touch of class, an indefinable lift in culture, brains, and personality."

Another wrote that he "talks like a Harvard graduate, looks like an actor, acts like a businessman, and impresses you as an all-around gentleman."

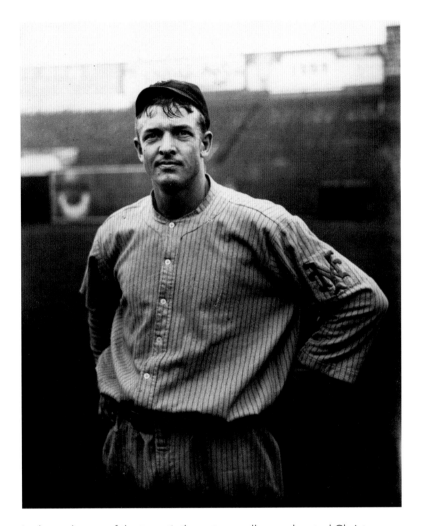

In the early part of the twentieth century, college-educated Christy Mathewson became the face of baseball shortly after reaching stardom with the New York Giants.

The irony to the mythmaking and publicity is that Mathewson was a very private person. Celebrity held no real importance to him. He would draw the curtain when his train pulled into a station, and Doyle said he "hated" how everyone rushed to him with their questions, though he added, "He was always courteous."

But Mathewson had the gift of being able to accept what he couldn't control, and he recognized he was the face of baseball. So even though he didn't like having his photograph taken, he posed for the cameras. And he smiled. Most photographs of that age show ball players with stern or unexpressive faces. Longer exposures required a still face, and it's easier to hold no expression at all than a smile. But Matty smiled.

One is struck by that smile, almost always the same: mouth closed, lips pulled back, smile lines between his nose and the ends of his lips. The right side of his mouth goes up just a little higher than the left. He squares up to the camera and looks directly into the lens. It's a smile brimming with confidence, but not arrogance; one that welcomes, assures, puts one at ease.

Charles Conlon, photographer of many classic images of baseball from the first half of the twentieth century, took his very first baseball portrait of Mathewson, and over the years, Matty became Conlan's favorite subject as well as a friend. He recalled that one day, he saw Mathewson from across the field. It was after practice on a hot day, and Mathewson was sweaty and tired. But he knew Matty wouldn't say no. The resulting image—with his smile maybe not quite as pronounced as usual—stands as one of the most iconic portraits in baseball history.

In January 1909, Mathewson's younger brother, Nicholas, after completing his first semester of college (and possibly having been diagnosed with tuberculosis), went into the family barn and shot himself. Christy, who was home visiting his family, found the body. Mathewson never spoke of it to any reporter, nor of another brother, Henry, who died of tuberculosis at thirty.

These tragedies, for Mathewson, were private. For the public, he smiled.

He won the 1905 World Series almost single-handedly: three complete game shutouts, giving up 13 hits and one walk in 27 innings, with 18 strikeouts. But Mathewson's Giants lost the World Series in 1911, 1912, and 1913. Still, no one blamed him (he went 2-5 in those Series, despite a 1.33 ERA); in fact, his sportsmanship was lauded.

One editorial read, "In victory he was admirable, but in defeat he was magnificent." Mathewson himself said, "You can learn little from victory. You can learn everything from defeat." The losses ate at the highly competitive Mathewson, but he smiled.

Across fourteen seasons from 1901 to 1914, only once did Mathewson record fewer than 20 wins; and four times he won at least 30 games. But in 1915, he struggled with his worst ERA in a full season and dropped 14 of 22 decisions. The next year, in mid-season, struggling again and the Giants below .500, he was traded to the Cincinnati Reds. He had spent sixteen years with the Giants, and though he was part of the negotiations and understood he would get a chance to manage the Reds, the trade must have been bittersweet.

"Why, it's alright," he reasoned. "It's a step upward, you know."

On his first day in Cincinnati, Mathewson dressed in his new uniform, went out onto the field…and smiled for the photographers.

In 1918, although Mathewson was thirty-eight years old and exempt from military service, he enlisted anyway. He caught the devastating 1918 influenza on the ship to Europe and had to be hospitalized for ten days. Then he served in the Chemical Warfare Service in the US Army, teaching soldiers how to put on gas masks in dangerous trials. Ty Cobb, who served with him, said an accident once exposed Mathewson to nearly lethal amounts of chemicals, damaging his lungs. In fact, when the armistice came, Mathewson was in the hospital again.

When he returned home, he still fought a painful cough. He also found out the Reds no longer had a job for him. But when asked to pose for a photograph, he squared up, closed his mouth, and pulled his right lip up just slightly more than the left, looking directly into the lens.

Mathewson took a job coaching with the Giants, but the cough didn't go away, and soon his side began to ache. In early July 1920, he was diagnosed with tuberculosis and was sent to a nationally renowned tuberculosis sanitarium at Saranac Lake, NY. The physicians who examined him said both lungs were infected and he might have six weeks to live. He was given absolute bed rest.

Months passed before he was allowed to sit up, and months more before he could stand. In early 1922, he was permitted to go outside and visit a local baseball game, where he threw out a ceremonial pitch. The press wanted updates.

"I try to keep cheerful, keep my mind busy, try not to worry, and I don't kick on decisions," he reported, "either by a doctor or an umpire."

Reporters wanted photos. Mathewson was very reluctant. Just the same, he'd stand in front of his residence and pose, with his lung deflated as part of his treatment, in considerable pain, leaning on a cane.

The healthier he became, the more anxious he was to return to baseball. Though his doctors considered his recovery nearly miraculous, they strongly advised against his return to the stressful life of baseball. Nevertheless, in 1923, he became part of a syndicate that bought the Boston Braves. He built a home in Saranac Lake. He continued to cough.

Down in Florida for Spring Training in 1925, he caught a cold that worsened quickly. He returned to Saranac. He fought for several more months, his body getting weaker and his pain getting worse, until he knew the time had come. He told his wife that it was over.

"Go into the other room and have a good cry," he told her. "But don't make it a long one. This can't be helped."

He died later that week, on October 7, 1925.

Earlier, while recovering at Saranac Lake, he had played catch with some boys. A reporter asked if he had any advice for them.

He stopped his throwing and said they should play baseball and learn from it.

Then he ended with six words that sum up his philosophy of life: "Be humble and gentle and kind."

Larry Brunt was the National Baseball Hall of Fame and Museum's Digital Strategy Intern in the Class of 2016 Frank and Peggy Steele Internship Program for Youth Leadership Development. This essay originally appeared in Memories & Dreams, *Issue 6, 2016.*

Paige in History
In 1971, Satchel Paige came to Cooperstown, opening the door for more legends
By Scott Pitoniak

Leroy "Satchel" Paige often preached about not looking back, "because something might be gaining on you." But as the legendary pitcher, showman, and civil rights activist approached the podium on the library steps outside the Baseball Hall of Fame the morning of August 9, 1971, he had no choice but to violate one of his most popular commandments.

For seven minutes, the Hall's first Negro Leagues inductee looked back, with humor and poignancy, on a four-decade baseball odyssey that had seen him barnstorm to every nook and cranny of the United States—and beyond. That Paige had finally arrived at a destination he never thought would open its doors to him totally blew his mind.

The man who had struck out Jim Crow and laid the foundation for Jackie Robinson to integrate a sport and a nation soaked in the applause of the 2,500 mostly white spectators who congregated in Cooperstown on that historic day. But, while basking in the limelight, the tall, slender sixty-five-year-old couldn't help but feel conflicted. Voices dueled inside Paige's head.

"Should he be grateful that the lords of hardball were finally acknowledging that blackball had brilliant players, or should he resent them—and all of America—for making him pitch his best ball in the shadows?" author Larry Tye explained in his award-winning biography *Satchel Paige: The Life and Times of an American Legend*. "Was what counted that he was the first vintage Negro Leaguer to be voted into this most exclusive club and the (first) pitcher ever to make it with a losing record in the (white) Majors? Or was it that the Hall had tried to banish him to a separate and unequal wing?"

Though Paige had every right to be bitter, he opted to express gratitude rather than regret when he arrived at the podium and was shown the bronze plaque that would hang near the ones immortalizing Babe Ruth, Walter Johnson, Bob Feller, Dizzy Dean, and Robinson.

"Since I've been here, I've heard myself called some very nice names," he began, grinning broadly beneath horn-rimmed glasses. "And I can remember when some of the men (enshrined in the Hall) called me some bad, bad names when I used to pitch against them."

Paige evoked more laughter when he talked about how former Cleveland Indians owner Bill Veeck had been lambasted for signing him to a contract in 1948 at the advanced age of forty-two. "They told him to 'get anyone but Paige—he's too old,' " Satchel said, pointing to his former boss in the crowd. "Well, Mr. Veeck, I got you off the hook today."

Paige mentioned how he once pitched 165 days in a row, and jokingly explained why he took his sweet time walking to the mound. "I never rushed myself," he deadpanned, "because I knew they couldn't start the game until I got out there."

His speech was interrupted by laughter thirteen times, but it was much more than a comedic monologue. There were touching moments, too, like when he spoke candidly about how he wished he—not Robinson—had been the one to break baseball's color barrier. But he added that, upon further reflection, he realized Jackie had been the right man for that enormous challenge.

Paige concluded by saying he "was the proudest man on the earth today," prompting a standing ovation. Ted Page, a former teammate, was among those springing to their feet.

"I cried a little, but I came away from that ceremony a lot taller," Paige told the *New Pittsburgh Courier*, a newspaper with a predominantly Black readership. "When Satch stood up to be inducted, he was standing up for all of us who had played the game during the days when we knew we were good but weren't recognized for being that way. His acceptance was vindication that we were as good as any man. I'm only happy that I was alive to see it."

Paige's unrivaled pitching and showmanship, particularly in interracial exhibition games against white aces like Dizzy Dean and Bob Feller, had paved the way for baseball integration. His induction into the Hall a half century ago would blaze trails, too. It opened the shrine's doors for Josh Gibson, Oscar Charleston, Cool Papa Bell, and other Negro Leagues legends whom history had forgotten. In the ten years following Paige's immortal moment, nine more of his Black contemporaries were enshrined. And in 2006, a special committee righted a bunch more wrongs, electing seventeen Black baseball pioneers, including the first female inductee, former Negro Leagues owner Effa Manley.

Writers from African-American newspapers had long lobbied for Paige's inclusion, but the campaign in the mainstream white media didn't really start until 1952, when *Sport* magazine's Ed Fitzgerald publicly championed the cause. But it took another decade before the movement gained steam. According to Donald Spivey's biography, *If You Were Only White*, a "Hall of Fame for Paige Committee" was formed in Connecticut in 1961, with founder John Henry Norton collecting letters of support.

Not surprisingly, Veeck became an ardent supporter, telling reporters: "If Paige had been brought up to the majors in his prime, today's Cy Young Award would be known as the Satchel Paige Award." Feller, who had waged mound duels with Paige in front of overflowing crowds, also jumped on board, calling Satchel's exclusion from the Hall "patently unfair."

The greatest impetus, though, would come from Ted Williams during his 1966 Hall of Fame induction speech. His unexpected comments pushing for the enshrinement of Paige, Gibson, and other Negro Leaguers prompted organized baseball to take action. Five years later, a special ten-man committee was formed to recommend which Black pioneers should be inducted. That Paige would be the unanimous first choice was not surprising, given his crossover popularity and achievements. In addition to his barnstorming tours, he had helped Cleveland win a pennant and World Series title, and he was the first Black pitcher ever to start a game in the white big leagues and pitch in a Fall Classic. By tossing three scoreless innings in a 1965 game for the Kansas City Athletics at age fifty-nine, Paige made good on another one of his adages: "Age is a matter of mind over matter. If you don't mind, it don't matter."

His pithy sayings and humorous names for his array of pitches (including "Bat Dodger," "Bee Ball," and "Hesitation Ball") contributed to the larger-than-life persona he had created, but the slapstick occasionally muddied the argument that he was the greatest pitcher of all time.

Though records are sketchy, the best information available suggests Paige had an overall Negro Leagues record of 146-64 with 1,620 strikeouts and just 316 bases on balls, and an American League record of 28-31, with a 3.29 earned-run average and 33 saves. Paige argued those stats significantly shortchanged him. He claimed he pitched in more than 2,500 games, winning roughly 2,000 of them, with 55 no-hitters and somewhere between 250 to 330 shutouts.

Numerous Hall of Famers vouched for his greatness. Dean said his fastball looked like a change-up compared "to that little pistol bullet Satchel shoots up to the plate." Joe DiMaggio said Paige was the best and fastest pitcher he faced. Slugger Hack Wilson claimed Satchel made baseballs look as small as marbles to batters struggling to see and hit them.

The announcement of Paige's unanimous election at a packed press conference in Manhattan on February 9, 1971, was supposed to be a crowning moment for him and for baseball. But the festivities took a sour turn when it was revealed his plaque would hang in a different room than previous inductees. Though Paige publicly accepted this "separate but unequal" decision–"I'm proud to be wherever they put me"–the media did not.

"The notion of Jim Crow in Baseball's Heaven is appalling," columnist Jim Murray wrote in the *Los Angeles Times*. "What is this–1840? Either let him in the front of the Hall–or move the damn thing to Mississippi."

Jackie Robinson suggested Paige boycott the induction.

Privately, Satchel seethed, telling friends, "The only change is that baseball has turned Paige from a second-class citizen to a second-class immortal."

On July 8, saner heads prevailed and MLB Commissioner Bowie Kuhn and Hall President Paul Kerr announced Paige's plaque would hang in the main hall. "I guess they finally found out I was really worthy," Paige told reporters. "I appreciate it to the highest."

Since then, thirty-four Negro Leagues legends have earned a plaque at the Hall of Fame.

Following his induction, he spoke frankly with reporters on a variety of topics, including his candidacy to become MLB's first Black manager. "I could manage easy–I've been in baseball forty years," he said. "And I would want to manage." But he also offered a reason why it wouldn't happen. "I don't think the white is ready to listen to the colored yet," he said. "That's why they're afraid to get a Black manager. They're afraid everybody won't take orders from him. You know there are plenty of qualified guys around."

Among them was Frank Robinson, who would topple that racial barrier four years later when he was hired to manage the Indians. Paige's comments had set the wheels in motion.

It was all part of his remarkable, trailblazing journey—a journey that saw him bust open some doors in Cooperstown fifty summers ago, clearing a path for Black pioneers to finally feel at home in the home of baseball.

Author and nationally recognized sports columnist Scott Pitoniak has written more than twenty-five books, including his most recent work, Remembrances of Swings Past: A Lifetime of Baseball Stories. *This essay originally appeared in* Memories & Dreams, *Issue 1, 2021.*

Chapter 4

The African-American Baseball Experience

Homers Defeat Hate

Hank Aaron overcame bigotry in his pursuit of Babe Ruth's record

By Terence Moore

Somewhere, tucked away in his southwest Atlanta home, Hank Aaron has memories that most folks would rather forget.

Those memories are letters.

Hateful ones.

"I saved quite a few of them," Aaron said recently, referring to the dreadful mail that dominated his life nearly five decades ago as much as the balls he routinely ripped over fences in Major League Baseball ballparks along the way to catching and passing Babe Ruth.

At one point during the 1973 season, with Aaron sprinting toward Ruth's record for career home runs (which he would break the following year), the US Postal Service announced he was receiving more daily mail than anybody in the country not named President Richard Nixon.

Aaron also was receiving something else.

Death threats.

Not only that, but some of those letters claimed they were written by kidnappers with designs on Aaron's children.

"When I think back to those years, yes, I'm disgusted by the things that happened to me that had nothing to do with playing the game of baseball," Aaron said, pausing to search for the right words.

Here was Aaron's problem for the moment: No matter how much you try, it's difficult to find the definitive thing to say when you're a naturally gentle soul who became a target of racists during much of the early 1970s as a Black man moving toward solidifying your stature among baseball's all-time elite with one of the greatest achievements in sports history.

After Aaron thought more about those times when his world featured armed bodyguards as much as pitchers and shortstops, he said: "Oh, many times I feared for my life—many, many times. I thought the safest place for me would be on the baseball field. Anywhere else, I didn't think I had a chance.

"I thought I was doomed, you know. But when I got in the batter's box, I never thought about anything but baseball. The good Lord took care of me in that regard. If it hadn't been for Him, I don't know what I would have done.

"Outside of myself, when it comes to going after a record, nobody else had to go through those kinds of things."

Nobody, indeed, and it began with this: To many, Ruth was the Great White Hope who made "714" not only magical but eternal in their minds. That was his final home run total, and it remained a baseball record from the moment he retired in 1935 with the Boston Braves—after his legendary stretch with the New York Yankees—through just before Aaron sent No. 715 over the wall in left-center field of Atlanta-Fulton County Stadium on April 8, 1974.

There was "The Chase" for Aaron before that. It involved nearly two years of seclusion in hotel rooms during road trips with his Atlanta Braves, handling those death threats and dealing with those letters.

Tons of them.

"I thought at that time, out of all the things I was doing, that I was only playing the little game of baseball, trying to make people enjoy the whole (experience) while I was out there," Aaron said. "Then I looked around and saw people were getting so irritated and aggravated, only because it was a Black man who was chasing a white man's record that he had for a long time."

Legendary slugger Hank Aaron endured racial bigotry and threats on his life as he chased Babe Ruth's career home run record in 1974.

Even so, Aaron spent his years before The Chase in the shadows, partly due to playing for average Braves teams in Atlanta after the franchise moved from Milwaukee before the 1966 season.

While in Wisconsin, well, that was a different story. Aaron began his major league career in 1954, with fellow Baseball Hall of Fame teammates Eddie Mathews and Warren Spahn, and they joined Aaron in taking the Braves to consecutive National League pennants in 1957 and 1958, including a world championship over the Yankees after the first one.

Aaron provided one of the most memorable of his 755 homers on September 23, 1957, at Milwaukee County Stadium, where he clinched a World Series trip for the Braves and NL Most Valuable Player honors with his walk-off shot against the St. Louis Cardinals.

The Atlanta years followed, and so did Aaron's home run milestones. Quietly, though.

Much of the baseball nation kept its focus during the summer of 1968 on things such as Bob Gibson's pitching for the Cardinals, Carl Yastrzemski chasing a batting title for the Boston Red Sox, or Mickey Mantle's last season with the Yankees, period. As a result, few noticed on July 14 when Aaron became the second-youngest player ever to rip his 500th career homer.

Speaking of Mantle, Aaron eased past The Mick with homer No. 537 on July 31, 1969, and two years later, Aaron got slightly more notoriety as only the third player at the time with 600 homers on his résumé.

Then came baseball's 1972 strike season, when Aaron surged past Willie Mays on the all-time homer list to have only one guy ahead of him—*that* guy.

Even though Aaron somehow swung his thirty-nine-year-old arms well enough to end 1973 with 40 homers for the season and 713 for his career, one shy of Ruth's record, that was the worst of the twenty-three major league seasons for the Braves' outfielder-turned-target for bigots everywhere.

"I had run-ins with racist people all the time.… The only thing I thought about when I left that dugout was baseball," Aaron said. "I've often tried to imagine over the years about how many home runs I would have hit if I didn't have all of those other things happening, but I was able to concentrate on what I needed to do at the plate and on the field."

Aaron had to leave the ballpark, though.

During those times, Black teammates Dusty Baker and Ralph Garr operated as Aaron's unofficial secret service men, because as Aaron put it, "They were young kids that I was really fond of, and they didn't fully understand what was going on, but any chance they got, they were right there with me."

Baker was in the on-deck circle at Atlanta-Fulton County Stadium when Aaron walked by on his way to the plate and said on that rainy night in Georgia that he was about to knock No. 715 into history. Aaron did just that against Al Downing of the Los Angeles Dodgers.

The Chase was over, but the hate mail continued.

Aaron still has the proof.

Terence Moore was a sportswriter for nearly twenty-five years with the Atlanta Journal-Constitution *and is the author of the book* The Real Hank Aaron: An Intimate Look at the Life and Legacy of the Home Run King. *This essay originally appeared in* Memories & Dreams, *Issue 6, 2020.*

Paper Trail

African-American publications provide much of the known record of the Negro Leagues

By Scott Pitoniak

While growing up in Florida in the 1910s and '20s, Buck O'Neil couldn't wait for Monday afternoons.

That's when the bundle of newspapers would arrive in the mail, and he and his friends would congregate to read about their baseball heroes in historically Black publications that included the *Chicago Defender*, *Pittsburgh Courier,* and *New York Amsterdam News*.

"My father subscribed to those weekly papers, mostly so I could learn about the Negro baseball teams," O'Neil wrote in his 1996 autobiography, *I Was Right On Time*. "When the mail arrived on Monday, all the kids were at my house, reading about Dick Lundy, who was from Jacksonville and was a great shortstop with the Bacharach Giants of Atlantic City. Or the legendary John Henry Lloyd, another fantastic shortstop from Palatka, Florida."

Those stories of local African Americans making good jumped off the pages. They provided O'Neil and his friends with role models and gave them hope during times when things seemed hopeless for Blacks, especially in the Jim Crow South.

"We'd read about these guys until we wore the paper out," O'Neil recalled. "Then, we'd go out and make believe we were Pop Lloyd and Dick Lundy until it got too dark to see the ball."

In that era, long before television, the internet, or even widespread radio availability, newspapers were the dominant disseminator of news and information, and baseball was the undisputed king of sports. The Black press played an integral role not only in boosting the collective spirits of Black Americans, but also in writing the rough drafts of Negro Leagues baseball history.

The Black newspapers and Black baseball franchises came to benefit from a symbiotic relationship that grew more complex over time, particularly in the 1930s and 1940s, when pioneering Black baseball writers Wendell Smith and Sam Lacy led the charge toward integration both on and off the diamond.

"The Negro Leagues would not have existed without the Black press—it's as simple as that," says Leslie Heaphy, a Kent State University history professor and one of the nation's foremost experts on Black baseball. "The leagues benefitted enormously from the publicity generated during a time when the mainstream white press ignored virtually anything of consequence to African Americans. And there's no doubt that the papers benefitted, too. Their coverage of Negro League baseball, which was a huge source of pride to their readers, sold newspapers."

Larry Lester, one of the driving forces behind the building of the Negro Leagues Baseball Museum in Kansas City, said the Black press' coverage of the Negro Leagues provided one of the few avenues of information available to Black readers.

"The Black press was the voice of the voiceless," Lester said. "It was essential in getting out the message of Black achievement, Black accomplishment. Its coverage of the Negro Leagues, in particular, had a huge impact on the collective psyche of the Black community. And the Black baseball writers, in addition to pushing for integration, played a big part in the creation of heroes and role models, and reminding us that we weren't inferior because of the color of our skin."

Lester cited columns and editorials putting Black stars on equal footing with white stars.

"The Black newspapers ran editorials saying, 'Hey, Spot Poles is just as great as Ty Cobb,' or 'Josh Gibson is just as great as Babe Ruth,' " said Lester, an accomplished author whose work with the National Baseball Hall of Fame and Museum's "Out of the Shadows" project unearthed huge amounts of data about the Negro Leagues. "Those comparisons to the white superstars had meaning to Black readers." Interestingly, white baseball writers would never compare white major leaguers to Negro Leaguers. In the 1930s and '40s, no one in the mainstream press was writing that Babe Ruth was the white Josh Gibson. Not surprisingly, white and Black writers covered exhibition games between white and Black teams differently.

"If Babe Ruth went 0-for-3, the white papers might write that Babe had to be under the weather or that the white players didn't care as much about the outcome as the Black players did," Lester says. "Meanwhile, the Black writers might celebrate just how good the pitcher who fanned the Babe three times was. It's interesting from a historian's perspective to read the contrasting points of view."

Negro League baseball was one of the most successful minority-run businesses of the 1920s, '30s, and '40s. And that success resulted in several of the owners being written about in the same glowing terms as star players like Gibson, Satchel Paige, and Cool Papa Bell.

"They became role models, too," said Ryan Whirty, a highly respected Negro League historian based in New Orleans. "People in the African-American community looked at National Negro League founder Rube Foster with great regard. His Chicago American Giants were a shining example of how a Black entrepreneur could succeed if he or she had the vision, determination, and savvy."

Slim newspaper budgets and once-a-week publication schedules left many Negro League games unstaffed, resulting in incomplete and inaccurate statistics. But the fuzzy numbers did not prevent the Black press from giving teams exposure extending far beyond their hometowns. Papers like the *Courier*, *Defender*, and *Amsterdam News* developed national circulations among Black readers.

"With a conglomeration of hyperbole, tongue-in-cheek humor, and endless similes, sportswriters such as Fay Young, Wendell Smith, Ric Roberts, and A.D. Williams made the Negro Leaguers heroes across the nation," author Janet Bruce wrote in her 1985 book *The Kansas City Monarchs: Champions of Black Baseball*.

Coverage, though, went beyond mythmaking and hero-worship. Injustices were regularly reported—and attacked in scathing commentaries.

"The writers would not hold back if they felt white major league owners were either denying Negro League teams use of their ballparks or trying to take advantage of them by taking an unfair percentage of the gate and concessions," Whirty said. "Business inequity was a huge topic. It was well-covered."

So too was the push for integration. As far back as the late 1860s, when the all-Black Philadelphia Pythians were denied entry into the National Association of Base Ball Players, there were stories in the Black press about the need for integration. Columns and editorials advocating the abolishment of baseball segregation would run intermittently in the ensuing years and decades, but the big push wouldn't come until the 1940s, and it would be led by Smith and Lacy.

"There were others who contributed to the charge, but, to me, Smith and Lacy were the godfathers of Black sportswriters," Lester said. "They were an essential part of the great experiment called Jackie Robinson."

They helped prove that the pen can be as mighty as the bat.

"Without their tireless crusading, Jackie doesn't break the color barrier in 1947, and integration in the game and in society winds up getting pushed back for years," Whirty said. "They were relentless and they were fearless and they were courageous. In addition to being shoulders for Jackie to cry on, they were out front and proactive, writing about how Jackie's story far transcended the sports pages."

Their historical impact did not go forgotten. In 1993, Smith became the first Black writer to receive the J.G. Taylor Spink Award from the Baseball Writers' Association of America (now known as the Career Excellence Award). Four years later, Lacy would join him in Cooperstown in the Museum's *Scribes and Mikemen* exhibit, which honors every Spink Award winner.

The advocacy journalism of Smith, Lacy, and other Black writers would ultimately lead to the demise of the Negro Leagues. Robinson's shattering of the color barrier with the Brooklyn Dodgers opened the doors for Black baseball stars to join the heretofore segregated major leagues. The loss of those outstanding ballplayers, coupled with scaled-back coverage by the Black press, proved to be a death knell for the Negro Leagues.

"Instead of devoting the lion's share of their coverage to Negro League stars, Smith and Lacy were traveling with Jackie, even in 1946 when he was in the minors (with the Montreal Royals)," Heaphy says. "This trend would continue when other Black stars, like Roy Campanella, Willie Mays, Hank Aaron, and Ernie Banks, joined the majors. They became the stories that readers of the historically Black press wanted to read about."

Negro Leagues owners found themselves in an impossible spot. They realized they couldn't argue against the integration that ultimately would put them out of business.

"Owners like Effa Manley tried to bargain with the Black press," Heaphy said. "She correctly pointed out that not every Negro Leaguer was going to make the white major leagues. In fact, only a small percentage of them would. So, she pled with Black sportswriters to keep covering the Negro Leagues, to not turn their backs on them. But they were in business to sell papers, and so they turned their attention to the Black players in the major leagues."

Over time, many of the historically African-American newspapers would fold, too. But their impact, like the impact of the Negro Leagues, continues to be felt long after they ceased publication.

"Those stories provided us with a treasure trove," Lester said. "So much of the history of Black baseball is based on those newspapers' accounts, and it becomes even more essential as more and more of the people who played in the Negro Leagues die off."

Adds Heaphy, "Those newspaper accounts are the primary foundation on which Negro League history is based."

Author and nationally recognized sports columnist Scott Pitoniak has written more than twenty-five books, including his most recent work, Remembrances of Swings Past: A Lifetime of Baseball Stories. *This essay originally appeared in* Memories & Dreams, *Issue 3, 2018.*

A Road To Equality

African-American barnstormers, led by Hall of Famer Satchel Paige, left a remarkable legacy

By Larry Tye

He was the nation's ringer, a barnstorming industry unto himself who learned to pitch not by the week but by the hour.

But while Leroy "Satchel" Paige was the best, he was hardly alone. For three generations of Black baseball players, barnstorming was more of a full-time job than a part-time tour.

They called the freewheeling freelance baseball they played across America barnstorming, to distinguish it from formal league games. Major Leaguers and Negro Leaguers both did it, but for the former, it was restricted to the postseason, whereas Black players squeezed in exhibitions year-round. The contests were set up by players, owners, or independent promoters, most of whom were white. Touring teams played each other or a local club. Admission was $0.75, and five hundred spectators was a decent turnout.

Players earned as much as $150 a day or as little as $15. Barnstormers dubbed themselves "All-Stars," although typically only two or three qualified. A more accurate description was Hungry Ball, since ballplayers needed the extra income to carry them through the year. Barnstorming brought baseball's icons to sleepy towns with no stoplights but lots of barns, and it gave hamlet heroes at least the fantasy that they might someday be discovered. In the East, games were fit in between the end of the World Series and the onset of winter; in the Midwest, they were scheduled around the harvest; in California, Florida, and the Caribbean, they continued until spring.

Black players had been barnstorming since the 1880s, generally in the no-budget, rag-tag fashion that characterized the rest of their play—but sometimes in style. Bud Fowler's All-American Black Tourists rented their own railroad car, and each game was kicked off with a parade led by players decked out in swallow-tail coats and opera hats and brandishing silk umbrellas. The American Giants entertained guests at Palm Beach's Royal Poinciana Hotel.

More typical, Giants infielder Jack Marshall said, were monotonous road trips where he ate sardines out of a Bell Fruit jar and was told by a shopkeeper he could not buy milk because it was white. Babe Ruth barnstormed, as did Dizzy Dean, Josh Gibson, Bob Feller, Cool Papa Bell, and other future Hall of Famers, white and Black, with that wayfaring way of playing continuing into the early 1960s.

No player barnstormed as wide or far, or for as long, as Paige. It suited his disposition: He was eager to follow the sun and money wherever they took him. Barnstorming let him live each day as it came, and days as a vagabond ballplayer offered boundless adventure and variety. He generated more offers than anyone, picking up as much as five hundred dollars for as few as three innings. Promoters knew he could fill the stands as well as mow down batters, so they booked him despite knowing he might not show. All of which makes feasible his fantastic claim to have pitched for as many as 250 teams over the course of his career.

His time on the road let him taste America at its least rehearsed. He sat on the porch and sang into the evening with a Black family that gave him a bed and meal in Dayton, Ohio, and ate ham and pumpkin pie with white ones in Iowa farm country. He thawed his hands over a fire next to the dugout in chilly Des Moines, rubbed his distended ankles after an all-night drive to Minnesota, and learned to spot a pool shark anywhere by the chalk in his breast pocket. In Harlem, he relished the Renaissance. In New Orleans, he savored the swing. He was what he called a travelin' man, logging 30,000 miles a year and visiting "every state in the United States except Maine and Boston." Among African Americans, only the Pullman porter saw more of America. To Satchel, that freedom and movement were more delicious than the sweetest chocolate.

That does not mean barnstorming was easy. As rough as conditions were in the Negro Leagues, that looked like luxury next to Satchel's early years on the road. He was away from home and family for months at a time. Driving all night and playing all day became his life. He learned to eat out of paper sacks and sleep three times a week. When he and his teammates could find and afford a hotel, it might be five to a bed, and "sometimes the whole club'd be in one room." He got to be an accomplished cat napper.

Bunny Downs, who drove the bus for a team Satchel barnstormed with, got a front-seat view of the strains and stresses: "Shucking corn, hoeing potatoes, picking cotton, ain't no tougher than this business. No, sir. For a real, hard-working business, day in and day out, you gotta take this here whatchacallit, tourist baseball."

A nationwide network of Negroes opened their homes to Satchel and other itinerant ballplayers. No need to post vacancy signs; word spread quietly, much as it had for runaway slaves in the days of the Underground Railroad. As for food, "we had to go in the colored neighborhood if we wanted anything hot at all," said Satchel. "If there was no colored in the town or no colored restaurant, then we went to the grocery store again for baloney sausage."

The more roadblocks they encountered, the more the gypsy ballplayers improvised. Having a lighter-skinned teammate like Wilmer Fields, the Homestead Grays pitcher, presented one such opportunity. Fields could order take-out or even rent a hotel room, with darker-hued teammates climbing through the window afterwards. Yet the ruse sometimes backfired, the way it did when Fields was in a whites-only café ordering sandwiches for a busload of Grays parked just out of sight. A darker-skinned teammate came in, intending to tease the pitcher. The restaurant owner was not amused, yelling at Fields, "Get the hell outta here."

During much of his career, Satchel Paige traveled thousands of miles each year as the star and main attraction for numerous Negro Leagues teams that barnstormed across America.

Spending so much time dueling with second-rate white teams and dodging the minefields of Jim Crow made Satchel and his teammates pros at using charm and humor to deflect tension. Batters hit one-handed or on their knees. Satchel took his warm-up throws sitting down, with his catcher stationed behind the plate in a rocking chair. Best of all was a riff called shadow ball. The hitter swung so hard, the fielders reacted so convincingly, and the runner tore down the line so fast that fans could hardly tell that it was pantomime. It was baseball so brilliant it could be played without the ball.

Black players knew it was best not to win by too many runs if they wanted to be invited back the next year. Oftentimes they did not record the score, which would have embarrassed the locals. They tried not to let racial animosities eat away at their humanity. Their stage might be shabby, but their performance remained regal. In the early 1930s, Satchel was hired to pitch for a Black high school team in San Diego that was challenging its white rival. Partway through the contest, he felt sorry enough for the white kids who were swinging without coming close that he let two of them get on base. Then he bore back down, striking out the San Diego players the way he always did when a game's outcome was in doubt.

Did clowning and cutting corners undermine their dignity? That was a touchy subject for Black ballplayers. While their tolerances varied on many topics, there was a consensus when it came to "Tomming:" It was taboo. Okay to put on a great display of baseball for white fans; okay, too, to make them laugh between pitches or innings. But not to behave like that old slave in Harriet Beecher Stowe's 1852 novel *Uncle Tom's Cabin*, who forever after symbolized subservience. So they calibrated their performances to ensure that the kidding never got in the way of their playing. They would do a lot to support their wives and kids, which was not easy for Black men in that era, but never to the point of compromising their manhood. When opposing players got cocky, the Black barnstormers challenged them to a wager, then showed how dominating they could be with cash on the line. In rare cases where the crowd turned nasty, said Satchel's Kansas City Monarchs teammate Connie Johnson, he and his teammates would "run twenty, twenty-five runs on 'em, so they'd leave the park whispering."

Ironically, it was the very integration of the sport that Johnson and Paige had dreamed of and battled for that ended up killing not just the Negro Leagues, but much of the barnstorming that defined that era. Why pay to see Black players in pick-up games on makeshift fields when you could see them at Ebbets Field or Municipal Stadium, or on television? What was the appeal of watching Black and white teams face off on a cold fall afternoon when they were doing it every night throughout the long regular season?

Obscured, too, would be the story of the epic and challenging world of Blackball—and all but its biggest legends. The National Baseball Hall of Fame and Museum is committed to preserving this history through its collections and its exhibit, *Ideals and Injustices: A Chronicle of Black Baseball*.

Larry Tye, a former reporter at the Boston Globe, *is the author of the Casey Award winning biography,* Satchel: The Life and Times of an American Legend. *This essay originally appeared in* Memories & Dreams, *Issue 2, 2010.*

Jackie's Rookie Season
In 1947, Jack Roosevelt Robinson became the first winner of the BBWAA's Rookie of the Year Award—and accomplished so much more
By Claire Smith

Alfred Surratt would never tell where, along the way, he was dubbed "Slick." It was a Kansas City Monarchs thing, a Negro Leagues thing, a baseball thing.

Brothers to the core, the men of the Monarchs kept one another's confidences, watched one another's backs, mourned teammates' losses and failed dreams, and cheered on their brothers'—and sisters'—achievements.

Never were the cheers louder, said Slick Surratt, then on April 11, 1947, the day Branch Rickey and the Brooklyn Dodgers signed Jackie Robinson, a one-time Monarch, to a major league contract.

Like so many Negro Leagues players who lived in the Kansas City area, Surratt was an auto assembly plant worker. The reserve outfielder, who passed away in 2010, was on the job on that historic date and, recalling the moment as if it were yesterday, said that the boisterous, instantaneous celebration spread through the plant as if on the assembly line.

The rest of the world had V-E Day; African Americans who'd dreamed of living long enough to see segregation eradicated now had a second Independence Day.

The joy within the black baseball community was palpable. The destruction of segregation within Major League Baseball was at hand. Four days later, on April 15, 1947, Jackie Robinson would debut with the Dodgers, his first step onto Ebbets Field in Brooklyn tromping out the National Pastime's odious color barrier forever.

As we all now know, it wasn't just signing on to be a baseball player. Those opposed to integration would push back, virulently, viciously, unrelentingly. Robinson, a former Army officer and one of the greatest athletes to come out of UCLA, was about to meet his greatest opponent: Jim Crow. And he would be asked to do so pretty much on his own: one Black man against a nation in which large swaths were steeped in segregationist policies.

Raised in California, Robinson and his bride would be asked to step into hostile territory where racism was not only codified by gentlemen's agreements but mandated by law. The ugly cultural divide they were about to experience were not only enforced by men wearing badges, but by night riders hidden beneath hoods and wearing sheets.

The Dodgers and Robinson, daring to change in 1947 what legislatures, Congress, and presidents had failed to do before—or after—the Civil War, knew both the risks and the responsibilities. Yet the man who carried the hopes of so many Slick Surratts, Hank Aarons, and Willie Mayses never shirked. Incredibly, Jackie not only authored one of the most impressive inaugural seasons the game had ever seen, he also gave lessons in heroism each and every day he stepped onto a major league field.

For the record, the first time Robinson stepped onto such a field, on that April 15 in 1947, the twenty-eight-year-old debuted against the Boston Braves before more than 25,000 fans at Ebbets Field. He played first base and went 0-for-3 at the plate. One hundred and fifty games later, Robinson had authored the first chapter of what was destined to be a Hall of Fame career.

Likely no other player ever traveled quite so treacherous a path to the Hall as did Robinson. In an article printed in the *New York Times* on May 10, 1947, it was revealed that Robinson had received "threatening letters of anonymous origin" from the day he'd broken into the big leagues that spring.

Said the un-bylined report: "This disclosure followed on the heels of a report that a strike of opposing players against the

Negro player had been spiked. Harassment of Robinson, the first of his race to make the major league grade in modern baseball history, by unidentified persons was confirmed in Philadelphia last night by Branch Rickey, president of the Brooklyn Baseball Club. 'At least two letters of a nature that I felt called for investigation were received by Robinson,' Rickey said. Robinson himself admitted receiving several such letters.… A high police official here disclosed that a letter warning Robinson to 'get out of baseball' had been turned over to the police department by the baseball club for investigation."

The article went on to describe a short-lived attempt by St. Louis Cardinals players to engineer a strike in protest against Robinson's playing that was put down by Cardinals team president Sam Breadon. The indignities heaped on Robinson by others in baseball uniforms included spikes-high slides and head-high knockdown pitches. Racist epithets were the rule of the day. What historians came to understand was that Robinson would not, could not, lash out, because he, too, had made a gentleman's agreement, with Rickey.

In his words, in an audio recording archived by National Public Radio, Robinson said: "I remember Mr. Rickey saying to me that I couldn't fight back, and I wondered whether or not I was going to be able to do this."

Nowhere was his resolve to honor his agreement with Rickey tested more than in Robinson's first games played against the Phillies in late April at Ebbets Field. The Phillies, led by manager Ben Chapman, infamously rained an unending torrent of racist slurs on Robinson, taunting the infielder about his physical features, telling him to go back to the cotton fields, and calling him the "N" word. The onslaught was so relentless and debilitating that Robinson later said it pushed him closer to breaking than any other humiliation suffered that season.

"For one wild and rage-crazed minute, I thought, 'To hell with Mr. Rickey's noble experiment,' " Robinson once recalled.

"He was physically and verbally abused, particularly when he was on the road, in certain cities," said Rachel Robinson, Jackie's wife, in an interview with *Scholastic* in 1998. "The taunts angered him, sometimes frightened him, but he turned away from them."

Said Robinson's teammate, center fielder Duke Snider: "He knew he had to do well. He knew that the future of blacks in baseball depended on it. The pressure was enormous, overwhelming, and unbearable at times. I don't know how he held up. I know I never could have."

Author Jonathan Eig wrote of Robinson's brutal season in his book *Opening Day*. In a 2016 interview with NPR reporter Hansi Lo Wang, Eig said the incidents with Chapman brought into focus what Robinson was being made to endure.

"It was so offensive that, for a lot of Americans, it was a wake-up call," Eig told Wang. "It made people, white people in particular, realize for the first time just what burden Robinson was shouldering."

As sportswriter Jimmy Cannon wrote: "Jackie Robinson is the loneliest man I have ever seen in sports."

Chapman would later try to explain away his actions by saying that he was bench-jockeying, and, in an effort to say he wasn't being racist, he described how he also hurled ethnic slurs at Italian-American players such as Joe DiMaggio and Jewish players like Hank Greenberg. Chapman told writer Allen Barra he was doing no less with Robinson, looking for a way to rattle a rookie.

"I can imagine the possibility that both things were true," Eig said of Chapman in an interview with the *New York Times*, "that he was deeply racist and he thought that by attacking a black guy with this racist language, he might make him snap, lose his composure, get the player to take the bait, get him thrown out for half a season, or get him to quit."

Robinson, though stung, did not crumble. "He knew this wasn't just symbolism," Eig told *The Times*. "He knew if he could integrate Major League Baseball, it would affect lots of people's lives. And he knew if he lashed out, he might lose the opportunity."

What Chapman could not envision was that his action eventually won Robinson sympathetic—and vocal—allies. As Eig wrote in *Opening Day*, in the second game of the initial Phillies-Dodgers series, the Dodgers' Eddie Stanky, a veteran infielder and native Philadelphian, called out Chapman and the Phillies, deeming them cowards for railing against a man who could not fight back.

"It was the first time a lot of white people and white reporters in particular noticed the abuse Robinson was taking," Eig told *The Times*, adding, "I interviewed a fan who had been a teenager who went to one of those games, heard the heckling, and was shocked."

By the time the Dodgers visited Philadelphia in May, Chapman, prodded by baseball, asked to have his picture taken with Robinson. The Dodger rookie would not shake his hand, so the two men grasped opposite ends of a baseball bat as photographers snapped away.

Off the field, many municipalities remained stubbornly unwelcoming. Even after Chapman's attempted truce, the Dodgers were not allowed to register at their chosen hotel in Philadelphia until other accommodations were made for Robinson. Sadly, this was nothing Robinson and the Dodgers had not experienced before.

Save for the Spring Trainings spent with the Dodgers in the Caribbean rather than segregated Florida and a minor league season spent in a welcoming Montreal, Robinson felt the hot breath of haters at every step, even as he broke the color barriers one ballpark, one town, one city at a time—with "Colored only/White only" signs on segregated water fountains and public bathrooms throughout the South, and meals delivered through restaurants' back doors and eaten in solitude on the back of buses.

"He faced it in Spring Training, in every town in Florida that he visited. He faced it in Pittsburgh and St. Louis and Cincinnati," Eig told NPR's Wang. "I doubt that he would've singled out Philadelphia as the worst place in the world."

Larry Doby, who became the first Black player to join the American League when he signed with the Cleveland Indians during the 1947 season, was often asked by youngsters of later generations why he and others, including Robinson, hadn't just refused to leave balking hotels, movie theatres, and restaurants.

"Because we didn't want to die," Doby told one such inquisitor during a seminar at Williams College in Massachusetts.

Yes, 1947 was that scary—and important. That Robinson not only survived but thrived during that grand experiment showed America that meritocracies had value. And his success inspired the architects of the Civil Rights movement of the 1960s.

Dr. Martin Luther King told Don Newcombe, Robinson's Dodger teammate and yet another star from the Negro Leagues, "You'll never know how easy you and Jackie [Robinson] and [Larry] Doby and Campy [Roy Campanella] made it for me to do my job by what you did on the baseball field."

Thus, more than seventy years after 1947, we still marvel at a rookie who—by any measure—refused to fail: Robinson, buffeted by societal ills, but steeled by the challenge of changing a nation, hit .297 in 151 games that season. He stole 29 bases, more than anyone else in the National League, scored 125 runs, and, with fellow future Hall of Famers Pee Wee Reese and Snider, helped Brooklyn win a National League pennant for only the second time since 1920. It would be the first of six league championships won by a Brooklyn team that featured a player Dr. King called "one of the truly great men of our nation."

For his efforts, as well as for the example he set, Robinson received the first-ever Rookie of the Year Award from the

Baseball Writers' Association of America, an award that now bears his name. In the words of Yogi Berra, some might say that Jackie Robinson made that award necessary.

Claire Smith, the winner of the 2017 BBWAA Career Excellence Award, is now on the faculty of Klein College of Media and Communication at Temple University, serving as the codirector of the newly created Claire Smith Center for Sports Media. This essay originally appeared in Memories & Dreams, *Issue 6, 2019.*

No Challenge Too Great
Hall of Famer Roy Campanella's strength in the face of racism and injury served as inspiration
By Neil Lanctot

Half-breed!

It was a term Roy Campanella often heard as a boy walking the streets of his Nicetown neighborhood in North Philadelphia in the 1930s. At times, the taunt goaded him into fistfights— where the chubby yet powerfully built youngster usually succeeded in silencing his loudmouthed tormentor, at least temporarily. But fighting did not answer the question that increasingly gnawed at him. If he was, as the kids teased, a "half-breed," why was that such a bad thing? One day, he finally mustered up the courage to ask his mother.

"Yes, your daddy's white and I'm colored, and it's nothing to be ashamed of," Ida Campanella explained. "You're just as good as anybody else, and don't you ever forget it."

Campanella never forgot his mother's words. If his biracial background made others uncomfortable, so be it. As he grew older, he never hid his joint Italian and African-American heritage and often boasted of his parents' long and happy marriage. But the difficulties he encountered as a mixed-race child in a less tolerant Depression-era America permanently soured him on the desirability of interracial relationships.

"Not a very good idea," he once told a reporter. "Too many problems."

The "problems" Campanella faced were innumerable. The racial arithmetic of his time dictated that one Black parent made Roy "colored" and subject to the cruel realities of Jim Crow, which were depressingly prevalent even in a northern city like Philadelphia. As a youngster, Campanella was openly barred from local boys' clubs, swimming pools, and even certain movie theaters.

Although some might look back bitterly on such degradation, Campanella never dwelled on the racism he faced as a youth. "Grin and bear it" was his philosophy.

"It is practically impossible," a reporter once remarked, "to get him to admit that any phase of his life was especially difficult or unpleasant."

Baseball allowed Campanella to escape the realities of his second-class citizenship. From an early age, he not only fell in love with the game, but proved to be almost freakishly gifted. At thirteen, he was already catching for the Nicetown Giants, a local Black sandlot team featuring boys several years his senior. Two years later, the semipro Bacharach Giants came calling, offering him twenty-five dollars to make a couple of upcoming weekend trips.

Just fifteen years old, Campanella was already a professional, but his stint with the Bacharach team would last less than two weeks. Plagued by injuries to their catching corps, the Washington Elite Giants of the Negro National League needed a backstop immediately. Their manager and regular catcher, future Hall of Famer Biz Mackey, had heard raves about Campanella and invited him to join the Elite Giants in June 1937.

Mackey was taking a considerable risk. Campanella was not only the youngest player in the league, but possibly the youngest player in Negro National League history.

Of course, Campanella, Mackey soon discovered, was different. The boy was obviously talented, but he also had the necessary personal makeup to handle whatever obstacles life threw at him.

Roy Campanella overcame prejudice and a tragic accident that left him a quadriplegic to serve as a role model for ball players on the field and a symbol of hope for the disabled.

Life in the Negro Leagues, as Campanella eventually learned, bore little resemblance to the major leagues. Brutal travel on a beat-up old bus was the norm, pay was pathetic in most years, and lodging in Southern locales was either segregated or nonexistent. On the field, he became accustomed to a steady diet of beanballs ("They'd fire at you like a duck," he once recalled), vicious collisions at home plate, and racial epithets hurled by fans at white venues. Still, he never once complained about the less-than-sterling conditions or the racism that had forced him into Black baseball in the first place. As a Black man with a ninth-grade education, he considered himself extremely fortunate to be making a decent living playing the game he loved so much.

After eight seasons of hard knocks in the Negro Leagues, Campanella knew he could play Major League Baseball, if only given the chance. The Pittsburgh Pirates had already toyed with the notion of offering him a tryout in 1942 before the team-backed owner, Bill Benswanger, backed out, an experience that left Campanella understandably cynical. When Branch Rickey approached him about joining the Brooklyn Dodgers organization in the fall of 1945, Campanella was dubious until the subsequent signing of Jackie Robinson confirmed that the offer was real.

The challenges ahead were considerable, far greater than those Campanella had faced as a fifteen-year-old trying to break into the Negro Leagues. In his two seasons in the minor leagues in 1946 and 1947, he had to contend with events such as dirt tossed in his face, a bigoted opposing manager who promised to run Campanella and Don Newcombe "out of the league in a week's time," and hostile players who peppered him with a nonstop volley of venomous racial insults.

"It was just as bad as [for] Robinson," recalled his teammate Butch Woyt. "He took all that 'N' stuff… It was hard to sit on the bench and hear the crap coming out of those guys."

Although some Black players in the early years of the "Great Experiment" proved unable to adapt to such an environment, Campanella's game continued to improve. In 1948, one year after Robinson's Brooklyn debut, the Dodgers promoted him to the majors and eventually made him their starting catcher. Not surprisingly, the transition was anything but smooth. He was beaned, perhaps intentionally, on his first major league pitch. Some Dodgers still openly recoiled at the presence of Black players.

But Campanella's determination to succeed never flagged. And with each season, his roly-poly build, lively personality, ready wit, and considerable personal charm won over almost everyone. What also won them over was his undeniable ability. In ten seasons with the Dodgers, he racked up three Most Valuable Player awards and nailed a phenomenal 51 percent of runners attempting to steal.

Perhaps most remarkable was his uncanny durability and resilience in the face of ongoing hand injuries, beanings, racial insults, and Jim Crow treatment during the Dodgers' excursions to Southern cities.

Campanella, one admiring sportswriter observed, seemed almost "indestructible." But on January 28, 1958, the sheer force of will he had summoned so many times finally failed him. Driving to his home in Glen Cove, New York, after a long day spent working at his liquor store and a nightclub, Campanella apparently fell asleep at the wheel. His rental car slammed into a telephone pole and turned over on its right side. The accident left him a quadriplegic, and he would never walk again.

The finality of the diagnosis hit Campanella hard in the years ahead. Baseball, the thing he loved most, had been taken from him.

"Why did it have to be me?" he asked a friend bitterly. "Why me?"

His already shaky marriage soon fell apart, and he even began drinking heavily. But somehow he pulled himself out of a profound depression. "I wanted to live more than I wanted to die," he later admitted.

His life was far from over. As one of America's first "celebrity" quadriplegics, Campanella became a symbol of what is now called the disabled or differently abled community, although rather less empowering terms were the norm in that era. And he embraced his position wholeheartedly, making frequent public appearances in a wheelchair and raising awareness

of the difficulties faced by the disabled. Campanella seldom
turned down a request, whether it was merely showing up at
the National Wheelchair Games or simply giving a pep talk to a
recently diagnosed quad.

Through it all, a smile never seemed to leave his lips, though
his "second" life as a quad was a never-ending ordeal. Each
morning began with a two-hour routine of being lifted out of
bed, bathed, shaved, and dressed by an attendant. Infections
and ulcers constantly posed threats, as did an America
then lacking even the most basic of accommodations for
wheelchair users.

But somehow Campanella, just as he had on the ballfield,
refused to give up. "He never, never complained," observed his
friend Raymond Ormand. "It was unbelievable."

In the thirty-five years he spent in a wheelchair, baseball was
never far from Campanella's mind, and he still believed he had
something to contribute. "The only thing affected by that crash
was my body, not my brain," he once remarked.

Eventually, he found his calling coaching the Dodgers' young
catchers at Vero Beach each Spring Training.

In the final years of his life, baseball seemed to be the only
thing keeping him going. Despite mounting health problems,
he somehow managed to attend most of the Dodgers' home
games and insisted on making the annual summer trek to
Cooperstown for the new crop of Hall of Fame inductees
following his own election in 1969.

In February 1993, he showed up at Dodgertown to work with
his latest protégé, a youngster named Mike Piazza, who had won
the starter's job after a sensational spring.

Campanella did not live to see Piazza achieve stardom. That
summer, he suffered a heart attack and was gone by the time
paramedics arrived. But his legacy, both as a ballplayer and as a
symbol of hope to the disabled, was more than assured.

"No one had more courage than Roy Campanella," former Dodgers owner Peter O'Malley said. "To me, he was the greatest Dodger of them all."

Neil Lanctot is a historian and author who has written extensively about race and baseball. This essay originally appeared in Memories & Dreams, *Issue 5, 2011.*

Color Between the Lines
On September 1, 1971, the Pirates put forth baseball's first all-Black lineup
By Claire Smith

Danny Murtaugh, the late, great Pittsburgh Pirates manager, once said that when it came to making out a lineup, "I'm colorblind, and my athletes know it."

If you know Murtaugh's story, then the American Optometric Association's definition of "colorblind" has to make you smile. For the AOA states in part that people who are totally color vision deficient due to a condition called achromatopsia can only see things as black and white.

Murtaugh famously did not see only black and white. He managed teams noted not only for their future Hall of Famers but also for their winning ways. He also successfully orchestrated teams that, unlike most any before or since, routinely resembled United Nations-worthy All-Star squads in their diversity.

Then, on September 1, 1971, Murtaugh managed his way into the history books. With one lineup and many strokes of a pen, Murtaugh did something no American or National League manager had before. He inked onto a lineup card a Pirates starting nine that consisted solely of players of color.

Murtaugh certainly had the diverse, as well as deep, roster needed to pull off that first in that night's game against the visiting Philadelphia Phillies, with thirteen Black American or

Hispanic players on it, according to the Society for American Baseball Research. Murtaugh also had enough Hall of Famers-in-waiting and perennial All-Stars to make color the least of any opponent's worries.

Anchoring that night's lineup were, of course, Roberto Clemente and Willie Stargell—two of the three future Hall of Famers Murtaugh managed on that Pirates squad. (Bill Mazeroski was the third.) Clemente and Stargell—the latter known as Pops—were in their usual positions that night, in right field and left field and batting third and cleanup, respectively.

Atop the lineup sat Rennie Stennett playing second. Fleet center fielder Gene Clines followed. After Clemente and Stargell came All-Star catcher Manny Sanguillén, destined to become later that fall the first Latin player to catch seven World Series games.

Dave Cash, a middle infielder, batted sixth. The kid out of Utica, New York (right up the road from Cooperstown), was in his first season as a regular, having taken over much of the play at second base from Mazeroski, the home run hero of the 1960 World Series. On this night, however, Cash played third, subbing for an ailing Richie Hebner.

Murtaugh also had pulled big Bob Robertson from the order, moving Al "Scoop" Oliver from the outfield to first base; Oliver batted seventh.

If there was any intrigue on that night, this was it. Robertson, a righty slugger, wielded one of the Pirates' biggest bats. Oliver, a lefty swinger, struggled against the Phillies starter, southpaw Woodie Fryman—yet Oliver was given the start. Eyebrows may have been raised, but no one wearing a Pirates uniform questioned the move, because no one questioned Murtaugh.

"When we looked him in the face, we could see he saw only Pirates," Sanguillén said. "He said he put his best nine players on the field every day. He was like that."

Rounding out the lineup were journeyman shortstop Jackie Hernández, batting eighth, and pitcher Dock Ellis, an undeniable and irrepressible ace, batting ninth.

Ellis was winding down a career-high nineteen-win regular season. His year's highlights featured an All-Star Game start for the National League and ended with a World Series championship after the Bucs defeated the Baltimore Orioles in the Fall Classic.

Ellis did not factor into the September 1 decision. The game was a rollicking affair favoring the hitters, and it reflected the Pirates' very good season—and the Phillies' very bad one—as Pittsburgh won, 10-7, in a crisp two hours and 44 minutes. All but two of the Pirates' position players had two hits each (Cash had one and Hernández did not have a hit). Clemente, Stargell, and Sanguillén each drove in two runs as the Pirates improved to 82-56.

Still, not the Pirates' win, their inexorable march toward the NL East title, nor Murtaugh's "first" drew much attention in the Steel City. The Pirates only attracted 11,278 fans to the mid-week game. The team, though wending its way to 97 victories and a magical postseason, existed in the shadows as Pittsburgh was in a news blackout due to a newspaper strike.

So it was left to the wire services and the Philadelphia papers to record history. *Philadelphia Daily News* reporter Bill Conlin wrote of Murtaugh's "all-soul" lineup but did not expand on it. The *Evening Bulletin* would publish an article headlined "Pirates Starters All Black." *United Press International* reported Murtaugh as saying: "They don't know it [his being 'colorblind'] because I told them. They know it because they're familiar with how I operate. The best men in our organization are the ones who are here. And the ones who are here all play, depending on when the circumstances present themselves."

We will never know if Murtaugh knew that the lineup would become one of the most famous in the game's history. The manager, who suffered health issues throughout that year, died in December, 1976, after suffering a stroke. The pride of Chester, Pennsylvania, was only fifty-nine at his passing.

To this day, Murtaugh's players know the significance of September 1, 1971, and celebrate it as if it just occurred yesterday. Just ask Sanguillén, the ebullient former catcher who still calls Pittsburgh home.

"I didn't have any idea until the second inning when Davey Cash said, 'Sangy, we're all black players out here!' " the soon-to-be seventy-seven-year-old Sanguillén said by telephone, laughing as he reveled in his memories. "I said, 'Praise the Lord!' I'd played my whole life hoping to see a day like that because I wanted to be appreciated for my hard work and not have people say 'no.' So that day was one of the best things that happened to me in baseball."

Did Murtaugh know that his lineup on that night represented both a glimpse of what was, and what would be, for baseball— the beneficiaries of Jackie Robinson's barrier breaking and the larger trends of diversity and opportunity?

Tectonic shifts were occurring not only in the game but in American society, and it was not always pretty. The fight for civil rights was being waged, and athletes often found themselves on the front lines. Clines and Cash had roomed with six other Black minor league players in a private home in Salem, Virginia, because segregation laws barred them from staying in the team hotel. Half a decade later, Clines stood on the field rewriting history.

Clines would tell the *Pittsburgh Tribune-Review* in 2011 that on that night, he heard a batboy say, "The Homestead Grays are playing tonight," referring to the famous Negro Leagues team based in Pittsburgh. He said he was thinking about the statement when it finally struck him while standing in the outfield. "Oh, wow," he thought.

For baseball, the ground was shifting in other significant ways. On the domestic front, the majors were in the midst of the Golden Age of Black baseball in 1971. The lineups Murtaugh penned throughout the '70s were chock full of products of Pittsburgh's good scouting.

Cash was a draft choice plucked from Utica, where he was a legendary high school basketball player. Oliver, an amateur free agent signing by the Pirates, hailed from Portsmouth, Ohio.

Then there were the California kids: Clines, Stargell, and Ellis, from San Pablo, Alameda, and Los Angeles respectively, also signed pro contracts with the Pirates. That trio's presence alone perfectly illustrated how the Pirates and other teams prospered in large part due to the contributions of the Golden State to that Golden Era.

Jackie Robinson, he of Los Angeles and UCLA, started it all after signing with the Brooklyn Dodgers and smashing baseball's segregation policy for good in 1947. In his wake came his California "descendants"—luminaries that included Stargell, Frank Robinson, Joe Morgan, Eddie Murray, Tony Gwynn, Vada Pinson, Dusty Baker, Bobby Bonds, Barry Bonds, Darryl Strawberry, and on and on and on…

That particular Golden Era is no more, as we now know. African-American representation on the field was less than 8 percent in 2020. The diversity gold rush is still on, however; it simply has moved south of the border. Again, the Pirates proved to have been ahead of the game as baseball turned to Latin America.

Clemente was the pride of Puerto Rico, a larger-than-life hero and the brightest star in that island's amazing crop of superstars who made up baseball's first wave of talent from Central and South America and the Caribbean. On that September night in 1971, he was joined on the field by Stennett and Sanguillén, both Panamanians, both from the city of Colon. Hernández? He was an émigré from the Central Tinguaro area of Cuba.

"Roberto was the most proud man in the whole world," Sanguillén said. "That day, he said he expected to see a lineup filled with Latin players and said he was just glad it happened while he was playing. And he said, 'Sangy, one day there will be so many more.' "

Talk about prescient. Still, on that September evening, it really was just young, athletic men doing what they loved for teammates they cherished.

"We really had no idea that history was being made," Oliver told Fox Sports. "It wasn't maybe as big as Jackie Robinson breaking into the major leagues, but it should be up there as far as baseball history is concerned. I think it's a day that really should be celebrated."

Call it history, but don't call it an aberration. Not if you understand Danny Murtaugh. After all, just look at the starting lineup he sent out to accompany pitcher Steve Blass and Robertson to victory in the seventh and final game of the 1971 Series: Dave Cash. Gene Clines. Roberto Clemente. Manny Sanguillén. Willie Stargell. José Pagán. And Jackie Hernández.

"He was a big Irishman, and he loved us all, no matter the color," Sanguillén said. "He made us winners. He made us a family."

Claire Smith, the winner of the 2017 BBWAA Career Excellence Award, is now on the faculty of Klein College of Media and Communication at Temple University, serving as the codirector of the newly created Claire Smith Center for Sports Media. This essay originally appeared in Memories & Dreams, Issue 1, 2021.

Chapter 5

Legendary Performances

Let's Play 2,632

Cal Ripken Jr.'s legendary durability had family roots

By Tim Kurkjian

Cal Ripken Sr. played soccer into his mid-fifties, and he would play the whole game without tiring.

More than once, he'd come home with a painful blood blister under his big toe. He would go to the basement, take out a power drill, and drill a hole into the nail, releasing the blood. His son, future Hall of Famer Cal Ripken Jr., would accompany him on these "surgeries."

"When the blood would spurt out," Cal Jr. recalled many years later, "he'd go, 'Ooooooooooh' in relief."

That's where Cal Ripken Jr. got his toughness. And it partly explains how a man can play 2,632 consecutive baseball games, breaking a seemingly unbreakable record set by an iconic figure—Hall of Famer Lou Gehrig—by more than five hundred games.

Now it's Ripken's record that is truly unbreakable, a feat achieved through a breathtaking combination of incredible strength and will, epic competitiveness, and a childlike love of play.

"Never once did I ever hear him say that he wasn't feeling good today," recalled first baseman Randy Milligan, one of Ripken's teammates. "I say that every day."

On Opening Day, 1985, before The Streak ever was relevant, Ripken rolled his left ankle on the second base bag.

He played the rest of the game, of course, but afterwards, the ankle swelled terribly, ringed in a hideous black and blue.

He went to the hospital, where the doctor gave him crutches and told him not to put weight on the ankle for two weeks. Ripken left the hospital, threw the crutches away before he got to his car, iced the ankle overnight, and played the next game…and every game after that for the next thirteen years.

Baltimore Oriole shortstop Cal Ripken Jr. broke Lou Gehrig's record for consecutive games played when he faced the California Angels in his 2,131st consecutive game. (Richard Lassner)

"I just taped it up real tight," Ripken said. "No big deal."
His pain tolerance was legendary. So was his competitive nature, and not just in baseball, but in any sport, any competition. The tunnel leading from the visitor's dugout to the clubhouse at the Metrodome in Minneapolis was long and steep—eleven steps, then a landing that's six feet deep, eleven steps, a landing, eleven steps, a landing, and, finally, eleven more steps. Every trip there, Ripken would finish pre-game infield and sprint up the stairs. The idea, which only he could concoct, was to reach the top in the fewest strides. He could do it in six strides, which was positively Bob Beamon-esque.

But before one game, teammate Rene Gonzales also made it in six. That was unacceptable to Ripken. He couldn't stand not to be the best, not even for one night, so he went back to the bottom and ran the steps again. This time, he made it in five strides.

The night before Opening Day in 1995—the year in which he would break Gehrig's record—Ripken and some teammates played basketball at a cookout at the house of former Orioles pitcher Rick Sutcliffe in Kansas City. Ripken's team won, and he dunked a few times, never bothering to mention that he'd played these pickup games in his street clothes and dunked while wearing loafers.

What if he had rolled an ankle? What if The Streak had ended at a barbecue? For Ripken, there was a competition that night; he had to play, and he had to win.

That's how he got to the night of September 6, 1995, at Camden Yards, the night he surpassed Gehrig's mark. It was an amazing night, one that was about much more than baseball. It was about commitment, family, neighborhood, loyalty.

Before that game, a writer from Toronto who didn't know Ripken and hadn't been part of the lead-up to the record-setting night said to me, "I don't feel it. I don't get it."

But after the bottom of the fifth inning, the banner was dropped from the top of the warehouse in right field: 2,131. Ripken, at the urging of teammates, took a lap around the ballpark, shaking hands with fans and pointing to others who, if he didn't know their names, he knew their faces. When he finally finished the lap—after a twenty-two-minute delay to the game—he hugged his wife and children, then looked at the fans, many of whom were weeping, and patted his heart.

The writer from Toronto, now with tears in his eyes, looked at me and said, "Okay, I get it."

Tim Kurkjian is a senior writer and analyst for ESPN and a former Orioles beat writer. He is the recipient of the 2022 BBWAA Career Excellence Award. This essay originally appeared in Memories & Dreams, *Issue 3, 2011.*

More than an "Average" Season
Seventy years after Ted Williams' feat,
baseball awaits its next .400 hitter
By Craig Muder

Impressive as it was, the number—at the time—seemed something less than an enduring standard.

But today, any player who comes within 30 points of Ted Williams' magical .406 batting average—even as early as June—is elevated to instant baseball celebrity.

It's a testament to the power of numbers in baseball…and to a mark that has not been equaled in seventy seasons.

"I think it can be done—and I think I would have done it if we had completed the strike-shortened season," said Hall of Famer Tony Gwynn, who was hitting .394—the highest final average since Williams in 1941—when the strike ended the 1994 MLB campaign. "When Ted and I talked about [hitting .400], we figured you needed between 240 and 260 hits. That's what it's going to take, unless you can walk 180 times."

Tony Gwynn never approached those walk totals. Williams, meanwhile, is one of only four players who ever drew more than 160 walks in a season. But in 1941, it was all about swinging the bat for the man known as Teddy Ballgame.

In just his third big league season, the Red Sox left fielder had already developed a reputation as one of the game's best pure hitters. He led the major leagues in RBI as a rookie in 1939 and in runs scored in 1940, then began the 1941 season on a tear that saw his batting average stand at .429 at the end of May. In June, he had his worst month of the season—hitting *just* .372—but he batted .429 in July and .402 in August to leave him with a .407 average as September dawned.

While the Yankees had gained control of the American League pennant race over the summer on the strength of Joe DiMaggio's 56-game hitting streak (en route to a 17-game final cushion over the Red Sox), the season dripped with drama as Williams pursued .400. Heading into the last day of the season, his average stood at .3995—which would be rounded up to .400—with two games yet to be played against the Athletics in Philadelphia. Tales have lived for seventy years that Red Sox manager Joe Cronin—himself a future Hall of Famer—suggested to Williams that he could sit out the final games to attain the mark.

"I'll play," Williams told Cronin that morning. "Hitting .3995 ain't hitting .400. If I'm going to be a .400 hitter, I want more than my toenails on the line."

Cronin later denied offering Williams the chance to sit out, saying, "We had an agreement made a week before that Ted would play every game no matter what happened. I never offered to let him sit any games out to protect his average."

Whatever the circumstances, the results were the same. Williams and the Red Sox were set to play a season-ending doubleheader against the A's on September 28 after being rained out the day before. As Williams stepped into the box for his first plate appearance against Philadelphia's Dick Fowler, catcher Frankie Hayes relayed what Hall of Fame manager Connie Mack had told his team: "Mr. Mack told us he'd run us all out of baseball if we let up on you. You're going to have to earn it."

Williams did…and then some. He began his day with a single to right. His next at-bat produced a home run. Porter Vaughan faced Williams in his third at-bat and surrendered another single. Yet another single followed against Vaughan in the seventh inning before Williams reached on an error in his last at-bat. His 4-for-5 effort left him standing at .4039.

To the surprise of many, Williams appeared in the starting lineup for Game 2, despite the fact that an 0-for-5 would drop him right back to where he started the day—at .3995. But his 2-for-3 performance put him at .4057 and forever in the country's sporting consciousness. The twenty-three-year-old slugger was well on his way to his goal of becoming the greatest hitter who ever lived.

"We were worried that Ted would be off on the final day, but he murdered the ball," Cronin said. "His last hit broke a piece off the public address horns."

The press celebrated Williams' achievement, but it was not considered a once-in-a-lifetime moment. Just eleven years earlier, Bill Terry of the Giants hit .401—the eighth different season of .400-or-better in the span between 1920 and 1930. Williams' .400 mark was the 13th of the modern era beginning in 1901, meaning that a .400 hitter appeared once every three seasons.

But following World War II, .400 hitters became extinct. In the 69 seasons since Williams' jewel, just four players have qualified for their league's batting title with better than a .380 average.

The first was Williams himself, who hit .388 in 1957 at the age of thirty-eight. After hitting .343 before the All-Star break, Williams hit an incredible .453 in the second half with 78 hits in just 60 games. In his final 12 games of the season, Williams batted .632—enough to close in on .390 but without enough time to approach .400. His average climbed as high as .393 on August 17, but he never crossed the .400 plateau after June 5.

Twenty years later, Rod Carew provided the next challenge. Carew virtually owned the American League batting crown throughout the 1970s en route to the Hall of Fame, and entering the 1977 season, the Twins first baseman had won five AL batting titles and missed out on a sixth in 1976 by a mere two points. But in 1977, Carew left no doubt about the title—hitting .388 while earning the American League Most Valuable Player Award.

Carew's run at .400 began early in the season. By July, he had pushed his average to .411 and found himself on the cover of *Time* magazine as the nation became captivated with his hitting skills.

"He has the best chance," said legendary hitting instructor Charley Lau of Carew's quest. "That's if anybody can do it."

But Carew dropped below .400 on July 11 and down below .380 by the end of August, with a late-season push returning him to .388.

Ted Williams of the Boston Red Sox, considered by many to be baseball's best pure hitter, was the last player to hit .400 in a season, batting .406 in 1941.

Three years later, the Royals' George Brett—a Lau disciple—came even closer. Brett was hitting .337 on June 10 when a right ankle injury sidelined him for a month. When he returned, a torrid month of July left him at .390, and he kept up the pace until he topped the .400 mark on August 17. He peaked at .407 with a 5-for-5 performance on August 26 and stood at .400 after the games of September 19—the latest anyone has been at .400 since Williams in 1941.

"I sure hope he does it," Williams said at the time. "Because I'm sick of people calling me every time someone gets close."

But in his final 13 games, Brett was a mortal 14-for-46 (.304), knocking him down to .390. Still, it was the greatest season of his Hall of Fame career.

"The media attention now might make it impossible to do," Brett said. "But despite the media that was there for me, I really thought I was going to do it. If you get close, you're not going to back down."

In 1994, a third future Hall of Famer—Gwynn—made his run at Williams. The Padres right fielder, who would hit .300 or better in 19 of his 20 major league seasons, had already won the NL batting title four times and was coming off a .358 campaign. His average hovered in the high .380/low .390 range throughout June and July, and he appeared ready to challenge .400 before the strike short-circuited the season August 12 with him at .394.

Since 1994, only one player—Larry Walker in 1999—has topped the .375 mark. 2010's AL and NL batting champions, Texas' Josh Hamilton and Colorado's Carlos González, hit .359 and .336, respectively.

Still, the quest for .400 continues. Meanwhile, Williams has ascended into the pantheon of great hitters. It was his destiny after that monumental weekend in Philadelphia.

"All I want out of life," Williams famously said, "is that when I walk down the street, folks will say, 'There goes the greatest hitter who ever lived.' "

Craig Muder is the director of communications for the National Baseball Hall of Fame and Museum. This essay originally appeared in Memories & Dreams, *Issue 3, 2011.*

The Great Home Run Race
Fifty years have passed since Roger Maris and Mickey Mantle chased the Babe
By Scott Pitoniak

Objects in orbit dominated the news during the spring and summer of 1961. The space race between the United States and the Soviet Union heated up as cosmonaut Yuri Gagarin became the first man to circle the earth and astronaut Alan Shepard became the first American to journey into outer space. And while new President John F. Kennedy was telling the world our goal was to put a man on the moon before the end of the decade, two muscular men in New York Yankees pinstripes were launching baseballs over outfield walls across the land at a prolific pace never witnessed before.

The great home run chase of 1961 between Bronx Bombers Roger Maris and Mickey Mantle—and the ghost of Hall of Famer Babe Ruth—became so enthralling that even non-baseball fans took notice. The "M&M Boys" were pictured on the cover of *Life* magazine, made appearances on prime-time television shows, and were asked to play themselves in the movie *That Touch of Mink*, starring Doris Day and Cary Grant. News organizations from Japan and England sent reporters to chronicle this very American sports phenomenon, and Walter Cronkite provided nightly updates about Mantle and Maris on the *CBS Evening News*.

"It really was a transcendent event," recalled Tony Kubek, the Baseball Hall of Fame's 2009 Ford C. Frick Award winner for baseball broadcasting excellence, who during that fateful season was the Yankees' All-Star shortstop. "As the summer progressed and it became apparent that one or both of them were going to break the Babe's single-season home run record, people couldn't wait to grab the morning paper to see if Mickey or Roger had added to their totals." And like any great drama, it gripped you to the very end.

At exactly 2:43 the afternoon of October 1, in the final game of the 1961 season, the story achieved its Hollywood ending as Maris smashed home run No. 61 into the right field stands at Yankee Stadium to eclipse by one the most hallowed record in all of sports. Kubek was in the dugout with his teammates at the time, and the scene remains as vivid as if it had happened fifty seconds ago rather than fifty years.

"Unlike Mickey or Ruth, who hit these high-soaring, majestic home runs, Roger tended to be a line-drive hitter," Kubek said. "So when he hit it, you didn't know if it was going to wind up being a single to right just over the second baseman's head or if it was going to rise and sail over the fence. It wasn't until you got off the bench and onto that first step of the dugout that you realized Rog had gotten all of this one and it was going to carry into the seats.

"While he rounded the bases, you felt so proud of him because we had witnessed firsthand the incredible pressure he had endured. The thing I'll remember most is that after he touched third and began heading for home, our third base coach, Frank Crosetti, shook his hand and slapped him on the back.

"Frank never did that before with anyone. He would clap, of course, when one of us hit a homer, but that was usually the extent of it. But this was such a historic moment that he couldn't resist doing more.

"And the thing that's really neat about that gesture is that Crosetti had been a teammate of Ruth's back in 1927 when the Babe set the original record," continued Kubek. "And Crosetti had been a Yankee ever since, so he was the thread connecting the two. History had come full circle."

Maris felt a great sense of accomplishment and relief.

"I couldn't even think as I went around the bases," he said, recounting his feelings after depositing a 2-0 pitch from Boston Red Sox hurler Tracy Stallard eight rows beyond the right field wall. "I couldn't tell you what crossed my mind. I don't think anything did; I was in a fog. I was all fogged out from a very, very hectic season and an extremely difficult month."

Teammates Mickey Mantle and Roger Maris captured the attention of the nation in 1961 as they battled each other chasing Babe Ruth's single season home run record.

The shy twenty-seven-year-old slugger from North Dakota had been forced to battle not only American League pitchers that season, but also the fans, sportswriters, and even baseball's commissioner, who appeared to be rooting against him from the moment in late June when it became apparent both he and Mantle had a legitimate shot at the record. The AL had added eight games to the schedule that season to accommodate two expansion teams. This prompted Commissioner Ford Frick, Ruth's former ghostwriter and friend, to decree in July that the Babe's record would have to be broken in 154 games or else there would be two marks listed in the record book. New York *Daily News* columnist Dick Young wrote that an "asterisk" would be used to distinguish the new record.

As the race gained steam, the media entourage chronicling the case swelled to nearly a hundred reporters, and competition for exclusive stories became fierce. This led to erroneous reporting, including fabricated stories that Maris and Mantle couldn't stand one another, when they were in fact great friends who roomed together with teammate Bob Cerv at a nondescript apartment in Queens.

"Yes, they both wanted to break the record, but it was a friendly competition," Kubek said. "The problem is that everybody is always looking for that storyline where you have a hero and a villain, and that just wasn't the case. I really believe it had its roots in the feud between Ruth and (Lou) Gehrig. They supposedly didn't shake each other's hands after homers. So some thought Mickey and Roger must not have liked each other either."

It got to the point where the M&M Boys would joke about their alleged feud.

"Roger would come to me in the morning with the newspaper in hand and say, 'Mick, you better get up and read this because it says we're fighting again,' " Mantle recalled years later with a smile. "It became a standing joke with us. I'd say, 'Hi Rog, I hate your guts.' And he'd say, 'Good morning, Mick, I hate your guts, too.' "

In reality, the competition spurred each of them on, like two thoroughbreds thundering neck-and-neck down the track while leaving the rest of the field in their wake. And the fans ate it up, as the M&M Boys attracted record crowds at home and on the road. Early that season, Yankees manager Ralph Houk approached Mantle about moving to the cleanup spot and putting Maris in front of him in the batting order. The future Hall of Famer agreed for the good of the team, and it resulted in Maris seeing more hittable pitches because no one wanted to walk him and have to face an even more-feared slugger. As a result, Maris went the entire season without receiving an intentional walk.

Mantle also helped Maris deal with the enormous demands of playing in New York. The Mick had been booed sporadically by Yankees fans who had expected him to eclipse the star of his predecessor, Joe DiMaggio. Near the end of the '61 season, the pressure became so fierce on Maris that he told Mantle, "I'm going nuts, Mick. I can't stand much more of this." The center fielder put an arm around Maris' shoulders and said, "You'll just have to learn to take it, Rog. There's no escape."

A hip infection took Mantle out of the race in September; he finished with 54 homers. But during the time he was sidelined, he would speak to the press about how he was pulling for his teammate. "Roger deserves to break the record," he told reporters. "I'm rooting for him. I want to see him do it, and I'm sure he will."

He didn't do it in 154 games, but that didn't matter to him or his teammates. Mantle called Maris' achievement the greatest feat in the history of sports.

The Baseball Hall of Fame preserves the memory of Maris' historic season with several artifacts, including the ball he hit for his 61st home run, the bat he used for home runs No. 59, 60, and 61, and a ticket from the October 1, 1961, game in which Maris broke Ruth's single-season home run record.

Maris' standard lasted thirty-seven years, three years longer than Ruth's mark. Mark McGwire established a new major league record of 70 in 1998; three years later, Barry Bonds extended it to 73. Maris, however, still holds the American League mark.

Kubek looks back on that summer fondly. "I had a front-row seat for one of the greatest seasons and moments in baseball history," he said. "It was truly unforgettable."

Author and nationally recognized sports columnist Scott Pitoniak has written more than twenty-five books, including his most recent work, Remembrances of Swings Past: A Lifetime of Baseball Stories. *This essay originally appeared in* Memories & Dreams, *Issue 3, 2011.*

Still a Miracle

The Amazin' Mets wrote what may be baseball's most incredible story

By Wayne Coffey

History was going to happen. To fans of the New York Mets, that seemed as certain as sitting in traffic after the game.

It was Opening Day of the 1969 season, April 8, a sunny Tuesday at Shea Stadium. The Mets had never won an opener in their previous seven tries, a span in which they'd lost with record-breaking regularity, dropping a total of 737 games and finishing every year but two in last place.

But the start of Year No. 8 would be different, wouldn't it? The Mets had their fresh-faced ace, Tom Seaver, on the mound, going against an expansion team, the Montreal Expos, a club outfitted in tri-color hats that might've been designed by Barnum & Bailey. It was the first international game in big league annals, in the game's first season with divisional play.

Already a two-time All-Star at age twenty-four, Seaver was widely regarded as the premier young pitcher in baseball, teaming with Jerry Koosman to give the Mets the best lefty-righty combination in the National League since the heyday of Sandy Koufax and Don Drysdale.

Shortstop Maury Wills was the first Expos hitter. Seaver struck him out looking. Subsequent outs did not come as easily. The Expos scored twice in the first and once in the third. They scored again in the fourth when a reliever named Dan McGinn, a former punter for Notre Dame, hit a ball that landed on top of the right field wall and plopped into the Mets bullpen. It was the only home run of McGinn's career.

Seaver was done after five innings, having yielded four runs, six hits, and three walks. The Mets lost, 11-10.

"My God, wasn't that awful?" Seaver said afterward.

Indeed it was, but things did not stay awful for long for the Mets, and that was principally because of Seaver, who would go on to win twenty-five games and the first of his three Cy Young Awards, the best season of a career that would land him in Cooperstown—one of just two Hall of Famers (with Nolan Ryan) on a fabled ballclub, one who may well be the most improbable World Series champion in history.

A year after they won 73 games under their new manager, Gil Hodges, the Mets finished 100-62 in 1969. They swept the Henry Aaron-led Atlanta Braves in the first National League Championship Series and then faced the mighty Baltimore Orioles, winners of 109 games, in the Fall Classic.

The Orioles were not terribly concerned about all the chatter surrounding the Mets and their charmed, providential journey.

"If somebody upstairs is guiding the Mets, as we're told, then all I can say is He is guiding us better, because we won 109 games to their 100," said Orioles manager Earl Weaver.

"We're going to whip the Amazin' Mets," added Frank Robinson, the Orioles' slugging right fielder and one of two Hall of Fame-bound Robinsons on the club (Brooks, of course, being the other). "The World Series might go five, or it just might go four.... The Birds haven't decided yet."

Such skepticism was nothing new for the Mets, who spent the whole season having to convince naysayers that these were not the Mets of yesteryear. From the moment he was hired, Hodges' top priority was to shed the club's culture of losing and convince his youthful ballplayers that they could turn things around quickly if they played crisp, fundamentally sound baseball and stuck together.

The message got through, and nobody carried it more passionately than Seaver. On May 21 in Atlanta, Seaver shut out the Braves on three hits to even the Mets' record at 18-18—the latest point in their history that they'd been at .500. Reporters descended on Seaver to get his reaction.

"What's so good about .500?" he said. "That's only mediocre. We didn't come into this season to play .500. Let Rod Kanehl and Marvelous Marv (Throneberry) laugh about the Mets. We're out here to win. You know when we'll have champagne? When we win the pennant."

Soon after, the Mets went on an eleven-game winning streak, moving into second place in the NL East and closing to within 5.5 games when the first-place Chicago Cubs visited Shea in early July. It was unquestionably the biggest series the Mets had ever played.

In the opener, trailing by two runs in the ninth against Cubs ace (and another future Hall of Famer) Ferguson Jenkins, the Mets rallied for three runs to win, 4-3. The next night, Seaver took the mound against Cubs left-hander Ken Holtzman and dominated from the start, striking out five of the first six batters he faced. The Mets, meanwhile, staked him an early lead. In the third inning, Mets pitching coach Rube Walker turned to Hodges in the dugout.

"[Seaver] has the stuff to throw a no-hitter tonight," Walker said.

Through five innings, Seaver had set down all 15 Cubs he'd faced. A 1-2-3 sixth made it 18 straight. When Don Kessinger, the Chicago shortstop, hit a liner to left to lead off the seventh, Seaver's heart sank before Cleon Jones made a nice running grab by the foul line. Seaver retired the next two hitters and got the Cubs in order again in the eighth.

Seaver had now faced twenty-four Chicago Cubs and retired every one of them. Only two National League pitchers in the twentieth century had pitched perfect games, both of them Hall of Famers: Jim Bunning did it on Father's Day in 1964 on this same mound, against the Mets, and Sandy Koufax did it against the Cubs the following season.

When Seaver came up to bat in the bottom of the eighth, the sellout crowd of 50,000-plus stood as one. One of those fans was Howie Rose, now a Mets broadcaster, but then a fifteen-year-old from Bayside, Queens.

Rose called it "the loudest sound I ever heard in my life."

"The sonic roar encapsulated the realization, at least to me, that not only had the Mets at long last 'arrived,' but that in

Tom Seaver, we as Mets fans had our very own Sandy Koufax or Mickey Mantle—a transcendent star who willed his team far beyond a newfound competitiveness; who allowed us to dream that the New York Mets in 1969 might actually be capable of something special," Rose said.

Seaver came out for the ninth, with the crowd still standing. Randy Hundley, the Cubs' catcher, dropped down a leadoff bunt, but the ball rolled right back to the mound. Seaver threw him out easily.

Twenty-five Cubs down. Two more to go.

Up stepped Jimmy Qualls, a twenty-two-year-old infielder/outfielder who had recently been activated after a two-week military stint and was playing in just his eighteenth big league game. He had made better contact than any other Cub in his previous two at-bats against Seaver, smacking a liner to right and a hard grounder to first. Seaver's first pitch was a fastball away. Qualls hit it solidly toward left-center. Jones and Tommie Agee, the center fielder, broke for it, but neither had a play. It was a clean single. The excitement and anticipation that had been building the entire night exited Shea Stadium faster than air from a punctured balloon.

"It was like a drain opened up under my feet," Seaver said later. "I just took a deep breath. I didn't say a word to myself. All the pressure, everything, was gone."

The crowd gave the right-hander one more thunderous ovation before he quickly got the final two outs. Seaver would forever more refer to that outing as "the imperfect game."

He and his teammates continued to chase the Cubs. Though a rough stretch coming out of the All-Star break left the Mets ten games behind in mid-August, neither Hodges nor his players lost heart, instead playing their best baseball of the season in the heat of their first pennant race.

The Mets went 38-11 over their final forty-nine games and zoomed past the Cubs to win the division going away. They clinched on September 24, scoring five times in the first inning to back Gary Gentry's four-hit shutout against the defending NL champion St. Louis Cardinals.

Overcome with euphoria, Mets fans tore up the field so completely it looked like something close to a war zone. They ransacked the field again after the Mets swept the Braves to advance to the Series. Even after Seaver dropped Game One in Baltimore, the Mets weren't shaken. Koosman carried a no-hitter into the seventh inning of Game Two as the Mets took a 2-1 decision, and back home at Shea in Game Three, Gentry pitched superbly and Agee had as great a game in the field as any outfielder in Series history, with two running catches in the gap that might well have saved five runs.

Seaver returned to the mound in Game Four, and this time he was in prime form, pitching a six-hitter over 10 innings to capture what would be the only Series victory of his career. He got a huge assist from right fielder Ron Swoboda, who made a spectacular grab of his own on a sinking line drive off the bat of Brooks Robinson.

Koosman closed it out a day later, getting the final out when Davey Johnson, who would later manage the '86 World Champion Mets, hit a fly ball to Cleon Jones in left. Jones went down to one knee as he made the catch, and soon Seaver and all the other Mets were pouring out of the dugout…as tens of thousands of fans poured out of the stands right behind them.

Six months after the Mets' 1969 season had gotten off to an awful start, it came to a sublime conclusion. And amid the spray of champagne and whoops of joy in the Mets clubhouse, Seaver may have put it best: "It's the greatest feeling in the world."

Wayne Coffey is a former sportswriter for the New York Daily News *and author of* They Said It Couldn't Be Done: The '69 Mets, New York City, and the Most Astounding Season in Baseball History. *This essay originally appeared in* Memories & Dreams, *Issue 2, 2019.*

The Sunday Manager
Burt Shotton faced challenges that no skipper ever had while leading the Dodgers to the 1947 NL pennant
By Steve Wulf

"He lives quietly. Since coming to Brooklyn about a month ago (he stays in the Hotel St. George), he has gone to one movie (The Best Years of Our Lives) and has not found it necessary to visit Manhattan, except on baseball business."
—Brooklyn Eagle, June 15, 1947

You wonder what Burt Shotton was thinking when the movie credits were rolling. *The Best Years of Our Lives* had to strike a chord. After all, it's about three veterans who must withstand a new ordeal after coming home to restart their lives. Wherever Burt was perched in the theater that day, he must have felt that he was sitting in their seats.

The story of how this unlikely but likeable man managed the 1947 Dodgers into the World Series—and the history books—is worthy of its own movie. When the season opened in Brooklyn, "Barney" was a sixty-two-year-old part-time scout living in Bartow, Florida, with his wife, Mary, content to hunt and fish for game—both in the wild and on the baseball diamond. In fact, he was down in Miami to talk about some Havana prospects when he was handed a telegram from the Brooklyn office. He didn't think it was crucial, so he put it in his pocket. Then he opened it at Mary's urging.

It read, "Be in Brooklyn tomorrow morning. See nobody. Say nothing. Rickey."

At the time, the Dodgers were 2-0 but were reeling. Right before Opening Day, manager Leo Durocher had been suspended by Commissioner Happy Chandler for conduct unbecoming of a manager. Jackie Robinson and Branch Rickey had just broken down the door to baseball's fortress of prejudice, only to find themselves surrounded by people who thought Robinson didn't belong—fans, owners, writers, players, even some of Jackie's own teammates.

The Dodgers were a pennant contender, but interim manager Clyde Sukeforth felt that he wasn't the man for the job. That's why Rickey asked his brain trust to come to his office to go over a list of candidates.

"I am falling out a window," he told them from the comfort of his chair. "I am on the ledge and going over! The sidewalk is twenty feet below! One name—one name can save me!"

One by one, the candidates were dismissed. But when Sukeforth made a case for a man who hadn't managed in the majors since 1933, Rickey backed away from the precipice…and sent a telegram to Burt Shotton.

The old scout had no idea what the cryptic message was all about when he stepped on the plane to LaGuardia Field on Friday, April 18. That's why he had only an overnight bag when Rickey met him and took him to breakfast at his home. It was then and there that "The Mahatma" dropped the bombshell: "I want you to manage the team the rest of the year."

As Shotton later said: "I didn't have a chance to refuse the job for the very good reason that you don't resist Branch Rickey."

They didn't discuss salary, but Rickey did agree to one of Shotton's conditions. When he had retired as an Indians coach a few years before, he promised Mary he would never again put on a uniform. Rickey was his boss, yes, but Mary was his partner of thirty-seven years. So Rickey agreed he could wear civilian clothes, the way Connie Mack did. Shotton then got in a cab to the Polo Grounds, where the Dodgers were scheduled to play the Giants. The driver got lost.

Shortly before game time, an announcement was made to the press while Sukeforth introduced this elderly gent in a fedora, glasses, and topcoat to the players. The Dodgers knew him from Spring Training, but really…Burt Shotton?

"You fellas can win the pennant in spite of me," he told them. "Don't be afraid of me as a manager."

With that, the Dodgers gave up six homers to the Giants and lost, 10-4. After the game, Shotton told the befuddled reporters: "As soon as I know something about the club and can help, I'll start to work. Until then, I'll just watch." Then he excused himself to call Mary to give her the news and have her ship him some clothes.

Red Barber, the legendary Dodgers broadcaster, summed up the situation this way: "It was a good thing Burt Shotton was already white-haired when he took over.... Otherwise, what he had to contend with would have turned his head the color of new-fallen snow."

So why did Rickey choose him? The answer goes back to 1913. According to *Burt Shotton, Dodgers Manager*, a 1994 biography by David Gough: "The pair first met in the lobby of a Philadelphia hotel...shortly after Rickey, fresh from attending law school at the University of Michigan, had joined the [Browns'] front office."

At the time, Shotton was a Browns outfielder and considered to be one of the fastest men in the game—he would steal 43 bases and score 105 runs that year. Indeed, he acquired the nickname "Barney" while growing up in Ohio because his speed afoot reminded people of Barney Oldfield, the famed auto racer who was also from Ohio.

Rickey, too, was an Ohioan, a former major league catcher whose intelligence for baseball was readily apparent. And he saw in Shotton a like mind. Late in the 1913 season, Rickey took over as manager of the Browns on one condition—he couldn't manage on the Sabbath because he had to go to church and teach Sunday school. So he needed somebody to run the team on the Sabbath, a "Sunday manager." Shotton was usually his choice.

How good a player was Shotton? When major leaguers were polled after the 1915 season to name an all-star team, the outfield was Ty Cobb, Tris Speaker, and...Burt Shotton. Four years later, he rejoined Rickey with the Cardinals.

When his playing days were over, Shotton became a coach for the Cardinals and then the manager of their Syracuse affiliate. That led to a six-year stint as the Phillies' manager (1928 to 1933). The only thing he won, though, was top honors in a 1929 target shooting competition.

Rickey brought him back into the Cardinals' fold in 1935 as a minor league manager, and he nurtured a new generation of stars for the team. Shotton then became the right-hand man for Cleveland Indians player/manager Lou Boudreau, while Rickey took over the Dodgers. They kept in touch.

In retrospect, it's little wonder that in April, 1947, when Rickey found himself in a bind after choosing to follow through on his beliefs, he turned to his old Sunday manager. But the job was far from a Sunday afternoon stroll.

"Shotton was handed by Rickey and by the fates the most upset, torn-apart ball club in history," said Barber.

After losing their first two games under Shotton, the Dodgers won six straight. It wasn't his genius so much as it was his patience—the team relaxed and played ball. Shotton owed a debt of gratitude to Durocher, who had put down a player revolt over Robinson in Spring Training. But he still had to win their trust, and they saw how well he handled the rookie first baseman during an early-season slump.

Robinson wrote of those struggles in *I Never Had It Made*. "As my slump deepened, I appreciated Shotton's patience and understanding. I knew the pressure was on him to take me out of the lineup.... Shotton, however, continued to encourage me."

Shotton had ditched the dugout attire of his debut for comfortable slacks, shirt, and a Dodgers baseball jacket. The more he learned about the team, the more he liked its chances. The lineup was solid, so his main area of concern was the starting rotation—he had to send Sukeforth out to the mound to change pitchers (only uniformed personnel could set foot on the field), and Sukey was doing a lot of walking.

Shotton wasn't just a cheerleader, though. He would call out his players if they disrespected the game. One of them was a brash rookie who struck out after being asked to bunt, then threw his bat and muttered, "What does that old so-and-so think he's doing, having a .300 hitter bunt?" Shotton overheard him and replied, "You'll find out tomorrow in St. Paul." Which is where Duke Snider was sent the next day.

The National League race was fairly tight for the first three months, but then the Dodgers rattled off seven- and 13-game winning streaks in July. By mid-September, they had built an insurmountable 10-game lead.

As Franklin Graham of the *New York Journal-American* wrote: "The name of Durocher is seldom heard in the borough. What particularly impressed…members of the press box was the way Shotton deployed his bench and every available arm."

Could the '47 Dodgers have won the NL pennant under Durocher? Barber didn't think so: "The coming of Jackie Robinson brought a seething turbulence that was waiting to explode. Shotton saw to it that serious internal trouble didn't break loose."

In his book *1947: When All Hell Broke Loose in Baseball*, Barber freely confided his affection for Shotton: "After an afternoon game on the road, after dinner, Shotton and I often walked, just the two of us…. Usually we found a place that served ice cream…. He had very simple habits, which made it very hard for certain city-wise writers to understand him."

One of those writers was Dick Young of the *Daily News*, who kept referring to Shotton simply as KOBS, an acronym for Kindly Old Burt Shotton. Well, he kindly got the Dodgers into the World Series with the New York Yankees.

"That's the true measure of a manager," said Branch Rickey III, the grandson of the man who had asked Shotton to do him a favor. "My grandfather always believed that what a manager did in the clubhouse was more important than what he did on the field."

An epic season ended with an epic World Series. Again, Shotton lost the first two games, and again, the Dodgers righted themselves, forcing a Game Seven. Two of their victories were directly attributable to Shotton moves.

In Game Four, pinch-hitter Cookie Lavagetto broke up Bill Bevens' no-hitter in the ninth and won the game, 3-2. In Game Six, with the Dodgers leading, 8-5, in the sixth, Al Gionfriddo was brought in to play left, and with two outs and runners on first and second, he robbed Joe DiMaggio of extra bases with a one-handed catch at the wall. The Dodgers held on to win, 8-6.

If life were a movie, they would have won Game Seven and carried Shotton off on their shoulders…but it's not. They lost, 5-2. Still, they had won over millions of doubters and opened the doors for thousands of players.

It was not only the best year of Barney's life, but it might have been the best year the game has ever had. It certainly inspired a movie—the 2013 film *42*, starring the late Chadwick Boseman as Jackie Robinson and featuring Max Gail as Burt Shotton.

Steve Wulf has been writing about baseball since Hank Aaron was active. He lives in Larchmont, NY, just up the hill from where Lou and Eleanor Gehrig once resided. This essay originally appeared in Memories & Dreams, *Issue 3, 2021.*

Mound of Effort
Fifty years ago, Juan Marichal and Warren Spahn
pitched a game for the ages
By Jim Kaplan

In retrospect, we might have expected a Hall of Fame pitching duel between future immortals Juan Marichal of the San Francisco Giants and Warren Spahn of the Milwaukee Braves on July 2, 1963.

Normally a slow starter, Spahn, 11-3 with a 3.12 earned run average, hadn't allowed a walk in 18 ⅓ innings and was facing the same eight position players he'd no-hit in 1961.

Marichal, 12-3 with a 2.38 ERA, had won eight straight and had no-hit Houston just seventeen days earlier. Moreover, they could not have asked for a better locale. Candlestick Park was invariably chilly because the wind came off San Francisco Bay. Balls don't carry as far in cold weather as they do when it's warm, and hitters don't fare as well when it's cold. Finally, the strike zone, enlarged before the 1963 season, now measured from the bottom of the knees to shoulder level.

Even so, what Spahn and Marichal accomplished that night fifty years ago was off the charts. Despite five other future Hall of Famers in the lineups—including Hank Aaron and Eddie Mathews of the Braves and Orlando Cepeda, Willie Mays, and Willie McCovey of the Giants—Spahn and Marichal threw more than 200 pitches apiece. They fought into the 16th inning and the next morning before a Hall of Fame moment ended the tilt with a single run before 15,921 exhausted fans.

It was arguably The Greatest Game Ever Pitched.

Marichal and Spahn, Juan and Warren, "Manito" and "Meatnose"—they were at once different yet much the same. An American and a World War II hero, Spahn, who was forty-two at the time, was left-handed with a receding hairline and a conspicuous nose that earned him several nicknames, "Hooks" being the most prominent.

A right-handed Dominican who'd served in his country's military, Marichal was twenty-five with a full head of hair and a round face with a proportionate nose—and cheeks so full that teammate Eddie Bressoud dubbed him "Popeye." He was also called Laughing Boy and, because of his light blue and cream-colored outfits, the Dominican Dandy—nicknames that forecast a more emotive, multicultural National Pastime.

Yet Marichal and Spahn had much in common. They were an inch or two taller than most pitchers of their time—with Marichal at six feet and 185 pounds and Spahn at six feet and 172 pounds—and both used signature, high-kicking deliveries that made their release points hard to pick up. Each threw an impressive variety of pitches and extended their careers by mastering the screwball. Moreover, both their life stories included formative experiences with a relative and the military.

Growing up in the farm community of Laguna Verde, Marichal would ride a horse to Monte Cristi, six miles away, to watch his older brother Gonzalo play baseball, then ride behind him on the horse peppering him with questions on the way home. Juan might have become just a good local pitcher were it not for the day when he pitched the Manzanillo team to a 2-1 win over Aviación, the Dominican Air Force nine, in the 1956 national amateur tournament. The next day he received a telegram reading, "Report Immediately to the Air Force team." He had been drafted to play baseball.

His first assignment was to head to Santo Domingo's Estadio Las Normal to qualify for a youth tournament in Mexico. After taking his first plane trip there, Marichal won one game and saved another against Puerto Rico to reach the final against the home team. There, he and his teammates encountered fans with knives and guns sitting directly on top of their dugout.

"When we went to the bullpen, they showed us their guns," he said. "We were so scared; we couldn't handle the pressure." The Mexicans won. The Dominicans escaped. And Juan never again viewed pitching as particularly pressure-laden.

Spahn grew up in Buffalo, New York, where his father, Edward, a shipping clerk, wallpaper salesman, and semipro baseball player, exhaustively taught him the game. Edward built his son a mound in the backyard and drilled him on the importance of control, by which he meant self-control as well as control over the strike zone.

"Don't pop off too much," he told Warren. "The guy who is noisy, always blowing off, is the guy who has an inferiority complex. Be yourself, be polite, respect other people's feelings, and treat them with deference."

After much schoolboy success, Spahn was signed by the then-Boston Braves, pitched well in the minors, and had a cup of coffee in Boston before enlisting for World War II. He eventually fought in the Battle of the Bulge and the fight over the bridge at Remagen, won a Purple Heart and a battlefield commission, and returned to the majors as a mature twenty-five-year-old.

Pitching? Pressure?

"No one is shooting at me," Spahn said.

And so Marichal and Spahn went to work on July 2, 1963. In a telling first inning, Marichal got Aaron on a foul to first and struck out Mathews, while Spahn got Mays on a called strike three and McCovey on a grounder to the mound. Four Hall of Famers, no balls out of the infield. Marichal was using his arsenal of pitches, perhaps most effectively his fastball. Spahn was spotting his fastball and subduing right-handers with his screwball and left-handers with his curve. Before the game went into extra innings, there was just one extra-base hit: Spahn's double off the right field fence.

Pitching classics often come with great fielding plays and some luck. With two outs in the Braves fourth and Norm Larker on second, Del Crandall singled to center for what looked like a sure run. But Mays fielded the ball on one hop and fired it home to nail Larker on what San Francisco sportswriters called "one amazing motion" and a "100 percent perfect peg." In the ninth, the Giants' McCovey hit one of his patented moon shots over the right field foul pole. Everyone thought it was a homer except first base umpire Chris Pelekoudas, who ruled it a foul ball.

As the game went into extra innings, those at Candlestick knew something special was afoot. Sitting on a long bench down the left-field line in a windbreaker, nineteen-year-old Giants rookie Al Stanek huddled with other relievers and bullpen catchers in what felt like a wind tunnel. Every once in a while, a reliever got up to throw, but only to stay warm.

"The feeling was that we'll be here for a long time," Stanek said.

While the Giants hit, Marichal sat on the bench chewing Bazooka bubble gum and studying Spahn. Neither man wanted to be relieved.

"Alvin, do you see that man pitching on the other side?" Marichal told Giants manager Alvin Dark. "He's forty-two and I'm twenty-five, and you can't take me out until that man is not pitching."

Only defeat could bench "that man" Spahn. With one out in the Giants 16th, he threw a screwball to Mays. The pitch hung. Mays swung. The ball headed over the head of third baseman Denis Menke, climbing inexorably, fighting the wind. At 12:31 a.m. on July 3, it crossed the fence after an eon in the cold night sky. Giants 1, Braves 0. The crowd rose and cheered: for the Giants' win, for Marichal, for Spahn, and for their own fortitude.

"JUAN BEATS SPAHN," blared a front-page *San Francisco Chronicle* headline. Ron Fimrite, later a *Sports Illustrated* legend, then a news-side *Chronicle* reporter at the park on a night off, wrote in an *SI* retrospective, "There were lesser Page One stories that day—something about a nuclear test ban and the

FBI smashing a Soviet spy ring. But for one day at least, an epic pitching duel dominated the news.

"It was, I told the guys in the office, a rare exercise of sound editorial judgment."

The Greatest Game Ever Pitched deserved no less.

Jim Kaplan is a former writer for Sports Illustrated *and the author of* The Greatest Game Ever Pitched: Juan Marichal, Warren Spahn and the Pitching Duel of the Century. *This essay originally appeared in* Memories & Dreams, *Issue 1, 2013.*

The Road Stockings
The 1869 trips by the Cincinnati baseball team made the game famous throughout the United States
By John Erardi

The greatest road trip in baseball history was arguably the one that was the most ambitious: the 20-game, June-long, 1,821-mile trip by the 1869 Cincinnati Red Stockings.

Three months later, they capped a 57-0 inaugural season with a 4,764-mile trip to San Francisco and back aboard the Transcontinental Railroad, which was completed only the previous May with the pounding of the Golden Spike at Promontory Summit, Utah.

One hundred and fifty years later—this season—Major League Baseball is celebrating the sesquicentennial of the birth of professional baseball with an "MLB 150" logo on each team's uniforms.

Two of those Red Stockings are in the National Baseball Hall of Fame: Shortstop George Wright, inducted in 1937, and his brother, center fielder/manager Harry Wright, inducted in 1953. Harry is known as the "Father of Professional Baseball," and his brother as baseball's first superstar.

The Wrights led the team to both coasts, foreshadowing baseball's expansion to the West Coast eighty-eight years later. Both of the Red Stockings' trips—East and West—turned out to be masterworks of planning, although the former was incredibly less well-financed than the latter. Both trips were full of all sorts of challenges along the way (the Red Stockings embraced risk-reward and on-the-go adjustments). Both trips laid a blueprint for what was to come in baseball.

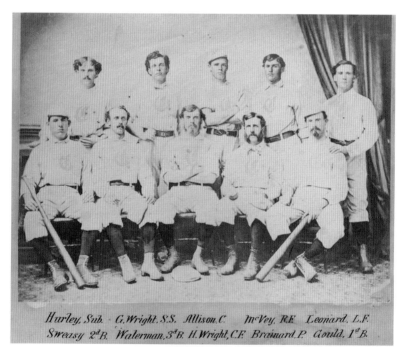

Hurley, Sub. G.Wright, S.S. Allison, C. McVey, R.F. Leonard, L.F.
Sweasy, 2ᵈ B. Waterman, 3ᵈ B. H.Wright, C.F. Brainard, P. Gould, 1ˢᵗ B.

The 1869 Cincinnati Red Stockings, led by Hall of Famers George and Harry Wright, helped spread the popularity of baseball, embarking on a nationwide road trip on their way to a 57-0 record.

The Eastern Trip

The Red Stockings' famous road trip began on May 31 at Little Miami Railroad Depot, today the site of Sawyer Point, an Ohio

River park three-quarters of a mile east of Cincinnati's Great American Ball Park.

The Red Stockings' thirty-two-day road trip was more like a rock 'n roll tour than a baseball trip. Huge crowds turned out to see the handsome young men in their crimson hose and white-knicker uniforms in Cleveland, Buffalo, Rochester, Boston, New York City, Philadelphia, Baltimore, and Washington, DC, where the Red Stockings received an audience with President Ulysses S. Grant.

They won all twenty games on the road trip, and every game thereafter, playing before 200,000 fans.

But things didn't start out so promising.

The day before the Eastern trip began, a game scheduled at the home park, Union Grounds, to raise money for the trip had been rained out. A shareholder in the club, Will Noble, had to borrow $300 ($5,575 in today's dollars) from his wife to get the trip started. It bought the team tickets as far as Boston. But the ten players and two club executives needed to eat and occasionally sleep in a real bed. That same night, club president Aaron Champion visited the players in their rooms at the Gibson House to ensure they weren't drinking. It didn't work. The next morning, Champion found that "Some of the members of the nine, forgetful of (their temperance) pledges, had touched the rosy too freely."

The Red Stockings, some grumpier than others, along with beat writer Harry Millar of the *Cincinnati Commercial* newspaper, boarded the train. Things didn't improve. It was pouring in Yellow Springs, located just outside of Dayton, Ohio. The boys headed northeast for Mansfield in the smoke-filled train.

Millar: "The boys, weary after riding so many miles, with the dampness of the misty atmosphere coming in the open windows, and at intervals almost suffocating, [were] again obliged to turn up coat collars and bind handkerchiefs around the [mouth, nose, and] throat to prevent catching a cold."

Some of the players tried to sleep. George Wright, armed with a long-legged wire spider, walked down the aisle and dropped it gently on the faces of the sleeping. Unsuspectingly, those who were pranked flicked the "spider" away, drawing laughs from Wright and those players who hadn't yet dozed off.

The Red Stockings were a team full of characters, including a pool shark who was a hypochondriac, a boxer turned right fielder, and a second baseman who couldn't stop partying. Eight of the ten were young, eighteen to twenty-three. Harry was thirty-four, pitcher Asa Brainard twenty-eight. All were ballers—ballers at the mercy of Champion and his right-hand man, John Joyce, who had to keep the trip financially afloat despite the rain—even accepting a loan from the beat writer. Champion knew Millar's family and knew that Millar's family had advanced their son a sizeable sum for his expenses.

Champion and Joyce gave Millar a promissory note Millar kept to his dying day: "Received of Harry M. Millar $245 as a loan to the Cincinnati Baseball Club, to (be) repaid out of New York receipts of gate money… Amount of loan guaranteed by John P. Joyce, A. B. Champion."

In Rochester, NY, the game had barely begun when rain soaked the teams and their eager fans. The Red Stockings broomed off the puddles, spread sawdust in the mud, and played on.

When the team arrived for their game in Syracuse, the outfield grass was a foot high and the fence was in a shambles. The Red Stockings had walked into the middle of a pigeon shoot. Harry couldn't find anybody who remembered scheduling the game, so the team settled for a salt bath at a local spa for 35 cents apiece.

The week that made baseball famous began on Tuesday, June 15, and ended six days later. But first it required a setup. That came on Monday, June 7, when the Red Stockings arrived in Lansingburgh, New York, a village on the north end of Troy, on the east shore of the Hudson River, eighty miles from Cooperstown.

It is a direct shot—175 miles due south down the Hudson—to New York City. Even in those days, one had to take Troy before one could take Manhattan. And the Red Stockings did, 37-31. In Boston, they whipped four Massachusetts nines.

The Red Stockings arrived at Earle's Hotel in lower Manhattan at eight o'clock on June 14. At one thirty the next day, officials of the New York Mutuals club called upon them, several elegant coaches at the ready, to ferry the impeccably clad Red Stockings across the East River to the Union Grounds in Brooklyn, Greater New York's most famous ballpark. The crowd was wired, eager to see the youngsters from Cincinnati who had defeated the team from Troy. The spectators roared at the first sight of red, bringing cap-tips from the players. The ensuing 4-2 game—with the Red Stockings scoring twice in the bottom of the ninth inning—had the crowd on its feet; even the newspapers crowed: "Bully for you, boys," wrote the *New York Gazette* reporter.

The low-scoring thriller, with defensive gem after gem and belying the underhand era in which scores of 40 and 50 runs were common, was immediately proclaimed an instant classic. It brought out a huge crowd for the next day's game at the Capitoline Grounds, estimated at 12,000 (by far the biggest baseball crowd to date). The Red Stockings walloped the powerful Brooklyn Atlantics, 32-10, then knocked off the Eckfords 24-5 the next day back at the Union Grounds: three victories in three days over the best teams in New York, birthplace of the pastime, with the Red Stockings pocketing a $1,700 share of the bloated gate receipts.

One huge foe awaited, the Philadelphia Athletics, adjudged by everybody as the strongest group of hitters anywhere, one through eight. The dizzying fame of the Cincinnati nine drew the attention of female admirers. As a light rain fell on the eve of the Athletics game, a group of young women passed in front of the Red Stockings' hotel. They lifted their long skirts to avoid the mud in the streets, many revealing a flash of red stockings. The Cincinnatis won the next day, 27-18.

Then home to a raucous parade, eight city blocks long, and a sumptuous banquet at the Gibson House. Club officials pondered what might come next.

The Western Trip

A key to the Red Stockings' decision to travel to the West Coast in September of 1869 was the earnestness of the invitation from W. L. Hatton, the proprietor of San Francisco's new, enclosed ballpark, the Recreation Grounds, a.k.a. "The Rec," on the corner of Folsom and 25th. The San Francisco clubs would pay all of the Red Stockings' expenses and give them half of the gate receipts. Hatton himself traveled to Cincinnati to handle the details of the trip.

On Tuesday afternoon, September 14, the Red Stockings departed for St. Louis, arriving the next morning; they played two games and then headed west, changing trains in Macon to the Hannibal and St. Joseph Railroad.

Millar: "The cars zig-zag (making it impossible) to stand erect... Not only do they zig-zag, they jump up from the track... In one place we counted seven freight cars in a triangular heap, with the locomotive about fifty feet in advance, alongside the track in a swampy hole."

In Council Bluffs, Missouri, a stagecoach awaited, the "whip" (driver) choosing the convivial and graceful George Wright and Cal McVey to ride the platform with him. Millar, Charlie Gould, and lone substitute Oak Taylor sat on top with the baggage while the rest of the party climbed inside. What a sight!—the champion ball club of America bumping and bouncing toward the next great adventure.

In Omaha, Nebraska, Harry and the boys boarded a special Pullman "Silver Palace" car on the Union Pacific Railroad. The operator of Cincinnati's grand Gibson House hotel catered a party in a large, private compartment at the rear of the car that Hatton had reserved. Millar reported everyone in "jubilant spirits," eating, drinking, and carrying on. Millar noted that the team's quartet of singers—Brainard, third baseman Fred Waterman, left fielder Andy Leonard, and the writer himself—had improved considerably since the team's Eastern tour.

As for the Transcontinental train ride itself, Millar wrote: "It is almost impossible to keep the boys inside of the car (so anxious are they) to get a glimpse of everything attractive or novel." Sightings of buffalo, antelope, and prairie dogs created an uproar and dash for the windows. Harry and some others carried pistols and rifles and, in the custom of the day, took potshots at this menagerie from the train windows. At each stop, the players would hurry outside and toss the ball about to keep their arms in shape, much to the astonishment of the locals, especially the Native Americans and the Chinese.

Darryl Brock, a painstaking researcher, described the scenery the boys would have seen in Utah Territory this way in his bestselling novel, *If I Never Get Back*: "We climbed through the rugged gorges of Echo and Weber Canyons, staring at thrusts of red sandstone towering hundreds of feet above—Devil's Gate, Devil's Slide, Witches' Rock—as we passed along the ledges barely wide enough for the tracks. The Weber River was spanned by a reconstructed bridge. The original had washed away. This one swayed alarmingly as the engineer stopped in midspan so we could look straight down into a chasm where the river flowed between rock walls."

Once in San Francisco, the Red Stockings routed the opposition in eight games over the course of eleven days, starting on September 25 with a 35-4 drubbing of the Eagle of San Francisco BBC. Among their other results were two wins over the Pacific BBC, one over the Atlantic BBC, and a 50-6 triumph over a local Picked Nine that closed out their stay. The "Frisco" clubs, however, had one custom the Red Stockings were not familiar with. At the end of the sixth inning, the teams observed a ten-minute intermission, "a dodge to advertise and have the crowd patronize the bar," Millar wrote.

Away from the ballpark, the Red Stockings enjoyed the sights of the Bay Area. There was no Golden Gate Bridge or Coit Tower, but there was Chinatown and the Cliff House overlooking the Pacific Ocean, where sea lions perched on the rocks.

On the Red Stockings' final night in San Francisco, they were feted at a splendid banquet, and the next morning headed for home.

The team's exploits were reported nationally. So familiar were the nation's ball fans with this team that in western Illinois, when the club stopped for a prearranged game with the Quincy Occidentals, they complained about the Red Stockings playing out of position. Harry had wanted to rest the sore hands of catcher Doug Allison. At the end of each inning, the fans called for Harry to put Asa in the pitcher's box and Allison behind the plate.

Finally, Harry relented, and the crowd cheered.

John Erardi, Greg Rhodes, and Greg Gajus are the coauthors of the new book, Baseball Revolutionaries: How the 1869 Cincinnati Red Stockings Rocked the Country and Made Baseball Famous. *This essay originally appeared in* Memories & Dreams, *Issue 3, 2019.*

Chapter 6

Latino Legacy

Roberto Clemente:
The Father of Puerto Rican Baseball
By Luis R. Mayoral

Major League Baseball is of great importance in the history of Puerto Rico. It has given the island unforgettable heroes with careers full of great accomplishments, headed by Hall of Famer Roberto Clemente, who played for the Pittsburgh Pirates from 1955-1972.

Clemente's days of glory coincided with a period of great social change in the United States as African Americans and Hispanics accelerated their causes for equality and better tomorrows. With resounding pride in his color and heritage, though never to the extent of demeaning others, all Clemente wanted was to make human beings aware of the strengths within themselves.

One Saturday afternoon during the spring of 1972, in his second-story Spring Training room in Bradenton, Florida, Clemente recalled how proud he was of having met with Dr. Martin Luther King Jr. in Puerto Rico years before. He also discussed how he admired the principles of President John F. Kennedy's Peace Corps program to benefit countries around the world.

All countries need heroes, and as a US colony since 1898, Puerto Rico is no exception. During the first half of the twentieth century, the country had few internationally known heroes, but

Major League Baseball paved the way for Clemente, Orlando Cepeda, Iván Rodríguez, Juan González, Bernie Williams, and so many others.

To Puerto Ricans, the national flag and Clemente are common denominators. He leads a very select group of islanders who by way of sports, arts, sociology, science, and politics touch millions around the world in attempts to contribute to the greatness of man.

On December 31, 1972, while on a goodwill mission to aid earthquake victims in Nicaragua, Clemente, thirty-eight, died when his plane crashed a few miles northeast of Puerto Rico's main airport. Today, I still recall the words of Elfren R. Bernier, a former president of the Puerto Rican Bar Association: "Puerto Rico has always been a country divided by religious, political, and social matters, but Puerto Rico was always united in admiring and respecting Roberto."

Years after his death, Clemente's friend Bill Guilfoile, who spent nearly forty years in public relations with the Yankees, the Pirates, and the Baseball Hall of Fame, wrote, "Here in the Hall of Fame, I think a lot, and, you know, Roberto died with the same dignity with which he played the game. No head of a mission of mercy, like Roberto in relation to Nicaragua, travels on December 31 to encounter death. Most leaders would send others, but not Roberto."

Imperfectly human as we all are, Clemente attained a legendary status not only for his triumphs on the playing field, but with simple deeds and thoughts. Maintaining a strong work ethic, helping others whenever possible, and keeping alive the family concept were several of his personal campaigns.

I think about Clemente frequently. His smile had something peculiar to it; it was difficult to decipher. If I spoke a truth about him that he did not want to admit, he would come back with that smile. He told me several times that he was so strong, that at six years of age, he could take a nail and bend it with his hands. Then he would offer that smile.

Sharing time with Clemente was fun. We hardly talked baseball. Most of the time, we would philosophize about life. He loved to tell stories.

Roberto Clemente was a hero in his native Puerto Rico and known throughout the baseball world for his accomplishments on the field, as well as his humanitarian efforts off it. (Don Sparks)

"Once in San Francisco," he said, "I hit a great shot to right-center field that appeared to be a sure home run, but the wind held the ball and Willie Mays caught it. I got so mad that I threw my helmet up in the air, and the wind blew it right out of the park!" He paused and said, "Ask Orlando Cepeda; he was there." Then he gave me that smile of his.

During the winter of 1970-1971, in the balcony of his home overlooking San Juan, he told me, "Late one night, an old lady knocked at the door. She was all bent over in pain and told me that God had sent her to me so that I could treat her with my massages." With a sense of great satisfaction, he added, "I gave her such a 'pop' of the back and a 'crack' of the neck, and she walked away just fine."

Helping that woman was a highlight to him. His large hands come to mind—to me they reflected his spirit. He would grip the bat with the strength of a tiger, but those same hands became extremely gentle when he saw a child and patted his or her head. With those talented hands, he made ceramic objects. He never studied music, but he played the organ quite well. Let us not forget that at the time of his death, he was caring for people by means of chiropractic methods.

In Major League Baseball, in Puerto Rico, and in the Hispanic culture of the game, Roberto Clemente equals number 21 and vice versa. The right field wall at PNC Park in Pittsburgh is 21 feet high in honor of the great Pirate.

Number 21 has a history of its own. Several nights after Clemente's plane crashed, I sat down with his dear friend Phil Dorsey in San Juan. Dorsey, now in his eighties, met Clemente in the spring of 1955 through pitcher Bob Friend. Dorsey was Friend's sergeant in the Army Reserve. Knowing that Clemente would need help in adapting to life in the USA, Friend asked Dorsey, an African-American postal employee, to assist the young player.

Dorsey recalled this apocryphal story: "During the 1955 season, Roberto and I would go to the movies. One night before the show began, he wrote his full name—Roberto Clemente Walker—on a piece of paper." Clemente then turned to Dorsey and said, "My full name is made up of 21 letters. I'm going to see if the Pirates will give me that number."

On the night of September 30, 1972, hours after reaching his 3,000th hit in a room in his Greentree, Pennsylvania, apartment, he told Dorsey and me after reflecting on his accomplishments, "Now, at last, they know me for the player that I am."

He did not use other adjectives to describe his abilities. He simply said, "the player that I am."

The recent World Baseball Classic, of which Puerto Rico was one of the hosts, brought Clemente to my mind repeatedly. Seeing so many fans enjoying major league caliber baseball in my country made me think of his legacy.

For Clemente, the Classic would have been a dream come true, a dream he shared with his longtime friend Bob Leith, a successful San Juan businessman.

Joe L. Brown, the Pirates general manager during Clemente's eighteen-year career, once said of him, "You could never capture the magnificence of the man."

Former MLB Commissioner Bowie K. Kuhn stated at the time of Clemente's death, "He had about him a touch of royalty."

In Puerto Rico, we remember Roberto Clemente as a national hero, an outstanding humanitarian, and an inspiration to the needy, as well as a man who was able to solve the human, social, and political challenges life presented to him.

He gave Puerto Rico a sense of identity, as well as new concepts of hope and respect; above all, his biggest legacy is that he remains an inspiration thirty-three years after his death.

A native of Puerto Rico, Luis R. Mayoral has worked as a team official with the Texas Rangers and Detroit Tigers. He is the author of five baseball books and a veteran of over two thousand MLB radio broadcasts. This essay originally appeared in Memories & Dreams, *Issue 3, 2006.*

Primero Player
The majors' Latin American roots reach back 144 years
to Esteban Bellán
By Jim Gates

As relations between the United States and Cuba show signs of a thaw, visions of Cuban baseball players coming to America dance in the heads of MLB general managers in the same manner that visions of sugar plums dance in the heads of children on the night before Christmas.

To modern fans, this stream of baseball talent may appear to be a twenty-first century component of baseball history, but it is in truth, a pipeline that can trace its roots back to the earliest days of professional baseball in North America. In fact, when the first professional league formed in 1871, one charter member, the Troy Haymakers, had a Cuban-born player. He was Esteban Bellán, a young man born in Havana, who is today recognized as the first Latin American player to appear at the big league level.

Bellán was born October 1, 1849, to a wealthy Cuban father whose name has been lost to history, and to Hart Bellán, his Irish-born mother. Cuba was a colony of Spain during this era and was beset with political turmoil as it struggled for independence. It therefore became common for upper-class Cubans to send their children to the United States to further their education. This helped get their children to a safer location, since the island often broke out in violence and conflict, but it was also a form of protest as the supporters of colonial rule were supposed to send their children to school in Spain.

Along with an older brother, Domingo, thirteen-year-old Bellán arrived in New York in 1863 to enroll in the preparatory department at St. John's College. A small Catholic school at Rose Hill Manor in the Fordham section of the Bronx, the college would eventually become Fordham University. In the 1860s, it was home to at least ten Latin American students. Under the auspices of the Jesuit priests, Bellán would begin his education with courses in English grammar; he would remain enrolled there through 1868.

In addition to his classroom education, Bellán also began a long connection to baseball, a career in which he would serve as a pioneer in two nations. St. John's College had supported a baseball program since September, 1859, and sponsored a team called the Rose Hill Club. Bellán's participation on the team as a catcher and leadoff hitter gave him a chance to play a variety of schools and other local teams, as well as offering their managers the chance to study this young ballplayer.

In 1868, at the age of eighteen, Bellán (then known as Steve Bellán) joined the Union of Morrisania baseball club, a program also located in the Bronx and one which provided him with greater exposure to the world of adult baseball. The Morrisania squad was a powerhouse in the National Association of Base Ball Players (NABBP), and just after Bellán joined the team, it went on a western road trip, offering Bellán the chance to play in most of the major Midwestern cities.

It is also of some interest to note that the NABBP had barred Negro clubs in 1867, after the Pythians of Philadelphia had applied for admission. Bellán's fair complexion, however, allowed him to escape the tyranny of racism.

Following his year with Morrisania, Bellán joined the Union of Lansingburgh club in Rensselaer County, near Troy, NY. Census records indicate that his mother and several sisters had taken up residence in the area, helping to explain his move upstate. This occurred at the time when the NABBP was debating the establishment of professionalism in the game, with Lansingburgh making the decision to join this new category. They would appear as the Troy Haymakers, a charter member of the National Association, the first openly professional major league in 1871.

Bellán played for Troy during the 1871 and 1872 campaigns and appeared as a member of the New York Mutuals of the National Association in 1873. As a third baseman, he was known for his slick, gloveless fielding skills, earning the nickname "The Cuban Sylph." The *New York Clipper* reported that he was "one of the pluckiest of base players." His arm, however, was described as erratic, and his hitting skills were average. Regardless, he was good enough to play at the highest level for those three seasons—batting .251 for his career—before heading back to Cuba.

Third baseman Esteban Bellán (back row, second from left) is recognized as the first Latin American player to play for a professional major league team when he joined the 1871 Troy Haymakers of the National Association.

Upon returning to his native island, Bellán discovered the population was more than ready to adopt his favorite sport. While there is some dispute as to who deserves credit for the introduction of the game, Bellán certainly played an important role in its further development. For Cubans, baseball became a form of rebellion against Spain. The colonial power favored bullfighting, and in some areas the game of baseball was banned. As such, it became a statement of independence, and Bellán was instrumental in helping to grow interest in the game, serving as player-manager in the first professional Cuban league at the end of 1878. He would remain active on the Cuban baseball scene for several years before disappearing from the historical record. His death occurred on August 8, 1932, but the final four decades of his life remain a mystery.

A postscript: Different accounts list Bellán as a Fordham graduate. However, this does not appear to be correct. A 1969 letter from a Fordham University archivist states, "He probably left in his sophomore year to become a semiprofessional baseball player, as they were then called. Estevan [sic] Bellan did not graduate and is not listed among the alumni. He did well scholastically in the beginning, but I guess sport caught up with him."

Jim Gates is Librarian Emeritus at the National Baseball Hall of Fame and Museum. This essay originally appeared in Memories & Dreams, *Issue 3, 2015.*

Besting the Bambino

Hall of Famer Cristóbal Torriente's story revisited through historic image of Babe Ruth in Museum's collection

By Alex Coffey

He was widely known as a franchise-type player, the sort of singular talent who could lead a team to victory in a number of ways. A powerfully built outfielder with a left-handed bat that could reach any fence in any park, he had a flare for the extravagant and for racking up mind-boggling statistics. He was as iconic as he was unforgettable.

"A tremendous guy," Hall of Famer Frankie Frisch once said of him.

"He did everything well," said former teammate Martín Dihigo. "He fielded like a natural, threw in perfect form. He covered as much field as could be covered. As for batting, he went [from] being good to being something extraordinary."

The sports editors of the *Pittsburgh Courier* called him a "prodigious hitter, a rifle-armed thrower, and a tower of strength on the defense."

Babe Ruth? Mel Ott? No.

His name was Cristóbal Torriente.

Torriente, a hard-hitting center fielder who hailed from Cienfuegos, Cuba, was one of the first Cuban baseball stars to play in the United States. A member of the Cuban Baseball Hall of Fame's first class of 1939, Torriente was posthumously inducted into the National Baseball Hall of Fame in 2006 by a Special Committee on the Negro Leagues and pre-Negro Leagues.

Torriente's fame began in earnest when the great Bambino himself came to Torriente's homeland, under the promise of a thousand dollars per exhibition game, to play against the Havana Reds and Torriente's Almendares Blues. In a game that has gone down in Cuban baseball lore as a "David and Goliath" story of sorts, Torriente, playing on his home soil, upstaged Ruth, bursting onto the baseball scene and capturing the attention of fans worldwide.

Recently, the National Baseball Hall of Fame and Museum has begun digitizing photos via its Digital Archive Project, providing fans with online access to its historic images. One of the many images now available at collection.baseballhall.org depicts Ruth batting in Havana, Cuba, in an exhibition game against Torriente's squad on November 6, 1920.

Years before Ruth ever set foot in Cuba, Torriente was rapidly developing as a coveted young player. While there isn't much in the written record about Torriente's baseball upbringing, it is widely believed that he started playing at an early age for the sugar mill baseball teams in Cienfuegos.

"The important thing about Cienfuegos was that the sugar industry was made for baseball," explained Roberto González Echevarría, a professor of Hispanic and Comparative Literature at Yale University and author of *The Pride of Havana: A History of Cuban Baseball.*

"The sugar mills developed company towns, and these small company towns around the sugar mills had baseball teams that competed against each other," González Echevarría said. "[Torriente] probably got his start there. Cuban Blacks could only get their start in sugar league baseball and in the amateur leagues."

After his tenure in Cienfuegos, Torriente began his pro career in 1913 with the Cuban Stars. He would play for them until 1916, when he briefly joined the Kansas City All Nations. His career would take off soon after that, when he began playing under Hall of Fame manager Rube Foster with the Chicago American Giants—the powerhouse of the Negro National League. Torriente was so highly touted and anticipated that fellow Hall of Famer Oscar Charleston was relocated from center field to left upon the Cuban's arrival. Torriente would help the Giants capture their first three Negro National League pennants, from 1920 to 1922.

During his seventeen seasons in the Negro Leagues, Torriente moved around quite a bit, as was characteristic of the time. After his seven-year stint with the Giants, he spent a season with the Kansas City Monarchs, then played two seasons with the Detroit Stars and a year with the Cleveland Cubs. During that time, he compiled a .331 batting average—and hit as high as .432 in 1920, the year he won the league's batting title. Stacked up against other Negro Leaguers, he ranks 11th all-time in RBI with 309, 12th in slugging percentage (.517), and 16th in total bases (1,055). He could even perform on the mound, posting a pitching record of 16-5 during his Negro Leagues career.

"Torriente batted cleanup for Rube [Foster] through 1925, but he was much more than a power hitter," wrote an unnamed scout in a report that is part of the National Baseball Hall of Fame Library's Ashland Collection, an archive of Negro Leagues history. "Unlike Louis Santop, Mule Suttles, and Heavy Johnson, all top sluggers of that era, Torriente was also a master at bunting, base running, and defense."

A five-tool player, Torriente could dominate the game with his bat, his arm, his legs, and his glove, but he was unfortunately playing at the wrong time. Prejudices of the era were alive and well, and racial bias prevented him from advancing to the big leagues, even though light-skinned Cubans of the time did.

"Why did the major leagues ignore the light-skinned Cuban, during a period when Latins Dolf Luque, Mike González, and Armando Marsans all went to the big time?" a scout named "Gardner" hypothetically asked in a report from the Ashland Collection. "He would have went up there, but he had real bad hair. He was a little lighter than I am, but he had real rough hair. He would have been all right if his hair had been better."

It meant that a man who had drawn comparisons to Ruth and other standout talents was relegated to the Negro Leagues for the entirety of his career—a fact that made a seventeen-day stretch in the fall of 1920 perhaps his most memorable time as a baseball player.

That fall, the New York Giants played a series of exhibition games against the Havana Reds and the Almendares Blues. The brainchild of the ever-economical mind of Abel Linares, the Cuban Stars' owner, the games were a huge attraction in baseball-crazed Cuba. Torriente, playing winter ball for the Blues at the time, had a chance to play against the Babe.

While Ruth wasn't a member of the New York Giants, he was interested in making an "easy" $20,000. And Linares was interested in drawing a big crowd.

"Linares searched his mind for the most compelling [way] to promote an exhibition that a year earlier had been reduced to second billing by a soccer match that received special attention because it was supported financially by Spain," wrote Yuyo Ruíz in his book *The Bambino Visits Cuba*. "…So he approached the game's biggest star, George Herman 'Babe' Ruth, and ultimately convinced him to come to Cuba."

The Giants arrived in Cuba in mid-October, led by manager John McGraw and then-assistant manager Johnny Evers. While the entire team didn't make the trek—the Giants were quite short on starting pitching, a factor sorely felt when facing Torriente in particular—about a dozen of them did. Meanwhile, Ruth arrived in late October, accompanied by his then-wife, Helen, and stayed for a number of weeks.

Already an iconic player who had just come off of a historic 54-home run season, Ruth's arrival was proclaimed far and wide in both American and Cuban newspapers. "Babe Ruth is playing winter ball in Cuba," read the *Daily Illinois*. "Reports have it that boats going from the US to Havana are putting on armor plates to escape being torpedoed by stray homers."

Because Cuban baseball was more driven by small-ball style of play, bombastic hitters like Ruth and Torriente were exciting and different. Expecting to see a show, people paid the high ticket prices set by Linares—high enough to pay off the $20,000 that would eventually make its way into Ruth's pocket.

"[Ruth's] feats were touted in the papers," González Echevarría said. "But Cuban baseball was not home run-centered. Black baseball was very prudent, very tactical."

With those expectations awaiting him, Ruth arrived at the park on October 30 to play in his first exhibition game of the tour. He doubled and tripled, but hit no home runs.

The real shock came in Ruth's third game on Torriente's turf. Because the roster was limited, McGraw opted to put in George "High Pockets" Kelly, as the starting pitcher, even though Kelly traditionally played first base. Torriente reportedly smacked a two-run homer to left-center field and came back for more in the third, with a solo round-tripper.

By the fifth inning, the Bambino decided to take matters into his own hands and stepped onto the mound. In a dramatic match-up between a world-famous slugger and a rising star, Torriente drilled a line drive to left field for a two-run double. He would finish the game with three home runs and six RBI in five at-bats, while Ruth would go hitless.

While the Giants would go on to narrowly defeat the Blues in the series, 5 games to 4, the Blues won that game, 11-4, led by the offensive prowess of their own Bambino.

Feeling pride in their hometown hero, the Cuban fans threw money onto the field for Torriente as a way of showing their admiration. Some fans reportedly even went as far as throwing cigars and gold watches. But what Torriente received in money that day was far exceeded by the high compliments he would earn from all who had witnessed the game.

"I was down in Havana in 1920 with Babe Ruth and about twelve of the New York Giants," Frisch recalled. "That's over fifty years ago, but I can still recall Torriente. He was a tremendous guy. I think I was playing third base at that time, and he hit a ground ball by me, and you know, that's one of those things—look in the glove, it might be there. But it wasn't in my glove.

It dug a hole about a foot deep on its way to left field. And I'm glad I wasn't in front of it!"

The Cuban newspaper *El Día* confirmed this account, with a prideful one of its own.

"Yesterday Cristóbal Torriente elevated himself to the greatest heights of glory and popularity," the editors wrote of their newfound hero. "His hitting will enter Cuban baseball history as one of its most brilliant pages."

And for all of the praise Torriente received, Ruth was criticized for not meeting expectations. Varying newspaper accounts from the time list his home run total between zero and three during his time in Havana, a disappointment for fans who went to see the home run king.

The *Evening World*, a New York City paper in circulation at the turn of the twentieth century, published a story entitled "Babe Ruth Returns Here from Almost Homerunless Junket on Cuban Soil," explaining that "the funny part of the trip to Cuba was that Babe was not able to live right up to the handle of his reputation as a home run hitter. Down there, natives were led to believe that Babe could knock out a homer whenever he wanted to."

A couple of weeks later, the same paper took it one step further, singling Torriente out as well. "[Babe Ruth] didn't make a single home run in the fifteen games, though he batted .500 on the trip. Torriente, the 'Black Babe Ruth,' on the other hand, hit three home runs in one game last week, and in a fourth trip to the plate made a two-bagger."

According to the Cuban newspaper *El Diario de la Marina*, fans started to boo Ruth when he came to the plate, frustrated that they weren't getting what they had originally paid to see.

But regardless of what the media was printing and how the fans were reacting, Torriente insisted his feat was small when sized up against those of the great Bambino.

"In summary, Torriente recovered quite a bit of change and three hundred cigars," reported the Cuban newspaper *Horacio Roqueta*. "Interviewed by journalists over his three-home run performance, he said it was purely an accident: 'Ask the Bambino what he does every day.' "

While these sensationalized newspaper articles gave varying descriptions of the game, a similar message seemed to ring true in most accounts—Cuba had found its Bambino, a hard-hitting slugger it could tout as its own. Yet it's important to note that today's historians have presented conflicting opinions on the level of competition during these games. Echevarría is of the mindset that this almost-mythical performance by Torriente could be accounted for by a number of factors, starting with the dearth of starting pitchers the Giants had to choose from.

"It became an iconic game, although it was really not a serious game," he explained. "It was an exhibition game. And so the Cubans wanted to best the Americans at anything they could and were very proud of the fact that [Torriente] had bested Babe Ruth."

Even *El Diario de La Marina* questioned the legitimacy of the game, comparing it to batting practice—"resulto una practica al bate del club alemendares"—and implying that certain players might have been drunk during the game.

Jorge S. Figuerdo, a historian who specializes in Cuban baseball, insists in his brief essay "November 4, 1920: The Day Torriente Outclassed Ruth" that the myth is not only true, but is an important part of Cuban history. "[Torriente] had the most unforgettable game of his career and surely one of the most memorable games in the history of Cuban baseball as he outclassed the incomparable Babe Ruth."

Regardless of the competition level, it was clear that by the end of his time in Cuba, Ruth was ready to get back to his normal self.

The day after he returned to the United States, the *Tulsa Daily World* published a photo of Ruth grinning, with a caption below that read, "Mr. George Ruth, known in ball-dom as Babe or the Bambino, returned yesterday from Cuba, radiating ambition and declaring he will establish a mark of seventy-five home runs next season."

Whether or not Torriente's acclaimed performance ignited a competitive spark in Ruth is up for debate. But what can't be denied is the lasting impact Torriente's performance would have on Cuban history.

In the image of Ruth in the Hall of Fame's Archives, he is captured mid-swing. Although the background of the photo is blurry, the enormous dimensions of Almendares Park, lined with palm trees in the distance that give it a tropical flair, are visible. As Ruth swings, it seems as if every spectator in the park is as still as the photo itself. Time is put on hold as the world waits to see the Bambino they have heard about from far and wide.

Cristóbal Torriente, of course, did not have the fabled career that Babe Ruth did, as segregation-era baseball, sadly, did not make that an option. For at least one game, however, he upstaged the great Bambino and gave a glimpse of the power and talent that would one day make him a Hall of Famer. Crushing three home runs and a double, Torriente, the Cuban Babe, put on a display that his fans would never forget.

Alex Coffey was the Communications Specialist at the National Baseball Hall of Fame and former Oakland A's beat writer at The Athletic. *This essay originally appeared in* Memories & Dreams, *Issue 1, 2017.*

Cuban Baseball Legacy Rich in American Heritage

By Adrian Burgos

Baseball arrived in Cuba in the 1860s amidst political strife and economic instability in the Spanish colony. Political tensions, especially during Cuba's Ten Years War (1868-1878), drove disenchanted members of the Cuban elite to send their children to US educational institutions and thousands of other Cubans to relocate to the States. As a result, many prominent figures in Cuban baseball received their indoctrination as émigrés or students.

Credited as "the father" of Cuban baseball, Nemesio Guilló returned to Cuba in 1864 after attending Springhill College in Mobile, Alabama, with a bat and baseball among his possessions. A January 1924 account in the Cuban newspaper *Diario de la Marina* labeled the equipment "the first to be seen in Cuba."

While Guilló has received credit for introducing the game, Esteban Bellán represents the island's most successful "graduate" of stateside baseball training. A varsity player at Rose Hill College at Fordham University, Bellán turned pro in 1869. Two years later he performed with the Troy Haymakers in the National Association as Cuba's first big leaguer. After returning to Cuba late in 1872, Bellán helped form the island's first baseball club, the Habana Base Ball Club. Brothers Carlos and Teodoro Zaldo shared a Fordham background with Bellán, having studied there from 1875 to 1877 and creating the Almendares Baseball Club upon returning to their native land.

Cubans organized a professional league in the winter of 1878-1879. Indicative of the island's fragile political situation, Spanish rulers closely monitored the baseball circuit, including the visit of the Rochester-based Hop Bitters, the circuit's first North American visitors. The club's publicity campaign, distributing American flags with "hop bitters" emblazoned on them, upset Spanish authorities who worried the flags "would encourage the Cubans to rebellion," said Hop Bitters manager Frank Bancroft. While it was unsuccessful financially and not overly competitive, the Hop Bitters' tour nonetheless initiated the first era of Cuban barnstorming by North American teams.

Cubans strove to improve their baseball through the incorporation of North American talent, direct competition, and importation of technical expertise. Several Cuban league teams sought out US professionals. In September, 1879, the Habana team advertised its interest in "importing" a pitcher for the 1879-1880 campaign in the *New York Clipper*. While Habana failed to sign a North American player, its starting lineup featured Bellán, Guilló, and Emilio Sabourín, all of whom had attended US educational institutions. The Colón team did sign two white North Americans, Warren "Hick" Carpenter and Jimmy Macullar.

Cubans debated the impact North American professionals would have on Cuban baseball. Some worried they would corrupt the Cuban game by encouraging playing for pay over virtuous competition. Cuban player Wenceslao Gálvez complained that hiring North American players gave clubs an unfair advantage. Despite such reservations, Cubans openly recruited North Americans and continued to welcome US barnstorming teams.

North American barnstormers observed firsthand the development of Cuban players. A frequent visitor to Cuba throughout his professional career, John McGraw's initial trip in 1891 piqued his interest in Antonio María García, a lighter-skinned Cuban nicknamed *"El Inglés"* (The Englishman), who starred in the Cuban circuit. García turned down McGraw's invitation to join Baltimore's American Association club, claiming his Cuban monthly salary (five hundred dollars throughout the year) was more than what the Orioles offered.

Cuban professional baseball gradually opened along racial lines in the late nineteenth century. On the heels of slave emancipation in 1886, Afro-Cubans formed their own baseball clubs, and in 1887, a tournament for the "colored" championship was organized in Havana. The entry of black Cubans would dramatically change the ranks of Cuban professional players. Whereas when the Hop Bitters toured in 1879, all the Cuban players came from Cuba's "white" elite, by the start of the twentieth century, the strongest teams in the Cuban league and those that barnstormed in the United States featured Afro-Cubans.

In July 1899, approximately six months after Cuba gained independence, the All Cubans initiated the first US tour by a Cuban professional team. The All Cubans dropped the majority of their games against semiprofessional, minor league, and black teams. The team did attempt to reclaim the Cuban name. Protesting the Cuban X-Giants "posing as representatives of Cuba," the native Cubans challenged the African-American impersonators but dropped both the challenge match and rematch. Tours by the Cuban X-Giants and the Brooklyn Superbas that winter initiated the first barnstorming era free of Spanish colonial rule.

Cuban teams grew increasingly competitive against barnstorming big leaguers, especially after 1907, when talented African Americans like Rube Foster and John Henry Lloyd started to formally participate in the Cuban league. Composed of American and National League players, the All-Leaguers who visited in 1907 won five of eleven contests versus Almendares and Habana. The following winter, the Cincinnati Reds mustered only six wins in thirteen games. The lackluster performance upset team president August "Garry" Herrmann, who expressed opposition to future barnstorming trips in *Sporting Life*, stating, "I find that the Reds are playing against certain men in Cuba against whom there is an unwritten law in the big leagues…

That is another reason why I am opposed to any future games in Cuba."

Cubans who entered the US playing fields learned the brutal reality of organized baseball's color line. Securing access involved scrutinizing family history and team officials providing "proof" of a player's racial eligibility. In 1908, New Britain signed Cubans Rafael Almeida, Alfredo Cabrera, Armando Marsans, and Luis Padrón. Connecticut League officials called into question the Cubans' racial eligibility, voting to forbid teams from contracting "black" players at their post season meeting. New Britain's manager traveled to Cuba and found that all his Cubans were "real Cubans" except Padrón, resulting in his expulsion from the circuit.

Cuban pitcher José Méndez endured a different fate. Clearly possessing major league caliber talent, evident in his compiling a 25-inning scoreless streak against the barnstorming Cincinnati Reds (1908), New York Giants manager John McGraw told sportswriters he would pay $50,000 for Méndez's release if he were a white man.

Rafael Almeida and Armando Marsans did successfully break into the majors with the Cincinnati Reds in 1911. This sparked a movement to revamp the Cuban professional circuit's cooperative system. League officials and team owners complained players enjoyed too much control. One league official told *Sporting Life* in February, 1912, that Black Cubans controlled the system "to such an extent that it failed to develop young players." Another official's remarks to sportswriter Bill Phelon unveiled a racial subtext to the reform movement, stating, "I wish…some big league team would whip us ten straight games. That would reduce the heads of the black players, make them listen to reason, and also give a better chance for white men to succeed them on the local teams." The campaign to change the Cuban league succeeded in implementing a contract system, but Black Cubans continued to dominate the Cuban professional scene.

The formation of the Negro National League (1920) and the Eastern Colored League (1923) increased the Cuban presence on the US playing field. The participation of white and Black Americans in the Cuban league likewise grew during this period. By the late 1940s, the integrated leagues in the Caribbean featured the sport's most talented players without regard to race. These players were showcased in the Caribbean Series, organized in 1948 with the Cuban league champion facing the winners of the Puerto Rican, Panamanian, and Venezuelan circuits.

The Cuban Revolution (1959) precipitated the end of open exchange between US and Cuban professional baseball. "Baseball Is Dying in Castro's Cuba," the *New York Times* declared in a November article that detailed the Cuban circuit's declining attendance and the Cuban government's efforts to rally support. Shortly thereafter, Fidel Castro declared the end of Cuban professional baseball, converting the circuit into an amateur national league, *serie nacional*.

Citing security concerns, Major League Baseball Commissioner Ford Frick prohibited US-born players from participating in Cuba. The turbulent political climate forced Orestes "Minnie" Miñoso, Tony Taylor, Mike Cuellar, and dozens of other Cubans to make the difficult, life-altering decision to leave the island not knowing whether they would be able to return or to stay in Cuba and give up their US professional career. In either case, Cuban professional baseball would never be the same.

Adrian Burgos is a professor of history at the University of Illinois-Urbana Champagne. He is the author of several books on Latino baseball including Playing America's Game: Baseball, Latinos, and the Color Line. *This essay originally appeared in* Memories & Dreams, *Issue 3, 2006.*

A Cuban Revolution
Hall of Famer Martín Dihigo left a legacy that still impacts the National Pastime
By Danny Torres

Since its inception, the National Baseball Hall of Fame and Museum has meticulously documented the historic achievements of the National Pastime. But there's a little-known performance by a Hall of Famer that only a few historians have shared.

Martín Dihigo, a native of Matanzas, Cuba, was born in 1906 and is widely considered to be the most versatile ballplayer who ever wore a baseball uniform.

And a feat achieved eighty years ago—on September 5, 1938—might have been the pinnacle of his career. That season, Dihigo, who played in the Negro and Latin American Leagues, led the Mexican League in wins, strikeouts, ERA, and batting average.

Under the unbearable heat of a relentless Mexican sun, he squared off against another outstanding pitcher from the Negro Leagues—Satchel Paige. According to baseball journalist and author Peter C. Bjarkman, an authority on Cuban baseball history, the two future Hall of Famers competed against one another in that year's Mexican League championship game.

Dihigo was on the mound for Águila of Veracruz. With an impressive record of 18-2, a league-best 184 strikeouts, and a jaw-dropping 0.92 ERA, he was fully aware of the challenge of facing Agrario of Mexico City with the incomparable Paige as their starting pitcher.

Through eight innings, the game was at an impasse, but Paige couldn't continue to pitch in this highly contested matchup, and the ball was handed over to Agrario's Cuban hurler, Ramón Bragaña. With the score 1-1 in the ninth inning, Dihigo stepped up to the plate.

The owner of a whopping .387 average, Dihigo ripped a monstrous blast over the center field wall to end this thrilling game with a walk-off homer. With that swing, Martín Magdaleno Dihigo Llanos achieved a baseball trifecta: hitting the game-ending homer, earning the win as a pitcher, and managing the pennant-winning team.

A lifetime .300-plus hitter and a four-time Cuban Winter League MVP, Dihigo began his playing career at age sixteen with the Cuban Stars of the Eastern Colored League. Dihigo's versatility would today be a manager's dream—he could play every position other than catcher.

Similar to that of Babe Ruth, Dihigo's pitching prowess was extraordinary; he notched no-hitters in three different countries (Puerto Rico, Mexico, and Venezuela) and finished with a combined 218-106 Winter League/Negro Leagues record.

Given that the game of baseball was still segregated until 1947, one could only imagine the records Dihigo and so many others would have broken if given the opportunity to play in the big leagues.

Although he passed away just short of his sixty-sixth birthday in 1971, his legend has grown larger than ever. Throughout Latin America, Dihigo was idolized and anointed with two distinct Spanish nicknames: "El Inmortal" (The Immortal) and "El Maestro" (The Teacher).

In his fascinating book, *Mi Padre, El Inmortal* (*My Father, the Immortal*), about his beloved father, Gilberto Dihigo takes readers on a narrative journey to discover who Martín Dihigo really was outside of his native country. For the author, this revelation didn't happen until he reached the age of twenty-four on a visit to the Dominican Republic. On that trip, Gilberto was stunned by the emotional outpouring as baseball fans stopped and asked him, "Are you the son of Martín Dihigo?"

"I knew my dad was a famous ballplayer because of how people spoke about him. But that was in Cuba. But for foreigners to idolize my dad in that manner is what struck me. For me, it was very impressionable," said the now sixty-five-year-old author from his home in Orlando, Florida.

Born in Cuba in 1952, Gilberto majored in history but was drawn to journalism and worked as a reporter and television producer at various news agencies throughout Latin America. Through his own research, his many travels abroad, and at one point interviewing those who knew and had played with his late father, he began to grasp his father's standing in the baseball world.

Gilberto describes his father, who was always impeccably dressed, as a great communicator and a "progressive" who delved into politics and social issues. He was a phenomenal chef (which he had to take up because restaurants during that era were segregated) and loved Cuban history.

"I inherited my father's passion for history. My father would play trivia games with me on various topics that I tried to answer. If I got it right, he would reward me with some money," Gilberto said.

When asked about what his father's opinion would be of baseball in 2018, Gilberto mentioned one of the hot topics in Major League Baseball today: the length of the game.

"One of the things that my father complained about was the pace of the game. He said something had to be done," Gilberto said. "For example, pitching changes add to the length of the game. This is something my father talked about for years. He said games should be two hours because fans don't have the patience."

On the mound, Dihigo frustrated hitters with his impeccable control, blazing fastball, and rocket of a throwing arm. Off the mound, he had strong views on pitching and conditioning.

"He said a pitcher doesn't have to throw hard. The pitcher needs control and [has to know] how to work the corners," Gilberto said. "As for conditioning, there was no such thing as lifting weights. Players during that era ran because that was the best exercise for a pitcher. It seemed to work because they played the entire year and they needed the money. He played every position out of necessity, just to have a job."

During the 1920s and 1930s, Cuban-born Martín Dihigo starred in the Latin American and Negro Leagues as a feared hitter and pitcher. He would eventually earn election to the Hall of Fame in 1977.

Alex Pompez, the intuitive executive/owner of the Cuban Stars and New York Cubans and a 2006 Hall of Fame inductee, played an instrumental role in the life of Gilberto's father and other Latin American and Negro Leagues players. So did future Baseball Hall of Famers Oscar Charleston, Pop Lloyd, and Cristóbal Torriente, who served as mentors to the Cuban sensation from Matanzas during his formative years.

Added Gilberto, "The book pays homage to a father, but also to all of those players who played with my dad. They were the pioneers for all Latinos and African-American players. They played in adverse conditions, for little pay, and with no medical benefits. Judy Johnson, Cool Papa Bell, and, of course, Josh Gibson [all of whom were eventually enshrined in Cooperstown] were friends of my dad."

In 1987, while Gilberto was traveling in Mexico, a man approached him and told an inspirational story about his dad's charitable side that few knew of.

"An elderly man looked into my eyes and gave me a hug. He said, 'This hug is not for you, but in the name of your father.' "

When the elderly man was a young boy, he worked as a shoe shiner and Dihigo was his customer.

Gilberto continued, "One day my father asked, 'Why aren't you in school?' "

"The young boy responded, 'I have to work for myself and my family.'

"My dad asked another question," Gilberto said. " 'Where do you live?' And within a week, my dad went to his home and said to his parents that their son was bright and [that he had] observed this while he was shining shoes. My dad ended up paying for the boy's entire education."

Similar to legends Roberto Clemente and Lou Gehrig, Dihigo wasn't able to celebrate his grand entrance into Cooperstown. He passed away six years prior to the Special Committee on the Negro Leagues electing him to the National Baseball Hall of Fame in 1977. In his place stood José Valdivielso, a former Washington Senators infielder who was from the same town in Cuba and also a distant cousin of "El Maestro." He would have the distinct honor of accepting Dihigo's Hall of Fame plaque.

But, as Valdivielso recalled, there's more to this touching story:

"I called the Commissioner's office. At that time, my dear friend, Monte Irvin, worked there," he said. "Rodolfo Fernández (former pitcher in the Cuban Baseball League), Bowie Kuhn, and a few others began to research Dihigo's career. Once it was decided he was going to be inducted, they asked me to receive his plaque. I said I would do this for my country and my hometown."

Another revered ballplayer, Atanacio "Tony" Pérez Rigal, played twenty-three seasons in the majors. As a two-time World Series champion, a seven-time All-Star, and a 2000 Baseball Hall of Fame inductee, he described his immense pride in meeting "El Inmortal" in Havana, Cuba. He credits Dihigo's oldest son, Martín Jr., for making the moment possible.

"I played with his son in the minors, and from everything I heard from my father and father-in-law, they said [Dihigo] was the best," Pérez said. "He was a super player, and what an honor it was to meet him. I became quite emotional in his presence. Keep in mind, I'm meeting a legend."

Dihigo's extraordinary impact as a player and manager, and even after his retirement as a commentator of Cuban league games, continues as succeeding generations of Cuban ballplayers leave their mark on the game.

Danny Torres is an educator and freelance writer from the Bronx, NY. This essay originally appeared in Memories & Dreams, *Issue 3, 2018.*

Kings of the World
In 1959, Havana-based Triple-A team ruled minor league baseball
By David Krell

The gold lettering has been worn down with time, but the words still speak to the unique story of Danny Morejon's championship ring from 1959. The word "mundiales"—Spanish for "world"—lets everyone know that the Havana Sugar Kings called Cuba their home. And they were the best team in the Triple-A International League that year.

The ring is now a part of the collection at the National Baseball Hall of Fame and Museum, and the story of the Sugar Kings—a Cincinnati Reds farm team that sent dozens of players to the big leagues from 1954 to 1960—is one of the ties that forever bind baseball and Cuba together.

In 1946, renowned scout Joe Cambria founded the Havana Cubans, a Washington Senators affiliate. The Cubans played in the Florida International League, which began operations that same year with five other teams: the Miami Sun Sox, Miami Beach Flamingos, Lakeland Pilots, Tampa Smokers, and West Palm Beach Indians. In the league's first three years, the Cubans won two league championships in 1947 and 1948.

Cambria's efforts in Cuba began in 1935, when the Senators assigned him to be their first scout in Latin America. His work led to the signing of more than four hundred players of Cuban origin to professional baseball contracts, including 1964 American League Rookie of the Year Tony Oliva and 1965 American League Most Valuable Player Zoilo Versalles.

Cambria refused to persuade his prospects with money. The *Associated Press*'s 1962 obituary for Cambria quoted his views on such tactics: "I never gave anybody a nickel bonus. I don't believe in making a boy a financial success before he starts. A big bonus puts too much pressure on the player and the scout."

By 1954, the Cubans had become the Sugar Kings and
had found a new home in the International League. Five years
later, the team achieved a rare feat—winning a tripleheader on
August 3, 1959, against the Toronto Maple Leafs. With future
big league manager Preston Gómez skippering the team to an
80-73 regular-season record (despite being outscored by more
than 50 runs), the Sugar Kings made the playoffs and upset
Columbus and Richmond to win the International League crown.
They then went on to capture the Little World Series against the
Minneapolis Millers.

Future big leaguers Luis Arroyo, Leo Cardenas, Elio Chacón,
Mike Cuellar, and Cookie Rojas were some of the nearly two
dozen Sugar Kings players who would play in the majors.

But changes were in the air during the Cuban Revolution.
Nationalization of US property and businesses became a high
priority under Fidel Castro's regime, which overthrew the Batista
government in January, 1959. The Sugar Kings, in turn, migrated
to New Jersey in 1960 amid increasing Cold War strife between
the two nations.

On July 8, 1960, International League President Frank
Shaughnessy authorized moving the Sugar Kings from Havana
because of the volatility in Cuba. Shaughnessy informed the
Sugar Kings' owner, Roberto Maduro, of his reasons.

"The message said that an emergency existed in Havana
because of tension between Cuba and the United States, and
that the safety and welfare of baseball personnel 'is or might be
endangered,' " the *Associated Press* reported.

It was unpersuasive to Maduro, who blamed the Continental
League, Branch Rickey's ultimately unrealized dream of a third
baseball circuit that would compete against the National League
and the American League.

"Toronto and Buffalo both want to go in the Continental
League," said Maduro in *The Washington Post*. "They are mad at
the International League for setting the value of the franchises

too high. They now are using the Cuban situation to torpedo the International League and open the way for their exit into the Continental League."

Further, Maduro exclaimed, "I don't know what to do. I can only say it's completely outrageous. I am not in politics."

Castro, a one-time aspiring pitcher who frequented Sugar Kings games, took to the airwaves with a televised speech laced with detestation of Shaughnessy's action. According to the *AP*, Castro said, "American players when they came here got nothing but respect and admiration. The people treated them cordially, and there is no record of attacks on players of any kind. But violating all codes of sportsmanship, they now take away our franchise."

On July 14, the team played its last game as the Sugar Kings, winning 7-3 against the Miami Marlins. The following day, Jersey City welcomed its new tenants with a motorcade that inspired joyous shouts. Now called the Jerseys, the team had a new manager. Napoleon Reyes took the reins after Tony Castano opted to return to Cuba.

The Jerseys lost their first two games, both against the Columbus Jets, by scores of 8-3 and 4-2. Though an inauspicious beginning, it did not dilute the enthusiasm of fans in Jersey City, just across the Hudson River from Manhattan. When the Dodgers and the Giants left for California after the 1957 season, the New York City metropolitan area suffered a baseball void of epic magnitude. With the Yankees offering the only professional baseball option, fans welcomed this alternative.

Robert L. Teague identified this passion in his description of the second Jerseys-Jets game for the *New York Times*.

"Today, the local heroes committed what would have been an unpardonable sin in the eyes of a less hospitable audience," wrote Teague. "They failed to hold a 2-0 advantage and finished the contest still under the .500 level for the season and at the .000 mark for their efforts in their new city.

"Despite the charitable atmosphere, however, the deposed Sugar Kings appeared determined to merit such loyalty in their new realm. They hustled on and off el diamente between innings and ran the bases as if hotly pursued by el Diablo."

The love affair between the Jerseys and Jersey City, however, was brief. Following the 1961 season, the team moved to Jacksonville and became the Suns. In 1969, Virginia became the team's home. First stationed in Portsmouth, the team changed its name to the Tidewater Tides. When Norfolk's Harbor Park opened in 1993, the team became the Norfolk Tides to honor its new home field and city.

David Krell is a noted historian and author of several books on baseball history, including his most recent work, 1962: Baseball and America in the Time of JFK. *This essay originally appeared in* Memories & Dreams, *Issue 3, 2015.*

Pirates of the Caribbean
The 1971 Bucs utilized a diverse lineup to help secure a World Series crown
By Danny Torres

In 1871, Esteban Bellán, by way of Havana, Cuba, and Fordham University, played in twenty-nine games with the Troy Haymakers of the National Association, becoming the first Latin American player in the big leagues.

One hundred years later, the Pittsburgh Pirates fielded the most culturally diverse team in Major League Baseball en route to the World Series title—led by future Hall of Famer and proud Puerto Rican Roberto Clemente. After a century of progress, the Latin American influence was fully visible in baseball.

Today, Hispanic ballplayers populate rosters throughout the majors, giving the Caribbean a commanding presence in the National Pastime. In 2015, the Dominican Republic leads the big leagues with eighty-three players, followed by Venezuela (sixty-five), Cuba (eighteen), and Puerto Rico (thirteen).

But in 1971, the Pirates were on the cutting edge of baseball diversity. Fans around the National League witnessed firsthand an intriguing lineup that included prominent Latino players such as Manny Sanguillén, Vic Davalillo, José Pagán, Jackie Hernández, Rennie Stennett, and Clemente.

"There was no question that Roberto Clemente was our leader," said Al Oliver, a seven-time All-Star and the Pirates' center fielder in 1971. "Undeniably, [Latin American players] brought the love of the game, an enthusiasm, and they played the game loosely. To this day, I love watching the Latinos play because they remind me of the Harlem Globetrotters on a baseball field. They're having fun, and that's how the game should be played."

Baseball historian/journalist Luis Rodríguez-Mayoral, who was a Spanish radio commentator during select games for the '71 Pirates, attributes the triumphs to the Latino players who, during an era of racial bigotry and segregation, transformed baseball into a sport of inclusion.

"Latino stars like Minnie Miñoso, Chico Carrasquel, Luis Aparicio, Vic Power, and Roberto Clemente paved the road for younger players and Latinos in all walks of life," Rodríguez-Mayoral said. "Up until the 1950s, we had few personalities to admire from afar. Baseball's magical power to unite gave Latino players the incentive to reach for the stars with their colorful artistry between the white lines."

Dave Cash, the Pirates' second baseman in 1971, recalled how Clemente, his Latino brethren, and team skipper Danny Murtaugh formed a camaraderie throughout the season that to this day still amazes him.

"Murtaugh was a player's manager. He knew the psyche of each player. He handled them perfectly and was a student of the game," said Cash, who grew up about forty-five minutes north of Cooperstown in Utica, NY.

If you took a survey of the best player on the 1971 Pirates, Clemente would be the obvious choice. But if you asked who was the second-best, the response might be a surprise: Many would answer it was Sanguillén, a catcher who batted .319 and threw out an impressive 50 percent of would-be base stealers.

Both Oliver and Cash agreed that if it weren't for Hall of Famer Johnny Bench, who overshadowed "Sangy's" clutch hitting and impressive defense, the Panamanian native might have been looked at during his own time in an entirely different manner.

With Sanguillén's World Series batting average of .379, the affable backstop—immortalized on film for his hug of Clemente during the Fall Classic, one that is often played on highlight reels—became one of the keys to the Pirates' victory against the Orioles. There was also Pagán's memorable double to drive in what proved to be the winning run in Game Seven, as well as Davalillo's tutelage of young players like Oliver.

And—of course—The Great One.

The maturation of Clemente's unforgettable career was truly one for the ages. It runs much deeper than his two World Series championships (including MVP honors in the 1971 Fall Classic) and an extraordinary lifetime .317 batting average. For those who knew Clemente inside the clubhouse, on the baseball diamond, or in his private life, the one common denominator that still resonates today above all his glorious achievements and accolades is that he cared about the dignity of the human race.

He worked tirelessly with charities, commented on social issues, and ultimately died trying to shuttle food and medical supplies to an earthquake-ravaged Nicaragua on New Year's Eve in 1972. Interestingly, his style of play and his life off the field were synonymous with a chess match.

Throughout the entire 1971 World Series, he seemed to calculate every move to perfection. And with that final out in Game Seven and the entire team celebrating their unbelievable win in the clubhouse, legendary Pirates sportscaster Bob Prince congratulated winning pitcher Steve Blass (who also was victorious in Game Three after the Pirates dropped the Series' first two games) and Clemente. After speaking with Blass, Prince turned to Clemente. But before they continued with the interview, which was broadcast live on NBC, Clemente modestly thanked Prince but respectfully asked if it was okay to say a few words in Spanish to his beloved parents who were watching:

"En el día mas grande de mi vida, para los nenes la bendición mia y que mis padres me hechen la bendición." ("On the most important day of my life, I extend a blessing to my boys and ask my parents to give me their blessing.")

Not only did a global stage witness one of the greatest performances in World Series history, but to hear Clemente take a moment to acknowledge his family in Spanish was truly unprecedented for a US national television audience. Through tears and immeasurable pride, Latinos were finally able to applaud one of their very own.

Less than two years later, Clemente became the first Latin American inducted to the Hall of Fame, chosen via special election when the five-year waiting period was waived following his death.

Over forty years after that World Series win, those heroics haven't been forgotten as Pirates fans still flock to hear heartfelt stories from Sanguillén, who can always be found by his barbecue concession stand greeting fans and signing autographs at Pittsburgh's PNC Park. Blass, who delivered the eulogy at Clemente's memorial service after his tragic passing, is now a broadcaster who does radio or TV color commentary at every Pirates home game.

Like all his teammates, Oliver will carry the memories of that 1971 Pirates team in his heart forever.

"If it weren't for the [Pirates'] Latino ballplayers during those years," Oliver said, "we wouldn't have had a chance to go to the 1971 World Series."

Danny Torres is an educator and freelance writer from the Bronx, NY. This essay originally appeared in Memories & Dreams, *Issue 3, 2015.*

Chapter 7

Baseball Goes to War

Battling on the Diamond
As the sesquicentennial observance begins,
we look back at baseball during the Civil War
By Steve Light

As the Baseball Hall of Fame's chief curator for twenty-eight years, Ted Spencer experienced history every day. But one day in the early 1990s, he was amazed to discover just how strong the tie is between baseball and America's history.

Spencer had seen a Currier & Ives lithograph—an original of which resides in the Museum's collection—several times before, but it wasn't until that day that it piqued his curiosity.

"When I looked at it, I started to wonder what it was all about," Spencer said. Spencer showed the lithograph to his eldest son, then in middle school. His son had a passion for American history and was able to decode the political cartoon for his father. The lithograph, published just months after the 1860 presidential election, depicts Abraham Lincoln playing baseball against his rival candidates: John Bell, Stephen A. Douglas, and John C. Breckinridge. Lincoln has hit a home run using a bat representing his party's platform, while the others have all been called out using much weaker bats.

"To me, it was an epiphany," Spencer said. "I began to appreciate the relationship between the game, our country, and our history. Currier & Ives were looking for a vehicle to explain a complicated political message, and they felt people would understand it best in baseball terms."

Even during the Civil War, baseball was a central part of American culture.

As the lithograph's portrayal suggests, baseball was not unknown to Americans in 1860. Bat-and-ball games in America arrived with the earliest European settlers, and the popularity of more modern versions of baseball began to spread across the country in the 1840s and 1850s. Throughout the 1850s, multiple regional variations of the sport coexisted, with the rules of the New York Game and the Massachusetts Game winning the most favor.

At the start of the American Civil War in the spring of 1861, baseball was a national sport, though it remained most popular in Northeastern cities such as New York, Philadelphia, and Boston. By this time too, the New York Game (or National Association Game, as it was known by then) had begun to assert its dominance over other variations. During the war, baseball served an important role in American culture. On the home front in Northern cities, it remained a popular leisure activity that entertained the masses. On the front lines, baseball became an important diversion for the more than three million Americans serving in uniform on both sides.

Civil War soldiers faced many hardships, including the possibility of death in battle or from disease. They also struggled with the tedious monotony of camp life. When not actively campaigning, soldiers on both sides sought diversions to pass the time. Many soldiers read newspapers and books, wrote letters home, or enjoyed music. They also participated in sports and games.

Commanders and Army doctors encouraged these physical activities, believing that they kept the soldiers fit and healthy, while also keeping them out of trouble. While soldiers frequently took part in foot races, wrestling and boxing matches, and occasionally even cricket or football, renowned Civil War historian Bell Irvin Wiley has stated that baseball "appears to have been the most popular of all competitive sports" in the camps of both armies.

Civil War veterans have left us accounts of playing baseball in letters, diaries, newspapers, memoirs, and regimental histories. These accounts indicate that Northern troops played the sport more often than their Confederate counterparts and that the sport garnered the most popularity among units from New York, Massachusetts, and New Jersey.

In addition, soldier accounts reveal that troops most frequently played baseball in the winter and spring months, with games peaking during the months of March and April. This served as an ideal time to play, as fair weather coincided with reduced army activity. Typically, the active campaigning season for Civil War armies began at some point in May and lasted through November. The armies stayed in winter quarters during the months of December, January, and February, and many roads became impassable in March and April because of heavy rains. During these months, soldiers sought to keep themselves occupied, and whenever the weather cooperated, they organized ballgames.

Reporting on camp life in the Army of the Potomac on November 18, 1861, a correspondent for the *Chicago Tribune* related that "a song, a light-hearted laugh…a wrestling match, a foot race, or a party at base ball are the leading variations on the more formal duties."

New Jersey veteran Camille Baquet recalled of camp life during these lulls: "Drill, dress parade, inspection, picket and guard duty, policing, [and] building roads were the usual occupations. Amusements were encouraged, and chess, checkers, baseball, and athletic exercises helped to while away tedious hours."

The armies frequently held competitive games that attracted crowds of soldier-spectators and generated a great deal of interest in the camps. Often the ballplayers of one company, regiment, or brigade would challenge the ballplayers from another. The rules for these games varied from regiment to regiment, and frequently the competing teams would have to iron out rules variations prior to the start of each match. Some accounts tell of baseball games taking place between soldiers from both sides, though these stories—like most involving Union and Confederate fraternization—are difficult to prove and likely mythical, or, at the very least, exaggerated.

Baseball also served as a popular diversion for soldiers held in prison camps, particularly early in the war. Otto Boetticher, a soldier in the 68th New York Regiment, preserved for history one of the more famous depictions of baseball during the Civil War when he sketched Union soldiers playing ball at Salisbury Prison in North Carolina as he awaited exchange in 1862. Others imprisoned at Salisbury also left accounts of baseball there. A doctor named Charles Gray recorded in his diary that prisoners played ball nearly every day that the weather allowed.

Until 1863, the Union and Confederacy operated an exchange cartel that allowed man-for-man exchanges—keeping the number of imprisoned soldiers relatively low. In 1863, this system broke down as a result of Confederate refusals to treat Black soldiers as prisoners of war. With no exchanges, prison populations swelled to beyond capacity, and living conditions for those incarcerated—particularly in Southern prisons—became abominable. Due to the resulting poor health of the soldiers and a lack of space, strenuous physical activities such as baseball became very rare in prison camps during the latter part of the war.

Baseball during the war wasn't limited to soldiers, however. Northern cities continued to teem with activity throughout the war, and baseball remained one of the prominent leisure time

activities on the Northern home front. By 1861, the sport had
built a significant following in many cities. The most successful
teams of the day attracted thousands of spectators to games,
and newspapers provided accounts of all the latest contests.
The start of the war understandably cast a shadow over the
sport, and several clubs disbanded as players deemed it
their patriotic duty to volunteer for the Union cause. Even the
clubs that remained active reduced the length of their playing
schedule in 1861.

Much like baseball in the twentieth century, however,
wartime could not halt the sport. Baseball continued and indeed
flourished in the North during the war, since many players did
not volunteer and were not drafted. Ballgames featuring top
competition continued to draw large crowds, and newspaper
accounts of these matches appeared alongside reports from
the front. On June 7, 1862, for example, with the Union Army of
the Potomac within a few miles of the Confederate capital, the
New York Times reported on a match between a traveling team
from Philadelphia and a team picked from some of Brooklyn's
best clubs, including the Atlantics and the Excelsiors. The Times
reported the crowd as "by far the largest assemblage which
has gathered upon any base ball ground during this season."
In a game the previous day, the Philadelphia squad had played
a team selected from the Eckford, Putnam, and Constellation
clubs—"organizations which are well known to fame for their first-
class players." The Times reported that spectators in the crowd
included representatives from New York and Brooklyn clubs, as
well as those from Philadelphia, Boston, Albany, Troy, and many
other locales.

Much like the nation, baseball was rapidly changing during
the Civil War years. In the 1850s, the sport was played by
fraternal organizations made up of amateurs mostly from the
middle and upper classes. Between 1861 and 1865, it began
a slow evolution from an amateur sport to one played by

professionals. In 1860, rumors circulated that the Excelsior Club of Brooklyn compensated their star pitcher Jim Creighton. Several years later, in 1865, Eckfords star, Al Reach, accepted a monetary offer to switch to the Athletics of Philadelphia.

In addition to introducing professional players, the early 1860s saw the beginnings of admission fees for spectators. The first known instance of admission fees for a baseball game dates back to a series that began on July 24, 1858, at the Fashion Race Course on New York's Long Island. The series featured a Brooklyn all-star team taking on a New York all-star team. After paying for the rent of the field and other costs involved with staging the series, organizers donated the remaining money to a firemen's fund for widows and orphans. Prior to the war, such fees for admittance to ballgames were the exception rather than the rule. This began to change during the war.

An 1863 color lithograph of Union soldiers playing baseball at a Confederate prison in Salisbury, NC. The lithograph was based on a drawing by Major Otto Boettcher, who was held prisoner at the facility in 1862.

In 1862, the Brooklyn Union Grounds became the first enclosed baseball field ever constructed. To make money, the owner of the grounds contracted with several teams to play their matches at the Union Grounds and began to charge spectators admission on a regular basis. Several other entrepreneurs followed suit. The war years laid the foundation for paying professional players and charging fans to watch. The stage was set for the Cincinnati Red Stockings and the formation of professional leagues in the late 1860s and early 1870s.

The game itself continued to evolve during the war as well. The National Association of Base Ball Players (NABBP)—the sport's first organized governing body, founded in 1857—met annually, though attendance at NABBP conventions dropped significantly. Those participating in these conventions frequently debated rule changes, and several important rules were altered during the war. In 1863, the NABBP altered several pitching regulations. Before the 1865 season, a new fly rule passed: A batter was no longer out if a fair ball was caught on one bounce; a fielder had to catch the ball on the fly (though the bounce rule remained for foul balls).

As we look back at baseball's role in the Civil War 150 years later, we can appreciate the growing strength of the bonds between baseball and American culture, even then. During a terrible crisis for the country, Americans at home and at war turned to baseball for comfort, distraction, and entertainment. "They played baseball continually throughout the war," Spencer points out. "There was something every week."

For Spencer, the Currier & Ives lithograph, "The National Game," exemplifies the bond between baseball and American culture. In fact, he recalls introducing the artwork to another history enthusiast and avid baseball fan during Hall of Fame Weekend in 2007.

While guiding her through the Hall of Fame's collections, Spencer offered Pulitzer Prize-winning author and diehard Red

Sox fan Doris Kearns Goodwin her first glimpse of the Currier
& Ives cartoon. Goodwin had recently published a bestselling
book, *Team of Rivals: The Political Genius of Abraham Lincoln*.

While in the book Goodwin recounts Lincoln's political skill,
it was at the Hall of Fame that she first learned of his ability to
"strike a 'fair ball.' "

*Steve Light was the Manager of Museum Programs at the National
Baseball Hall of Fame and Museum and is currently the Director
of Education and Visitor Programs at the Thomas Jefferson
Foundation. This essay originally appeared in* Memories &
Dreams, *Issue 1, 2011.*

Evers Goes to France
Kept from combat by injury, Johnny Evers still served
his country in The Great War
By Jim Leeke

Hank Gowdy, Rabbit Maranville, and Johnny Evers combined
to lead the Boston Braves to one of baseball's most improbable
championships in 1914.

Three years later, the trio had a bigger battle in mind as
the United States entered World War I. But while Gowdy and
Maranville were able to serve on active duty, Evers was kept
sidelined by nerve inflammation in his right arm. The hero of
the Miracle Braves, however, eventually found a way to serve
his country and spread the gospel of baseball throughout
the world.

Evers, Gowdy, and Maranville had helped the 1914 Braves
rally from last place in the National League in July to defeat the
heavily favored Philadelphia Athletics in the World Series. In
1917, all three were still with Boston—but soon headed in vastly
different directions.

Gowdy, a catcher, was the first active major leaguer to enlist, signing up with the Ohio National Guard that June. Maranville, a slick-fielding shortstop who like Evers would one day be inducted into the Hall of Fame, entered the naval reserve following the 1917 season.

By the summer of 1918, Gowdy was in France with the 42nd "Rainbow" Division and Maranville was on board the battleship USS Pennsylvania. But second baseman Evers, out of big league baseball after sixteen seasons, couldn't enlist because of the pain in his arm.

"I remember how low in spirits Johnny was when he failed to pass the physical examination," Gowdy said. "But the outstanding thing to me was his determination to serve his country. There was no one more violently patriotic than Johnny Evers. 'Hank,' Johnny told me after I was accepted, 'I will be over there some way.' "

In June 1918, Evers joined the Knights of Columbus, a Catholic service organization, to become what one newspaper called the "generalissimo of baseball in France." Similar to the YMCA, Salvation Army, and Jewish Welfare Board, the "K. of C." supported the health and welfare of the US Army in France. The Knights were busily enrolling two thousand volunteers, ages thirty-five to fifty, to work overseas. The organization called them all secretaries.

"I was never more enthusiastic about anything in my life," Evers said of his new assignment as an athletic director. He wore an officer's uniform with K. of C. patches and insignia, moving the *Sporting News* to poetry:

When Johnny Evers goes to France
And starts to wag his chin.
Old Kaiser Bill will look askance
And beat it to Berlin.

Forty-six new secretaries marched on July 27 from the Knights' headquarters to a farewell ceremony at the nearby New York Public Library. Baseball fans recognized Evers and cheered.

"We're not going to do any of the heavy slugging ourselves," he told reporters. "They're just sending us in to bunt. But maybe we'll help advance some of them a base or two at that."

Evers added that when he reached France, "I hope to get two good nines together and stage a game for the boys well up at the front."

The contingent sailed three days later, though news of their departure was withheld under wartime censorship. Evers traveled with his assistant athletic director, Daniel J. McGrath, a physical trainer and longtime friend from his hometown of Troy, NY—about eighty miles east of Cooperstown. Their transport docked at Liverpool on August 13, and Evers and McGrath spent time in London before traveling to Southampton and crossing to Le Havre, arriving in Paris on September 15. German bombers raided the city that night.

"Well, you can take it from me that it was not very encouraging," said McGrath, who quickly followed a crowd of Parisians forty feet underground. Evers simply wrote that "a lot of German bombs missed me." Amazingly, he bumped into Hank Gowdy the next day, the color sergeant on furlough in Paris following hard fighting at Château-Thierry.

"What, Johnny Evers! You here!" Gowdy exclaimed. "You darned fool! Go back!"

French newspapers had hailed Evers, who starred for the Cubs dynasty of the early 1900s before playing for Boston, as "*Monsieur Jeannot Evers, ancien champion de baseball de Chicago.*"

"All right, if they say so, but what did they want to tack on that *ancien* business for?" said Evers. (Speaking about fifty words of French, he didn't realize they only meant "former.")

French General Paul Vidal soon arranged to have Evers teach his poilus (French soldiers) how to play the US National Pastime. Married to an American, the general loved sports and marveled at how far and accurately his baseball-loving allies could toss hand grenades.

Evers and McGrath reported to Vidal at Besançon in eastern France. They spent two weeks instructing military cadets, who in turn instructed ordinary soldiers.

"Even with my bum throwing arm, I could show them how it is done, and after they watched for a while, they cut loose and began heaving in the regular style," Evers wrote.

Vidal, a vigorous sixty-four, sometimes donned a mitt for a game of catch.

"We left the young officers playing games every afternoon, with four regular teams and with dozens of others waiting for the chance to challenge them, and with thousands of officers and soldiers learning the game and throwing the ball as part of the daily routine," Evers wrote.

The war now entered the crucial forty-seven days of the Meuse-Argonne Offensive, the immense Allied push that would end the conflict. Evers threw himself into hard, dangerous duties. He and other K. of C. secretaries worked close to the fighting, sometimes venturing into the front-line trenches. Evers wrote of the experience:

"We are making a tour, riding in big motor vans or in anything going our way, from camp to camp, hospital base to hospital base, and we have discovered that the fellows want to see us, to talk baseball, and to talk about back home, and so every morning I get up early and go visiting the boys in the hospitals, carrying a little bag full of cigarettes and chocolate hung from my shoulders."

Rambling about from his Paris headquarters, Evers was often greeted by soldiers he'd known back home. Many hailed from Chicago and remembered the stellar "Tinker to Evers to Chance"

double-play combination. Evers met a former Cubs batboy, the
son of the club secretary, a younger brother of an old teammate,
one fellow who had lived just a few blocks away, and another
who had ridden downtown with him every day. He chatted with
Yankees co-owner Lieutenant Colonel Tillinghast Huston of the
Army engineers, sportswriter Lieutenant Grantland Rice of the
field artillery, and ballplayers he'd known in the major and minor
leagues. One big fellow just introduced himself as "the guy that
fired a pop bottle at you on the Polo Grounds once."

Evers occasionally came under fire and once got "a few
faint whiffs" of mustard gas. He met Lieutenant Joe Jenkins,
a White Sox catcher, in a trench only two hundred yards from
German lines.

"While we were talking, a shell burst within a short distance
of us and neither of us moved," according to Evers' newspaper
column. "He (Jenkins) just waited until the jarring buzz died out
of our ears and then went on talking baseball and asking the
news from home."

Evers offered a more honest account once back in the states.

"Right in front of me a soldier, a young lad, ducked like a
scared rabbit into a dugout. I followed just like that rabbit's
brother. I was picking myself up from the bottom of the dugout
when Jenkins stuck his head in the doorway and laughed, 'Ha!
Ha! Ha! Johnny! What're you afraid of! Don't you know that shell
is gone! You never see the one that hits you!' "

The pair solemnly shook hands when the catcher left with his
men. "Goodbye, Crab," Jenkins said, addressing Evers with his
nickname. "I'll see you back in [Chicago] when this is over."

An army chaplain once sought out Evers to show him a
soiled baseball he'd found in the overcoat of a dead doughboy.
Moved, Evers said he'd like to have it.

"Not for a million dollars," the chaplain answered. "I'm too big
a fan, and this is too precious to me. It will be more precious to
others. If I can find them when we get back, that boy's baseball

belongs to them. If not, then I'll keep it as one of the biggest prizes of my life."

Evers was back in Paris for the Armistice on November 11, "the biggest day in the world." He sailed for home with McGrath the next month, reaching Troy six days before Christmas.

"My experience in France did not last long so far as time is concerned," Evers wrote, "but there were more things crowded into those three months-and-a-half than ever happened to me before in a whole year."

He hoped to return to professional ball, but added, "I shall never have any other experiences as interesting as my work in France when I under took to teach the Poilus how to play baseball."

Jim Leeke is the author of several books on baseball during World War I, including his most recent The Best Team Over There: The Untold Story of Grover Cleveland Alexander and the Great War. *This essay originally appeared in* Memories & Dreams, *Issue 2, 2017.*

Playing with All Their Heart
For those who served our country, this 1948 Indians-A's matchup wasn't just another game
By Paul Dickson

On May 18, 1948, Cleveland Indians rookie pitcher Gene Bearden was scheduled to make his third start of the season. He was set to pitch against the Philadelphia Athletics at Cleveland Stadium in the first night game of the year for the Indians. The opposing pitcher would be Lou Brissie.

On paper, a rather unremarkable game, but for the men who played that day sixty-four years ago, baseball meant a return to normal—and triumph over unthinkable tragedy. The National Baseball Hall of Fame and Museum remembers the character and courage of the men who played in what became known as The Purple Heart Game.

Bearden and Brissie were both large, tall (six-foot-three and six-foot-four respectively) southpaws with a strong common bond: Both men had been awarded the Purple Heart given to those wounded in combat. Both had struggled mightily to overcome the injuries they had sustained half a world apart during World War II.

Ten days before the matchup, Bearden had made his season debut and pitched in his first major league start after throwing just a third of an inning while giving up two hits and three runs in his big league debut and lone appearance of 1947. But 1948 would be different, as he began his turn in the rotation with a masterful 6-1 three-hitter fueled by his devastating knuckleball, defeating the Washington Senators. This was also the day on which Bearden revealed publicly for the first time that he had been severely wounded in the war. He told his story to Harry Jones of the *Cleveland Plain Dealer*.

On the early morning of July 6, 1943, Bearden's ship, which was part of an American task force battling the Japanese, was struck in the Kula Gulf in the South Pacific near the Solomon Islands. Bearden was in the engine room when the first torpedo hit and the order was given to abandon ship. As he scrambled up the ladder leading out of the engine room, a second torpedo hit, and the ladder crumbled, hurling him to the deck. With his knee twisted and crushed and his head split open by flying shards of metal, he lay unconscious in the pit of a sinking ship.

"Someone pulled me out," he told Jones. "They told me later that it was an officer. I don't know how he did it. The ship went down in about seventeen minutes. All I know is that I came to in the water some time later."

In a semiconscious state, he spent the next two days in a rubber life raft until he was finally rescued by a US destroyer and shipped back to the United States. He was operated on in

August at the US Naval Hospital in Jacksonville, Florida. For the better part of the next two years, he was in the hospital; a silver plate was inserted into his skull to fill up the part that had been gashed out, and a metal hinge was inserted into his damaged knee. Bearden was told he would never play baseball again. It certainly seemed out of the question, a conclusion held by everyone but Bearden himself.

He still had an aluminum plate and screw in his knee and an aluminum plate in the back of his head but kept this to himself until after his first big game, "because they might get the idea that I'm not strong enough to pitch."

Brissie's story was no less compelling. He had been wounded on December 2, 1944, when his infantry unit suffered an artillery barrage while fighting in Italy. He was hit with twenty-one shell fragments, shattering his left shinbone. Army doctors wanted to amputate his leg, but Brissie refused. After two painful years and twenty-three major operations, sporting a metal brace over his damaged tibia, he returned to baseball. The Philadelphia A's signed him on December 15, 1946. That next season, he won twenty-five games with Savannah in the Southern League. Later that year, the A's called him up, and on September 28, 1947, he made his big league debut.

So on the unseasonably cold night of May 18, 1948, as Cleveland Indians owner Bill Veeck recovered at the Cleveland Clinic from a second amputation on a leg wound infected in a combat zone in the South Pacific, and before a crowd of 44,231, the game was under way. The crowd included Dr. William Brubaker, the surgeon who had performed the first of the twenty-three operations on Brissie's left leg and a Cleveland fan. He was in the stands to cheer for his patient, but to no avail. Bearden pitched the full nine innings, giving up only six hits, and won 6-1—putting the Indians in first place with a .004 margin over the A's to regain the lead they had ceded to the A's two weeks earlier. Brissie faced only 10 batters before being relieved.

The story didn't end there. The A's reliever was Bob Savage, who himself had three Purple Hearts, the first for a shrapnel wound in the back in Italy on November 5, 1943—making him the first Major League player to be wounded in World War II. The second was for wounds on his leg, wrist, and face from an artillery shell fired during the invasion of the south of France in 1944, which put him in the hospital for eight weeks. He was awarded a third Purple Heart for an injury he received in a victory celebration after the war, when a spent bullet knocked his helmet off.

Savage came into the game that night in May with a hunk of shrapnel still in his shoulder. He in turn was relieved by Charles "Bubba" Harris, who had served in the US Navy at the end of the war.

Bearden, Brissie, and Savage—and Veeck, for that matter—were not alone in prevailing over their war injuries and disabilities. Indians first baseman Eddie Robinson was in the Navy when, in 1945, a bone tumor paralyzed his right leg. He was operated on and wore a brace, which he tossed away on the first day of Spring Training in 1946. Like Bearden and Brissie, he was told at one point that he would never play baseball again.

Unlike Savage, whose baseball career had actually peaked earlier, Bearden and Brissie went on to greater fame after the game. For Gene Bearden, the 1948 season was a masterful one—with a 20-7 record in the regular season and a league leading 2.43 earned run average, six shutouts, and 15 complete games. He led the Indians to the 1948 World Championship by beating the Boston Red Sox in a one-game American League playoff, and then won a World Series game and protected the lead as a relief pitcher in another victory. Brissie's best year was 1949, when he was named to the American League All-Star team and won 16 games.

But as with so many others, their level of service and courage was not unusual for that era. Hall of Famers Yogi Berra and Leon Day took part in the D-Day invasion of Europe, and Monte Irvin went in after the initial assault. That operation at Normandy also claimed the lives of five minor league baseball players: Lefty Brewer, Sylvester Sturges, Elmer Wright, Ordway "Hal" Cisgen, and Joe Pinder.

The powerful symbolism of the May 18, 1948, game was barely noted at the time and almost immediately forgotten, but the Purple Heart veterans who pitched and played on that cold night game so many years ago were heroic in the truest sense of the word.

Former US Navy officer Paul Dickson is a freelancer from Maryland. His most recent book is Bill Veeck—Baseball's Greatest Maverick. *This essay originally appeared in* Memories & Dreams, *Issue 5, 2012.*

The Games Must Go On
Seventy-fifth anniversary of Green Light Letter offers insight on baseball's role in World War II
By Alex Coffey

There is a seventeen-hour time difference between the Solomon Islands and St. Louis, Missouri. But that didn't stop Corporal Young Man Kwon and Private First Class Louis A. Repetto, members of the Public Relations staff for the 298th Infantry Regiment in Guadalcanal, from reporting on the highly-anticipated outcome of the 1944 World Series between the St. Louis Cardinals and the St. Louis Browns.

"It was 2:00 in the morning across the International Date Line," Repetto wrote in a letter to the National Baseball Hall of Fame. "For the next three hours, [we] listened, recorded, and then issued *The Warrior's* World Series Extra of the St. Louis

Cardinals winning the Series from the St. Louis Browns. By 5:30 a.m., Headquarters jeeps were delivering copies throughout the regiment."

World War II affected the daily lives of most Americans, whether they were stationed on a southwestern Pacific island or selling war bonds at home. But regardless of their involvement, one thing *all* Americans needed was consistency. And thanks to the foresight of President Franklin Delano Roosevelt and Commissioner Kenesaw Mountain Landis seventy-five years ago, baseball was able to provide that.

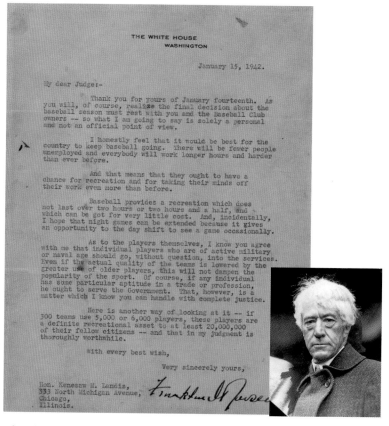

After the attack on Pearl Harbor, Franklin D. Roosevelt's "Green Light" letter encouraged commissioner Kenesaw Landis to continue with the upcoming 1942 baseball season.

On January 14, 1942, a mere five weeks after Japanese Imperial forces had attacked the American naval base at Pearl Harbor, Hawaii, Landis wrote Roosevelt about baseball's future as the US entered the war: "The time is approaching when, in ordinary conditions, our teams would be heading for spring training camps. However, inasmuch as these are not ordinary times, I venture to ask what you have in mind as to whether professional baseball should continue to operate."

The handwritten inquiry penned by Landis is preserved at the Franklin D. Roosevelt Presidential Library and Museum in Hyde Park, NY—115 miles away from Cooperstown. The Hall of Fame recently acquired digital images of the letter for research purposes.

"When it comes to understanding history, seeing only the transcripts or excerpts of documents places us all on the outside looking in," Baseball Hall of Fame Curator of History and Research John Odell said of Landis' letter. "Studying real documents (including their digital images) gives us a personal tie to the processes of history."

While Roosevelt was not much of a baseball player himself—referred to as a "notorious scatterarm" in one newspaper, he once hit the lens of a *Washington Post* photographer while trying to throw out a first pitch in 1940—he was a huge fan of the game. The President had served as manager of Harvard University's baseball team while he was a student there, and he used to sneak off and watch the New York Giants play at the Polo Grounds while working as a lawyer in the city.

But personal preferences aside, Roosevelt understood better than anyone that in a tumultuous time of change, the nation needed a steady source of entertainment—a respite from the turmoil of World War II. And what better to serve that role than America's most popular sport?

Despite being thrown into the midst of a worldwide crisis, Roosevelt got back to Landis as quickly as one could by mail, with his "Green Light Letter" dated January 15, 1942. His response to the Commissioner is now preserved in the Hall of Fame's collection:

> I honestly feel that it would be best for the country to keep baseball going. There will be fewer people unemployed, and everybody will work longer hours and harder than ever before. And that means they ought to have a chance for recreation and for taking their minds off their work more than ever before.
>
> Here is another way of looking at it. If 300 teams use 5,000 or 6,000 players, these players are a definite recreational asset to at least 20,000,000 of their fellow citizens—and that in my judgement is thoroughly worthwhile.

The correspondence between the President and the Commissioner made front-page news nationwide.

"Stay in There and Pitch—F.D.R." proclaimed the *Sporting News*, while the *New York Times* headline read, "Roosevelt Urges Continuation of Baseball During War and More Night Games." Baseball fans, executives, and players rejoiced that the National Pastime would continue on despite the oncoming World War.

"The President's letter confirms the conviction held by all baseball men that the national pastime has a definite place in the welfare of our country," American League President Will Harridge said to the *New York Times*, "particularly during times of stress."

The transition from non-wartime baseball to wartime baseball was not seamless; adjustments were made to accommodate the changing schedules of fans and players alike. Night games became more prevalent during the war so that fans who worked day shifts could still see their favorite teams play. Exhibition games were scheduled to raise money for war bonds. Meanwhile, an estimated 1,400 major league players, umpires, managers, and coaches served in the Armed Forces during the War. But the National Pastime continued on during those long four years and fulfilled the purpose that President Roosevelt had envisioned.

After the correspondence between Landis and the President had been made public, the Commissioner began receiving letters from servicemen both from overseas and nationwide, weighing in on the importance of baseball as the nation entered its second World War in thirty years.

"The men in service and the public at home want baseball to continue and want it in the conviction that the statutes operative for the rest of the country will operate upon us," Landis said to the *Herald Tribune*. "I can promise to the men in [the] army that they won't be let down."

Alex Coffey was the Communications Specialist at the National Baseball Hall of Fame and former Oakland A's beat writer at The Athletic. *This essay originally appeared in* Memories & Dreams, *Issue 2, 2017.*

Jackie's Battle

As a member of the US Army, Jackie Robinson fought for equality before he reached Ebbets Field

By Claire Smith

Seventy-five years ago, on September 2, 1945, Japan officially surrendered to the Allied Forces, ending World War II with the stroke of a pen.

That moment, acted out with pomp and circumstance on the deck of the USS Missouri on that day, is etched in history. Etched also in many minds are the oft-told stories of all those who served.

Among the millions who set aside lives and livelihoods to help secure that peace were countless ballplayers. This included thirty-four future Hall of Famers who joined up to fight for their countries. With peace secured, they exchanged military uniforms for team uniforms again, not knowing how much their stories would help to shape the narrative of their generation.

Ted Williams, an aviator with the Marines, set records for gunnery scores while training, thanks in part to his remarkable 20/10 eyesight. Commissioned in the Corps on May 2, 1944, he trained other pilots until 1946. When America went to war again, this time in Korea, Williams flew thirty-nine combat missions, serving at one point as wingman for the future legendary astronaut John Glenn.

Warren Spahn fought for the US Army in the Battle of the Bulge and received a battlefield commission. Later wounded in the battle for the only bridge crossing the Rhine, he received a Purple Heart.

Yogi Berra at age nineteen manned a machine gun on a US Navy rocket boat off the coast of France on D-Day. He would earn a Purple Heart, a Distinguished Unit Citation, two battle stars, and a European Theatre of Operations ribbon.

But while fighting for their country, Black Americans also fought the same war for civil rights.

Leon Day, the standout pitcher for the Newark Eagles, and power-hitting Willard Brown of the Kansas City Monarchs both served in the Army in the European Theatre. Day, a member of the 818th Amphibian Battalion, was at Utah Beach on D-Day. Both were elected to the Hall of Fame following their playing careers.

Hall of Famer Jackie Robinson also wore the uniform of his country during World War II. It was no surprise to those familiar with his fighting spirit that Robinson was as successful in the service as he was on the athletic field. After joining the Army in 1942, Robinson attended officer candidate school, and in January 1943, twenty-five-year-old Jackie Robinson was commissioned as a second lieutenant.

It was then that the newly minted lieutenant joined the multitudes of Black Americans in the segregated armed forces. Raised in California, he was about to meet Jim Crow, the umbrella rule of law and Southern mores that enforced segregation below the Mason-Dixon Line.

Long before he broke baseball's color barrier, Jackie Robinson fought prejudice in the military as a second lieutenant with the US Army during World War II.

Down South, racism was overt. One's blackness was treated with scorn and, all too often, with deadly hatred. It did not matter that Black servicemen and women were being asked to die for their country if needed. Large swaths of that country still literally or figuratively divided hotels, public transportation, schools, and even water fountains with "colored only" and "whites only" signs, laws, and attitudes.

Robinson, raised in diverse Southern California, bristled in Jim Crow country. Hadn't he played for, and excelled on, integrated teams at UCLA, where he had lettered in four sports? Hadn't he set collegiate records against white and Black athletes, some of which still stand today?

When assigned to Fort Riley in Kansas, Robinson—placed in charge of morale—pushed back against the segregation on the base, particularly protesting a rule that made it all but impossible for Black soldiers to secure more than a couple of seats at the Post Exchange (PX).

"Robinson telephoned the base provost marshal, Major Hafner, to protest this situation; the major said that taking seats away from the white soldiers and giving them to blacks would cause a problem among the white troops," wrote historian Jules Tygiel in *American Heritage* in 1984. "Furthermore, he could not believe that the lieutenant actually wanted the races seated together.

" 'Let me put it this way,' Robinson remembered the officer as saying: 'How would you like to have your wife sitting next to a n*****?'

Robinson exploded. " 'Major, I happen to be a Negro,' he shouted, 'and I don't know that to have anyone's wife sitting next to a Negro is any worse than to have her sitting next to some of these white soldiers I see around here.'

" 'I just want you to know,' said Hafner, 'that I don't want my wife sitting close to any colored guy.'

" 'How the hell do you know that your wife hasn't already been close to one?' asked Robinson as he launched into a tirade against the major. The provost marshal hung up on him, but Robinson's protest was not fruitless: Although separate areas in the Post Exchange remained the rule, blacks were allotted additional seats."

By the summer of 1944, Robinson moved further south to Camp (now Fort) Hood in Texas,. Life around a base named for a Confederate hero (Lt. Gen. John Bell Hood) had not evolved favorably for Black Americans in the decades after the Civil War.

"The prejudice and discrimination at Camp Hood made [other bases] seem ultraliberal in attitude," Harry Duplessis, one of Robinson's fellow black officers, told Tygiel (*American Heritage*, August–September 1984). "Camp Hood was frightening.... Segregation there was so complete that I even saw outhouses marked White, Colored, and Mexican."

Initially assigned to a Black tank unit, Robinson was prevented from deploying overseas with the 761st Tank Battalion because of a flare-up of lingering issues related to broken ankle injuries suffered as a football player.

"My CO sent me to the hospital for a physical checkup," Robinson told *Yank* magazine on November 23, 1945, "and they changed my status to permanent limited service."

Robinson would go on to receive a medical discharge on November 28, 1944, but not before he most famously refused to bow down to Jim Crow. His final act of defiance against the segregated Army began on a bus ride on July 6, 1944.

One month after D-Day, Robinson was returning to a hospital thirty miles from Camp Hood to collect test results. He sat up front, where he was confronted by the driver, who told Robinson to move farther back from where he sat, which was next to a fellow officer's light-skinned wife. In essence: Move to the back of the bus.

That one simple thing—sitting in a front seat—had become an often-dangerous flashpoint for Black servicemen and women across the South. After one soldier was shot and killed by a driver, the Army, under pressure from the National Association for the Advancement of Colored People (NAACP), skipped around segregated public transportation by starting its own nonsegregated bus service on bases. Still, as Robinson found out that day, the rules too often were ignored or violated.

Robinson, though, knew the regulations. Eleven years before Rosa Parks' refusal to move sparked the historic bus boycott in Montgomery, Alabama, Robinson did not yield. As he wrote to the NAACP two weeks later, "I refused to move because I recalled a letter from Washington, which states that there is to be no segregation on army posts." In his autobiography, Robinson stated that boxers Joe Louis and Ray Robinson had also influenced his actions by their refusals to obey Jim Crow regulations at a bus depot in Alabama.

But nothing in the rule books could prevent Robinson from having to run a gauntlet of racist abuses from that point on. He not only had angry face-offs with the bus driver and a depot dispatcher, but also encountered a military policeman who dropped the "N" word on the lieutenant, a reportedly hostile assistant provost marshal, and even a civilian stenographer (who reportedly interrupted Robinson to add her own opinions about why he should have moved).

After his camp commander refused to court-martial him, Robinson was soon transferred away from the 761st. The camp commander of the 758th Tank Battalion did not hesitate, levying charges of insubordination, disturbing the peace, drunkenness, conduct unbecoming an officer, insulting a civilian woman, and refusing to obey the lawful orders of a superior officer.

"The people have a pretty good bunch of lies," Robinson wrote to the NAACP. "When I read some of the statements of the witnesses, I was certain that these people had got together and [were] going to frame me."

While admitting that he had cursed after the bus dispatcher had called him a "n*****," he denied "calling the people around all sorts of names."

Though some charges were eventually dropped, a guilty verdict based on the insubordination accusation alone could have resulted in a dishonorable discharge. Fellow Black soldiers began raising concerns with the NAACP that Robinson was being set up. Black newspapers with large readerships in big cities in the North started to weigh in. The US Army was about to prosecute a known celebrity. Black America, including allies like Joe "The Brown Bomber" Louis, was watching.

In early August 1944, a four-day trial began, filled with testimony from many a prosecution witness. Finally, nine judges, in a vote by secret ballot, ruled that Jackie Robinson was "not guilty of all specifications and charges."

"My father took a bold stand with the Armed Forces and against Jim Crow," Sharon Robinson, daughter of Rachel and Jackie Robinson, said in a recent interview. "Ultimately, he won."

Like Bob Feller, Yogi Berra, Larry Doby, and others, Jackie Robinson eventually got to take off the uniform of his country—with honor. Then he donned baseball uniforms with pride, first for the Negro Leagues' famed Kansas City Monarchs, then in history-making fashion for the Brooklyn Dodgers.

With that last uniform change on April 15, 1947, Jackie Robinson joined with Dodgers owner Branch Rickey to shatter baseball's color barrier.

Would that last iconic stand have been possible had Robinson lost to Jim Crow and those who tried to court-martial him?

"I believe this show of leadership and self-confidence," said Sharon Robinson, "was one of the factors in Branch Rickey's decision to interview and hire Jackie Robinson."

Claire Smith, the winner of the 2017 BBWAA Career Excellence Award, is on the faculty of Klein College of Media and Communication at Temple University, serving as the codirector of the newly created Claire Smith Center for Sports Media. This essay originally appeared in Memories & Dreams, *Issue 5, 2020.*

Return Policy

Big leaguers showed in 1945 that their baseball skills would survive their time at war

By Phil Rogers

Buddy Lewis was in a hurry, which surprised almost no one. He had always liked traveling fast, and his Washington Senators somewhat unexpectedly found themselves with something to play for in the second half of the 1945 season. So Lewis—like many players who returned from military service that summer—wasted no time in resuming his baseball career.

Lewis was interested in aviation. He had taken some flying lessons before World War II, which at times worried Clark Griffith, the Senators' owner.

A combat assignment in North Africa awaited Lewis when his orders came through for the Army Air Corps flight school in 1942. Lewis, who famously buzzed Griffith Stadium in Washington before shipping out for the China-Burma-Indian Theater, said later the change in roles was the best thing to happen to him after he was drafted.

Lewis became a decorated pilot of transport planes after being drafted in 1941. He amassed 1,799 flying hours on 392 missions, including more than 600 hours that were classified as combat. But by 1945, Lewis was on dual missions—to help the United States win the war and to get back to the Senators, for whom his sweet swing from the left side had made him a lineup fixture since he was nineteen years old. He moved amazingly fast to return to Washington after Allied troops had finished the job in Burma in early 1945.

Lewis was officially discharged from the Army Air Corps on July 23; four days later, he cracked manager Ossie Bluege's lineup for a game against the Red Sox at Fenway Park. The twenty-eight-year-old Lewis was in right field, where he had been a regular since relocating from third base in 1940. The Senators were in second place in the American League, only three games behind Detroit despite counting on rookies and journeymen in Lewis' stead. Bluege not only threw Lewis into the lineup but batted him third.

It was exactly the homecoming Lewis had dreamed about while he was serving his country. He took a few flights overseas with Browns manager Luke Sewell, who visited troops one off-season.

"Everybody agreed he was the best transport pilot in the CBI theater," Sewell told the *Washington Post*. "He set his big transport plane down on tiny strips that didn't look big enough for a mosquito to land on. And he did it while he was talking baseball to me."

It's historically accurate to view 1946 as the year that Major League Baseball returned to normal following World War II. But the 250 big leaguers who traded in military uniforms for woolen baseball threads that year were preceded by an advance guard the previous summer, impacting both the pennant chase and World Series in 1945.

Germany surrendered in May. The battles continued in the Pacific until the United States bombed two Japanese cities, Hiroshima and Nagasaki, in August. Most of the ballplayers who were away with military units—those in combat as well as the large number who spent the war playing baseball and helping raise the morale of soldiers—were not discharged in time to get back on the field for the '45 season.

But Hall of Famers Hank Greenberg, Bob Feller, Red Ruffing, and Luke Appling joined Lewis in a group of about twenty players who wrapped up their military obligations in time to raise the level of baseball's diluted talent pool.

For fans, it was a sign of things to come. They would have to wait a little longer to welcome back Ted Williams, Joe DiMaggio, Stan Musial, Warren Spahn, Bill Dickey, and other future Hall of Famers who served in the military, but the return of the first wave of war heroes made the '45 season special in its own right.

It was fairly common for players to trickle back from military service throughout World War II. Four players returned in time to be in uniform on Opening Day 1945: the Cubs' Peanuts Lowrey, the Tigers' Al Benton, the Giants' Van Lingle Mungo, and the Braves' Tom Earley—each after missing one or two seasons.

Lowrey, who had hit .292 as a twenty-five-year-old for the Cubs in 1943, spent the following season at military police candidate school in Michigan before receiving a medical discharge late in '44 because of bad knees. They did not stop him from jumping right back into things with a 98-win Cubs team that rode Stan Hack, Phil Cavarretta, and Andy Pafko to the NL pennant. A regular in left field, Lowrey hit .283 and struck out only 27 times while playing 143 games, with Wrigley Field's outfield grass apparently providing a balm for his aching knees.

Benton's return was a similar blessing for the Tigers, and he followed a similar path back as well. He was invaluable to the Tigers because he had a rubber arm, which served him well as a starter or a reliever. Del Baker, Detroit's manager, said the Tigers wouldn't have won the pennant in 1940 without him.

Greenberg won the AL MVP that season, hitting 41 homers and driving in 150 runs. Benton backed up that performance with consecutive All-Star seasons. He joined the Navy after the 1942 season and served two years but was discharged at the end of '44 due to migraine headaches.

Benton, then in his early thirties, had spent the two years mostly playing baseball. He reportedly won 39 games for Navy teams and indeed seemed to have learned a few new tricks when he got back to Tiger Stadium (then known as Briggs Stadium). He started the third game of the season, throwing a four-hit shutout against the Browns, and finished May 5-1 with an 0.47 ERA, helping the Tigers position themselves for Greenberg's triumphant return.

Greenberg served two stints in the Army during World War II. He was included in an early wave of players who were drafted and left the Tigers in May, 1941, but then was honorably discharged on December 5, two days before Japan's attack on Pearl Harbor, when Congress prematurely released all men twenty-eight and over from service. He reenlisted as a sergeant in February, volunteering for the Army Air Corps, and figured his baseball career was ending.

After serving two stints in the US Army during World War II, Hank Greenberg returned to the Detroit Tigers in 1945, helping to lead the team to a World Series victory over the Chicago Cubs.

"We are in trouble and there is only one thing for me to do—return to the service," he told *Sporting News* in an interview revisited by Gary Bedingfeld's Baseball in Wartime website. "This doubtless means I am finished with baseball, and it would be silly for me to say I do not leave it without a pang. But all of us are confronted with a terrible task—the defense of our country and the fight for our lives."

Greenberg missed the next three seasons. He climbed to the rank of captain and learned to fly B-29 Superfortress bombers, eventually serving in the China-India-Burma Theater, largely in an administrative role.

He was recalled to New York to work in morale-boosting ways midway through 1944 and then in June, 1945, was placed on the military inactive list, allowing him to return to the Tigers.

A stream of players began arriving back to major league teams in August and September. Outfielder Charlie Keller rejoined the Yankees on August 19, Feller struck out 12 Tigers in his first game back with the Indians on August 24, and pitcher Hugh Mulcahy was back on the mound for the Phillies on August 26. Appling was back at shortstop for the White Sox on September 2, getting hits in both games of a doubleheader at Comiskey Park.

Mulcahy, who was then thirty-one, had pitched 280 innings and had been an All-Star in 1940. Then he had the distinction of becoming the first big leaguer drafted into the military before the United States entered World War II. He was packed to go to Spring Training for the '41 season but instead found himself in the Army, headed to basic training.

"Hugh Mulcahy was a hero in the minds of all ballplayers at that time," longtime player and manager Bobby Bragan said.

Although Mulcahy didn't see combat, he still missed four-and-a-half years of his career before being sent home from the Philippines in August, 1945. He had lost thirty-five pounds while battling dysentery and had completely lost his fastball while in the service.

Shortstop Cecil Travis, who had been Lewis' roommate in previous seasons, rejoined Lewis and the Senators on September 8. He had been with Washington for eight seasons before entering the Army and being assigned to the infantry shortly after Pearl Harbor.

Travis fought alongside his fellow Allied soldiers after the 76th Infantry was sent to Europe in late 1944, with the war in its final chapters. He served as a reinforcement for the Battle of the Bulge. Then he joined the 76th in advancing more than four hundred miles against German resistance, capturing more than 33,000 prisoners.

Travis received a Bronze Star and four battle stars from his time on the front line. He also suffered a bad case of frostbite that would require surgery. Travis was at his home in Georgia on leave when Japan surrendered; he was given his discharge on September 6. It took him only two days to travel to Washington and join the Senators, who were only 1.5 games behind Greenberg's Tigers.

There would be no magical ending for Travis and his teammates, including Lewis. Travis was never as successful as a hitter as he had been before the war—he attributed this to a lost sense of timing, not the frostbite—and the Senators couldn't catch the Tigers. Lewis, however, hit an impressive .333 in 69 games after returning and was named to the AL All-Star team in 1947, showing that his baseball skills had survived the war.

It was the last of the soldiers to return in 1945 who perhaps had the most impact. Virgil Trucks, who had gone into the Navy the previous year, had hoped to be back with the Tigers by midseason after applying for a medical discharge due to a knee he had injured on Guam, but he wouldn't end up putting on a uniform to pitch until September 30, the last day of the campaign.

Manager Steve O'Neill saw enough from the twenty-eight-year-old Trucks to slot him into his World Series rotation behind only Hal Newhouser, among starters that included Stubby Overmire and Dizzy Trout. The Cubs defeated Newhouser in the Series opener, but Trucks earned a complete game 4-1 victory in Game Two, with Greenberg smashing a three-run homer in front of a Detroit crowd of 53,636.

Lowrey hit third for the Cubs in the Series. He had two of the seven hits off Trucks in Game Two (and nine in the series) and two more in a 9-3 loss in the deciding Game Seven. Trucks had a chance to finish off the Cubs in the sixth game but got knocked out in the fifth inning.

It would be the last of four World Series for Greenberg and his most memorable. He went 7-for-23 at the plate, driving in seven runs and scoring seven times. And he did it after two tours of duty for his country.

He had been willing to sacrifice the rest of his career to the war effort, but it turned out he played three seasons after his service—all with a hard-earned sense of pride that had nothing to do with turning on a fastball.

Phil Rogers is a freelance writer who has covered baseball since 1984 for several newspapers, including the Dallas Morning News *and the* Chicago Tribune, *also serving as a national correspondent for MLB.com. This essay originally appeared in* Memories & Dreams, *Issue 5, 2020.*

Chapter 8

Women in Baseball

Saluting the Girls of Summer

**Women have starred on the diamond and contributed
to the game for more than 150 years**

By Debra Shattuck Burton

The 2017 baseball season is in full swing. Before it is finished, millions of baseball fans will root, root, root for the home team at major and minor league ballparks throughout the country and watch games on televisions, smartphones, and iPads. Millions more will gather on groomed fields, vacant lots, or wherever they can lay out a baseball diamond to recreate their own field of dreams and play the game they love.

The sport we know as baseball has a rich history, stretching back into antebellum America and sharing a family tree with myriad bat and ball games played in England and Europe as early as the Middle Ages, as well as with games like One Old Cat, Trap Ball, Wicket, Rounders, and Town Ball in the early American republic. What many fans of the modern sport do not realize is that girls and women have played baseball alongside boys and men ever since promoters first began touting the game as the National Pastime.

During the 1850s, male and female students at Eagleswood School in Perth Amboy, NJ, played baseball; so did their counterparts at rural schools in western New York. In the 1860s, girls and women played baseball on college teams in New York and Illinois, on school teams in California, Connecticut, and Maine, and on civic and pick-up teams in Michigan, Florida, New York, Ohio, New Jersey, and Indiana.

By 1869, some male baseball players were being paid to play; by 1875, so were some female players. As men's professional baseball teams multiplied during the latter third of the nineteenth century, so did women's professional teams. The first took the field in Springfield, Illinois, in August of 1875, and folded just two months later. Four years later, young women joined professional baseball troupes in Manhattan and Philadelphia. The Philadelphia group did particularly well, traveling more than three thousand miles and drawing more than 34,000 spectators to the 23 of 28 games for which attendance statistics are available. The team drew more fans to those 23 games than five of the eight National League teams drew to all 40 of their home games that season. African-American women played baseball too, on teams like the Dolly Varden 1, Dolly Varden 2, and Captain Jinks clubs of Philadelphia and Chester, Pennsylvania, in 1883.

Though many of the early female baseball troupes had a theatrical cast and featured female teams playing each other, by the late nineteenth century, male baseball entrepreneurs were fielding teams of talented female athletes who went head-to-head against men's teams. One of the most successful of these was the female Cincinnati Reds, organized in 1891 in New York City. The team featured ace pitcher Lizzie Arlington, who was only fourteen when she signed her first contract. During her second season with the Reds, Arlington, whose real name was Elizabeth Stride, was joined by another standout pitcher, Clementina Brida (who played as Maud Bradi and later, Maud Nelson. Players often used aliases during the early days of the game).

Arlington and Nelson both had stellar baseball careers. Arlington played on women's barnstorming teams like the Reds,

Young Ladies Base Ball Club of New York, and the New England Bloomer Girls before being signed by Atlantic League president (and future New York Yankees president and Hall of Famer) Ed Barrow to pitch for Atlantic League teams during the Spanish-American War in 1898. In 1899, Arlington returned to female baseball teams and played on into the early twentieth century.

Nelson's baseball career spanned four decades. After two seasons with the Reds, she played on several other women's squads, including the popular Boston Bloomer Girls and Chicago Star Bloomer Girls. Between 1910 and 1927, she co-owned and played on the Western Bloomer Girls, All-Star Athletic Girls, and All-Star Ranger Girls baseball teams.

While women like Arlington and Nelson were stars on barnstorming female baseball teams, countless girls and women continued to play on civic, pick-up, scholastic, and college teams throughout the country. During the 1870s and 1880s, Minnesota, Kansas, Iowa, New Hampshire, North Carolina, Kentucky, Missouri, Wisconsin, Rhode Island, Alabama, Montana, Colorado, North and South Dakota, West Virginia, New Mexico, and Texas got their first home-grown female baseball teams. By 1900, Nebraska, Wyoming, Georgia, South Carolina, and Arizona had female teams, too.

While the majority of girls and women played on all-female baseball teams, some talented players joined men's teams. In 1905, Ruth Egan of Kansas City drew rave reviews from local media for her baseball prowess as captain and pitcher for her youth team, the Bellevue Blues. Egan played baseball for the next seventeen years—including a stint with the Kansas City Bloomer Girls in 1906. Pitcher Carrie Viola Moyer, of Macungie, Pennsylvania, earned money and accolades pitching on boys and men's baseball teams as early as 1906. Her notoriety was eclipsed by Ohioan Alta Weiss, whose pitching exploits for the Vermilion Independents (1907) and Weiss All-Stars (1908) were proclaimed in newspapers across the country.

Weiss's reputation for excellence was confirmed by Cleveland Naps player-manager Nap Lajoie, who saw her play at League Park and admitted, "I was surprised to find that she could pitch so well."

Weiss had a relatively short-lived baseball career; she used her earnings to put herself through medical school. A decade later, first basewoman Mary Elizabeth Murphy began a twenty-year career playing for men's teams in New England, including the Providence (RI) Independents and Ed Carr's All-Stars of Boston. She retired in 1935.

Chattanooga Lookouts pitcher Jackie Mitchell became famous after striking out Babe Ruth and Lou Gehrig back-to-back in a 1931 exhibition game against the New York Yankees.

During the 1920s and 1930s, public opinion began to solidify around the notion that baseball was for boys and men, even though girls and women had been playing the game for decades. Well-meaning physical educators promoted baseball surrogates like softball and "women's baseball" and actively discouraged girls and women from playing genuine "hardball." Despite the obstacles, some girls and women refused to give up on their baseball dreams.

In 1928, fourteen-year-old Margaret Gisolo helped her Blanford, Indiana, American Legion men's baseball team win county, district, sectional, and state championships. Gisolo hit .429 and notched 10 putouts and 28 assists in the field with no charged errors. When opposing teams protested her presence on the field, the American Legion's National Americanism Commission referred the matter to MLB Commissioner Kenesaw Mountain Landis, who determined that American Legion rules did not ban female players. Gisolo's team kept its championship.

Landis addressed a similar situation in 1931 when the "Barnum of Baseball," Chattanooga Lookouts manager Joe Engel, signed seventeen-year-old Virnett "Jackie" Mitchell to a contract. Mitchell, who had received pitching tips from future Hall of Famer Arthur "Dazzy" Vance as a youngster, developed an impressive breaking ball. She is forever immortalized in baseball history for striking out Babe Ruth and Lou Gehrig back-to-back during an exhibition game between the Lookouts and the New York Yankees on April 2, 1931. Baseball purists still debate whether the whole affair was a set-up or not, but there is no question that Mitchell was a highly skilled baseball player. Although Commissioner Landis voided her contract just days after her pitching debut, Mitchell continued to impress crowds as she toured the country with exhibition teams for the next several years.

Babe Didrikson, a highly talented athlete and Olympic gold medal winner, pitched for several major league baseball teams in preseason exhibition games in 1935. On March 20 of that year, Didrikson pitched a scoreless inning for the Philadelphia Athletics against the Brooklyn Dodgers; two days later, she surrendered three earned runs to the Boston Red Sox while pitching for the St. Louis Cardinals. She redeemed herself on March 25, pitching two shutout innings for the Cleveland Indians against its minor league affiliate, the New Orleans Pelicans. Didrikson recorded two assists in the field and one base hit in the game.

By 1940, the popularity of softball drove most Bloomer Girl baseball teams out of business. Fortunately for young women who enjoyed playing baseball, World War II brought them an unprecedented opportunity to play for a women's professional baseball league. Initially organized by Chicago Cubs owner Philip Wrigley in 1943 as a softball league to entertain war workers, the All-American Girls Professional Baseball League gave more than six hundred young women the opportunity to earn a living playing baseball during its twelve-year existence. The League drew millions of fans to games in cities like South Bend and Fort Wayne (Indiana), Kenosha and Racine (Wisconsin), Peoria and Rockford (Illinois), and Kalamazoo, Battle Creek, and Muskegon (Michigan).

The talented athletes of the AAGPBL not only entertained fans, but they inspired subsequent generations of female players like Ila Borders, Carey Schueler, Justine Siegal, Tiffany Brooks, Sarah Hudek, and Kelsie Whitmore, who persevered on the field even when detractors railed against them for playing a "man's game."

There were no Black women in the AAGPBL, although there were countless supremely talented Black players in the country at that time. Three of them, second basewomen Toni Stone and Connie Morgan and pitcher Mamie "Peanut" Johnson, earned roster spots in the men's Negro Leagues in the early 1950s. Like many white players, these women grew up with a deep love for the game and worked hard to find opportunities to play baseball at a time when most girls were steered into softball. Their perseverance paid off and helped open doors to subsequent generations of female players.

The future looks bright for women in baseball. More and more Americans recognize that baseball and softball are two different games and that girls and women should be allowed to play whichever game appeals to them most. The Colorado Silver Bullets, a touring team that was in existence from 1994 through 1997, gave dozens of women the opportunity to play professional baseball again; a number of former players, like Julie Croteau and Lee Anne Ketcham, continued to play on men's baseball teams.

Girls and women around the world are embracing baseball too. Since 2001—when the United States, Canada, Japan, and Australia competed in the first Women's Baseball World Series—the number of teams competing in the biennial Women's Baseball World Cup has grown steadily. The 2016 competition featured women's teams from twelve countries, including the United States, Japan, South Korea, Australia, Cuba, Venezuela, India, Pakistan, and the Netherlands.

Groups like Baseball for All, the International Women's Baseball Center, the New York Women's Baseball Association, and Girls Travel Baseball are working tirelessly to give girls and women the opportunity to play baseball and to preserve the artifacts of women's baseball history.

Dr. Debra Shattuck Burton is provost and associate professor of history and leadership at John Witherspoon College in Rapid City, SD. She is the author of Bloomer Girls: Women Baseball Pioneers. *This essay originally appeared in* Memories & Dreams, *Issue 3, 2017.*

Woman's World
Hall of Famer Effa Manley blazed a trail
for female executives in baseball
By Scott Pitoniak

It didn't take long for Effa Manley to ruffle a few feathers.

At her very first Negro Leagues owners meeting in 1937, she voiced unflattering comments about the way Black baseball was being run. As we learned in Bob Luke's compelling biography, *The Most Famous Woman in Baseball,* Manley's audacious opinions at a time when many Americans believed women should be seen but not heard went over like a lead baseball. Once the meeting ended, angry Pittsburgh Crawfords owner Gus Greenlee grabbed Manley's husband, Abe, by the arm and told him, "Next time, keep your wife at home."

Abe, who co-owned the Newark Eagles with Effa, shrugged off the advice. He had no desire to muzzle his wife and business partner—nor would he have been able to even if he had wanted to do so, because Effa Manley was a force of nature. Stopping her would be like stopping a tornado.

During the next decade, she would storm through the racial and gender barriers of the time and help the Eagles and Negro League baseball to thrive. She also would become an influential civil rights crusader, launching a successful "Don't Buy Where You Can't Work" campaign that compelled Harlem retailers to hire Black employees. Combining savvy entrepreneurial skills, an ocean-deep passion for baseball, and dogged determination, the headstrong Manley blazed a trail for Black and female executives in her sport and beyond.

In an era when a woman's place supposedly was in the home, Manley made her place in a ballpark. And in 2006, twenty-five years after her death at age eighty-four, she found a permanent place in Cooperstown when she became the first woman inducted into the National Baseball Hall of Fame.

From Philadelphia to Newark

Manley's complicated life got off to a complicated start. Reports differ, however, many indicate her mother was white and her father was Black; Effa later discovered she had been conceived from an affair her seamstress mother had with a white stockbroker. Her parents would divorce and her mother remarried another African-American man. Effa, who was born in 1897 in Philadelphia, Pennsylvania, wound up being raised by a Black father and white mother and had mixed-race siblings. She and everyone else just assumed she was a light-skinned African-American girl. Manley said she didn't learn about her biological father until she was a teenager, and by that time, her racial identity had been formed. Leslie Heaphy, a Kent State University history professor and leading black baseball scholar, believes Manley's challenging childhood shaped her into becoming an aggressive businesswoman and reformer.

"She learned early on not to be overlooked," Heaphy said in a 2006 *New York Times* interview.

After graduating from high school, Manley moved to New York City, where she worked in the fashion industry and fell in love with baseball—and Abraham Lincoln Manley. A big fan of Babe Ruth, Effa met Abe at a game at Yankee Stadium. They were married in 1935, and a year later they bought the Brooklyn Eagles, a Negro National League team, and merged with the Newark Dodgers. Abe had made his money in real estate and racketeering. Although he funded the Eagles and was voted treasurer of the league, he would hold titles in name only. His flamboyant, outspoken wife became the brains and face of the franchise and also oversaw the league's finances. Effa ran the Eagles' day-to-day business operations, arranging game schedules, planning travel, managing payroll, negotiating players' contracts, purchasing equipment, and coordinating publicity and promotions.

"She was unique and effervescent and knowledgeable," said Monte Irvin, one of several Hall of Famers to play for the Eagles. "She ran the whole business end of the team."

Helping the Eagles Soar

A fiery competitor, Manley could be impatient and impetuous. After the Eagles lost, 21-7, in the 1935 season opener at Brooklyn's Ebbets Field (a game in which she convinced New York Mayor Fiorello LaGuardia to throw out the ceremonial first pitch), Manley was beside herself. That inauspicious start was a harbinger of a losing season. Following the final game, she demanded first baseman George Giles replace Ben Taylor as manager.

"When she was displeased, the world would come to an end; she'd stop traffic," Giles recalled years later. "Mrs. Manley loved baseball, but she couldn't stand to lose. I was a pretty hard loser myself, but I think she took it more seriously than anybody."

Legend has it that Manley occasionally would meddle during games, instructing her players to bunt by signaling to them by crossing or uncrossing her legs from her box seat. She also was a strict disciplinarian. "She would call you in and tell you how to dress, what to do, who to associate with," said Eagles pitcher James Walker. "When you had problems, if they were personal, you went to Mrs. Manley, and she was very understanding—as long as you toed the line."

As author James Overmyer explains in his book, *Queen of the Negro Leagues*, Manley believed her team had an obligation "to uphold the black community's best standards." She often used Eagles games to promote civic causes. In 1939, she held an "Anti-Lynching Day" at the ballpark and also devoted ticket and advertising revenue to fund the Booker T. Washington Community Hospital, which was one of the few institutions in

America offering training for Black doctors and nurses. She also gave thousands of free tickets to inner-city youth.

Though she could be demanding, the majority of her players adored her because she was their biggest advocate. Unlike most owners, Manley believed the players deserved decent salaries and working conditions. She and her husband eventually bought an air-conditioned luxury bus for team travel and sponsored a ball club in the Puerto Rico winter league so their players would have off-season work. She also became godmother to Larry Doby's first child, and she lent money to Irvin for a down payment on his first home and to Lenny Pearson to open a tavern.

Manley had the business sense to realize the Eagles would not be able to compete with Major League Baseball's Dodgers in Brooklyn, so she convinced her husband to move the team across the river to Newark, New Jersey, in 1936. The Eagles flourished there, thanks to Manley's marketing acumen and eye for baseball talent, which included signing star players Irvin, Doby, Don Newcombe, Leon Day, and Mule Suttles. The apex would come in 1946 when Newark beat the legendary Kansas City Monarchs to win the Negro League World Series.

Over time, several of the hardline owners, including one who initially groused that "baseball ain't no place for women," grudgingly praised her, adopting her proposals for an independent commissioner and a new constitution that helped Black baseball run more professionally. "Negro baseball can take a few tips from the lady member of the league," acknowledged Homestead Grays owner Cumberland Posey, who also was inducted into the Hall in 2006.

Changing History

Branch Rickey's signing of Jackie Robinson to a Brooklyn Dodgers minor league contract in 1945 was the first step in the integration of MLB and the demise of the Negro Leagues, which had become one of the most successful Black-run businesses in America. Manley took on Rickey for "poaching" Robinson and, soon after, Newcombe without compensating their Negro League clubs. She wound up receiving $15,000 from Bill Veeck when the Cleveland Indians signed Doby, and an agreement was struck where Black teams would receive a minimum of five thousand dollars per signing. As Luke states in his biography, these were times of mixed emotions for Manley and others who wanted to see Black stars finally receive their due but realized it would lead to the death of their business.

Effa Manley blazed a trail for women baseball executives as co-owner of the Newark Eagles of the Negro National League. She would be recognized for her contributions to baseball with her election to the Hall of Fame in 2006.

Declining attendance forced the Manleys to sell the Eagles in 1948. After the sale, Effa became more active with the Newark chapter of the National Association for the Advancement of Colored People (NAACP). She would have loved to continue her career as an executive in the major leagues, but that wasn't going to happen, even though she had proven herself eminently qualified.

During the final decades of her life, she wrote letters to Baseball Hall of Fame executives and media outlets advocating enshrinement for numerous Negro Leagues players and managers. In 1976, she cowrote a book titled *Negro Baseball… Before Integration,* in which she listed seventy-three players she believed to be Cooperstown-worthy. She also spent many a day poring over the enormous Negro League scrapbook she had assembled, now a part of the Library and Archives' collection. "People say, 'Don't live in the past,' " Manley said in an interview a few years before her death. "But I guess it depends on how interesting your past is."

Her past is compelling. And so much of it was devoted to the game that became her life. The epitaph on her gravestone at Holy Cross Cemetery in Culver City, California, reads: "She loved baseball."

Author and nationally recognized sports columnist Scott Pitoniak has written more than twenty-five books, including his most recent work, Remembrances of Swings Past: A Lifetime of Baseball Stories. *This essay originally appeared in* Memories & Dreams, *Issue 3, 2017.*

A Sacrifice of Their Own
AAGPBL players faced wartime hardships
just like their MLB counterparts
By Carroll Rogers Walton

As the world commemorates the seventy-fifth anniversary of the end of World War II, the natural inclination is to look back at what the war cost baseball.

How many wins would Bob Feller have had if he hadn't enlisted in the Navy just days after Pearl Harbor and missed the better part of four big league seasons? How far up the hit list would Ted Williams be if not for the three seasons he missed in his mid-twenties, serving as a US Marine fighter pilot? The Splendid Splinter is at No. 77 with 2,654.

But the war didn't just take away from baseball, it added to the game's history, too. Because of World War II, the first women's professional baseball league was created. The All-American Girls Professional Baseball League, depicted years later in the blockbuster movie *A League of Their Own*, served as a precursor for all women's professional sports.

The AAGPBL, which played a hybrid between softball and baseball, was the brainchild of Chicago Cubs owner Phillip Wrigley, who was looking for a stopgap if the war forced Major League Baseball to shut down. The chewing gum mogul used his vast scouting resources to scour the US and Canada for the best female softball players and narrowed the field from five hundred to sixty players among four teams at a tryout at Wrigley Field in 1943.

Wrigley strategically located teams in mid-sized Midwestern cities—Racine and Kenosha, Wisconsin, Rockford, Illinois, and South Bend, Indiana—that were also home to wartime manufacturing plants. The league was created as a nonprofit and marketed as entertainment for war factory workers looking for something to do after their shifts. Due to gas and tire rations, as well as limits on travel, these workers were in need of entertainment options close to home.

Ultimately, with the blessing of President Franklin D. Roosevelt, Major League Baseball played on as well, despite losing a host of talented players to deployment overseas. For the big league players left behind, the game had some new challenges: Travel restrictions, rubber shortages that affected the quality of the baseballs, and limited access to ash wood that diminished bat supply.

The women of the AAGPBL, while facing similar limitations, were mostly just grateful for the chance to play baseball for money. They pulled in between forty-five and eighty-five dollars a week, which meant some players—like South Bend outfielder Betsy Jochum—made more than their fathers did working at blue collar jobs.

"It was a wonderful experience," said Jochum, ninety-nine, who played six seasons for the South Bend Blue Sox from 1943 to 1948. "We got paid to travel. And any time you get paid to play the game, it's nice."

For the first two years during the war, teams traveled on trains rather than buses. Players had to carry their own baggage and equipment as they changed trains.

The women often wore men's spikes—some stuffed the toes with newspaper—and had to cut down ill-fitting men's catching equipment. Jochum said she bought her own bats from the local sporting goods store "and hoped they didn't break."

The standard league uniform was a skirted tunic, which meant players had to slide on bare legs. Sliding pads were available but weren't practical or attractive to players who were encouraged to show off their femininity.

"It was slide or get out, so we slid," said Jochum, who didn't bother with sliding pads. "They were cumbersome."

With fifteen-player rosters, the AAGPBL played 112-game schedules from the end of May to September, with very few off days and doubleheaders on Sundays. They played almost all of their games at night so factory workers could see them play, and they traveled either after games or early the following morning.

But for women who had grown up during the Great Depression, the hardships—both war-related and not—didn't seem overly daunting, especially when looking back on it seventy-five years later.

During World War II, "Mickey" Maguire was a catcher with the Milwaukee Chicks of the All-American Girls Professional Baseball League while her husband served as a pilot in the Army Air Corps.

"Oh, it wasn't that bad really," Jochum said.

There was one aspect of the war that affected some women of the AAGPBL in a unique and personal way, and that was playing while their husbands fought overseas.

The movie *A League of Their Own* featured an example of that in a scene believed to be based loosely on Milwaukee Chicks catcher Dorothy "Mickey" Maguire Chapman. In the movie, a player received a telegram from the war department before a game saying her husband had been killed. She broke down in tears and was escorted away by the team's chaperone.

In actuality, what happened to Chapman might have been too hard for moviegoers to believe. According to newspaper accounts, Chapman—then Dorothy Maguire—got a call from her mother before a game that her husband, Thomas Maguire, had been killed in action in Italy while serving as a pilot in the Army Air Corps. Chapman asked that the media not be told until after the game. She stayed and played.

According to more newspaper accounts, two months later, Chapman received letters from her husband, who was in a hospital in Italy. He'd been shot down and was badly burned but was alive. Chapman had suffered unspeakable grief unnecessarily.

Her son, Rick Chapman, pieced together the story from articles he found in scrapbooks and by talking to people who knew her, because she never told him or his siblings about it. The story he got was that his mother ultimately divorced Maguire because he wanted her to quit baseball and help support his extended family in Cleveland.

"Growing up, she didn't talk about her playing ball and didn't talk about her being married to Tom Maguire," said Rick Chapman, one of six children his mother had with her second husband, George Chapman.

In that way, AAGPBL players seemed to share something in common with soldiers coming back from World War II. After the league folded following the 1954 season, many quit talking about their playing days—not because it was traumatic, but because they thought no one would believe them.

"As a kid growing up, we found this funny looking baseball," Rick said, referring to an AAGPBL ball that measured 10 ⅜ inches in circumference. "It wasn't a softball; it wasn't a baseball. It had names on it. Our goal playing as a kid was to hit one of them over the barn. That was a home run. And we ended up losing them. We didn't know where they came from, other than they were in the attic somewhere."

Rick said his curiosity wasn't piqued until he was a teenager and his younger brother Terry decided he wanted to be a catcher.

"My mom said, 'This is how you play catcher,' and she showed him, and she could throw that ball," Rick said. "We said, 'How do you know how to do that?' She said, 'I played ball,' and then walked away."

It wasn't until twenty years later, on a visit to see her in LaGrange, Ohio, that he learned the extent of his mother's playing past. He saw a newsletter sent by an AAGPBL alumna and asked her about it. The AAGPBL was holding its first-ever reunion in Chicago the following summer, in 1982.

He offered to drive her to Chicago when the time came because she suffered from rheumatoid arthritis and couldn't drive. Rick said she was excited to go. But within a week or so of that conversation, his mother died suddenly of a heart attack at age sixty-two.

She was missed at that reunion and the twenty-nine that have been held since. She never knew about the PBS documentary that came out in 1987, the *Women in Baseball* exhibit that opened at the Hall of Fame in Cooperstown in 1988, or the movie *A League of Their Own* that hit theatres in 1992.

Rick now serves as board president of the Players Association of the AAGPBL. His job is to help keep the legacies of women like his mother alive. He said the organization has tracked down five hundred or so of the six-hundred-plus players believed to have played at least one game in the AAGPBL. He said fewer than sixty-five are still living.

The 2020 reunion was scheduled to be back in Chicago this year for the first time since 1982, but it was cancelled because of COVID-19. The seventy-fifth anniversary of the end of the World War II gives them another reason to look back, though, and acknowledge what they accomplished.

"After the league ended, (players) found that if they tried to tell people they played professional baseball, people would say 'Oh, you mean softball,' " said league historian Merrie Fidler, who turned a thesis paper into the book *The Origins and History of the All-American Girls Professional Baseball League.* "And they'd say, 'No, baseball.' Pretty soon they got tired of trying to explain that it was really baseball, so they didn't... Some of them didn't even talk to their kids or grandkids about it until the movie came out and they all came out of the background. That was the neatest thing about the movie; it gave them the accolades they hadn't gotten."

Carroll Rogers Walton is a former sportswriter for the Atlanta Journal-Constitution *and a freelance writer who coauthored* Ballplayer *with Chipper Jones. This essay originally appeared in* Memories & Dreams, *Issue 5, 2020.*

Equal Chance
Women barnstormers blazed a trail for future players
By Tim Wiles

The life of a barnstorming baseball player was often exciting, adventurous—and a lot of hard work.

But this challenging job has attracted players, both male and female, for more than a hundred years. And throughout history, women have proved to be just as capable as men when it came to entertaining fans and playing the game.

The earliest known barnstorming women's teams appeared in 1875, originating in Springfield, Illinois. Male promoters realized early on that baseball was so popular that customers would pay a premium to see unusual games, and thus women's touring teams were born. "The Blondes" and "The Brunettes" traveled together playing one another, and the concept caught on to the extent that several Eastern promoters imitated the idea into the 1880s. They were quickly followed by the "Young Ladies Base Ball Clubs," a series of as many as eight teams organized by the same man—who operated under several names.

These teams traveled up and down the East Coast as far north as Canada's maritime provinces and as far south as New Orleans and even Cuba. Some of these early teams featured literally homeless and orphaned teenage girls swept up off the street, costumed colorfully, and sent off to play the game—whether they knew how to or not. Typical press accounts denounced the players as "immoral" and "disgraceful," or focused on the comic aspects of their inexperienced play, as in this from the *New York Times* on September 23, 1883:

> Four of the girls had become expert—for girls. These were Misses Evans, P. Darlington, Moore, and Williams, comprising the batteries. The others, however, had original ideas... At the bat most of them preferred to strike at the

ball after it passed them. Then it generally passed the catcher... The girls displayed an alarming fondness for making home runs on three strikes, too. It was original and excited rapturous applause.

Soon, however, women themselves took control of their own teams, and the long tradition of Bloomer Girls teams, so named because they often played in the short pants popularized by reformer Amelia Bloomer, was born. Bloomer Girls teams— there were many—roamed across America setting up their tents, putting up temporary fences so that they could create an enclosed ballpark anywhere, and challenging the local teams, made up—almost always—of men.

These operations, often run by an athletic woman, such as Maud Nelson of the Boston Bloomer girls, capitalized on the novelty factor successfully discovered by the earlier male promoters, but with a few differences. Many of these women and girls were skilled athletes and could play the game. It was not unheard of for the Bloomer Girls to leave town with swelled coffers and a victory under their belts. As an added subterfuge, the teams often featured a couple of skilled male players in women's clothing, perhaps playing positions such as pitcher, catcher, or shortstop. These baby-faced youths could often pass for female, but the Bloomer Girls were not beyond employing a husky bearded lad in a wig and a dress—it just made the crowds more interested in forking over their dough.

In fact, a couple of great players got their start on Bloomer Girls teams: Hall of Famer Rogers Hornsby and the great pitcher Smoky Joe Wood.

The Bloomer Girls teams lasted from the 1880s all the way up to the 1930s. They died out in part because of the rise of softball for women, and also perhaps due to the Great Depression and the coming of the Second World War.

The war itself opened the door for women to play ball in a different way: against each other, rather than against males. The All-American Girls Professional Baseball League, well known as the subject of the 1992 hit movie *A League of Their Own*, began play in 1943. The league was the brainchild of Cubs owner Philip Wrigley, who had a little rarely cited assist from baseball innovator and future Hall of Famer Branch Rickey. The AAGPBL was the golden age of women playing baseball. While most of its teams were solid citizens of Grand Rapids, South Bend, Peoria, and other Midwestern cities, there were two teams of barnstormers associated with the league—teams which never had a home plate. The Chicago Colleens and the Springfield Sallies were touring teams, often featuring players a year or two younger than the mother league, who toured throughout the country playing each other in an attempt to both generate interest in the league and to scout local young ladies who might have the talent and interest to play in the league someday.

While the AAGPBL itself featured long bus or train trips, the Colleens and Sallies had it even worse—their road trips never ended. The chaperone-managers of the two teams, Barbara Liebrich and Pat Barringer, each donated scrapbooks and photo albums to the Baseball Hall of Fame's Library and Archives, chronicling life on the road. The stories they told include rolling into towns in the middle of the night, looking for late night laundromats to wash the uniforms, and also searching for inexpensive but decent housing. The Sallies and Colleens played around a hundred games a season, traveling throughout the south, the east, the Midwest, and Canada. Their games were often set up as benefits for local charities.

"To see the United States and Canada, to play baseball, and to get paid for it was my dream come true. I felt like I was in a dream world and would wake up any minute," noted former player Pat Brown in her autobiography. These tours even included exhibition games at Griffith Stadium and Yankee Stadium.

The AAGPBL lasted until 1954, eventually folding due to the reversion of women's social roles back to prewar standards, as well as the game-changing influences of television, air conditioning, and the automobile—all of which gave fans different options than sitting outside on summer evenings watching baseball. However, the league didn't fully die.

Manager Bill Allington, who led the Rockford Peaches to four league titles, assembled some of the best players in the league into a touring team, Allington's All-Stars, which barnstormed on until 1958, playing nearly a hundred games a season against men's teams from Michigan to Idaho and from West Virginia to Texas. Former player Katie Horstman recalled the league in a recent book by historian Merrie Fidler:

"We'd play in one city and then drive maybe three or four hundred miles, [sometimes] sleep in the car until we hit the next town and played again. It wasn't easy, but we all enjoyed it. We just loved to play baseball."

From 1959 up until recent times, the concept of female baseball teams, especially those who would play against men, went into hibernation. But in the 1980s, former Atlanta Braves executive Bob Hope had a dream about women enjoying the National Pastime as players. For a few brief, shining years, he made that dream a reality. Hope first tried to create a home team for female baseball players, petitioning the Florida State League to admit a new franchise, the Florida Sun Sox, made up entirely of women. When that didn't fly, he went back to the drawing board and came up with the concept of an all-female touring baseball team.

In 1994, Hope and the Coors Brewing Company announced the formation of the Colorado Silver Bullets, who would embark on a modern barnstorming odyssey that called to mind the romantic glory days of women's baseball. It is interesting that this concept—which began in the 1870s—still seemed a bit controversial about 120 years later. While the veteran players of the AAGPBL enthusiastically supported the Bullets, they often made no secret of their disapproval of the Bullets' opponents—men's semiprofessional baseball clubs.

"They had the right idea, but I think they went about it the wrong way. They could have put together two women's travel teams and toured the USA. Playing against men is not what I thought was good for women's baseball," noted former AAGPBL player Shirley Burkovich in an online interview.

The Bullets, made up mostly of former softball players, were managed by future Hall of Famer Phil Niekro and coached by his son John and brother Joe, also a former big league pitcher.

These baseball fanatics learned "inside baseball" from the Niekros and depended on pitching, defense, hustle, and out-thinking opponents to claw their way toward respectability and competitiveness. In 1997, their fourth and final season, the Bullets finished at 23-22, proving that they could play with and against the men. They played to large crowds, and the fans were on their side, win or lose.

While the fan support made it seem that the time had come for women's baseball, corporate support eventually dried up; the players went back home, playing in regional women's leagues and occasionally playing for men's independent and semipro teams. Part of their legacy is the ultimate home team—a women's USA national baseball team—which represents the nation in international play and has been in existence since 2004, winning Women's World Cup championships in 2004 and 2006.

Tim Wiles was the Director of Research for the National Baseball Hall of Fame and Museum. He is currently the director of the Guilderland Public Library in Guilderland, NY. This essay originally appeared in Memories & Dreams, *Issue 2, 2010.*

Second to None

**Toni Stone broke barriers as the first woman to play
in the Negro Leagues**
By Carroll Rogers Walton

A lifetime before the Marlins hired Kim Ng to become the Major
Leagues' first general manager, before the Red Sox made Bianca
Smith the first Black woman to coach in the minors, and even
before the Giants sent Alyssa Nakken out to coach first base in
a Spring Training game—there were three women who did one
better than that.

Toni Stone, Mamie Johnson, and Connie Morgan actually
played bigtime professional baseball, in the Negro Leagues.

Six years after Jackie Robinson left the Negro Leagues to
break Major League Baseball's color barrier, the Indianapolis
Clowns signed Toni Stone to play second base. She replaced
Hall of Famer Hank Aaron, who had just signed with the
Boston Braves.

Mamie Johnson joined the Clowns later in 1953, becoming
the league's first female pitcher, and Connie Morgan joined
them in 1954, taking over at second base for Stone, whose
contract was purchased by the Kansas City Monarchs.

"Here's a league born out of exclusion that became perhaps
this nation's most inclusive entity," said Bob Kendrick, president
of the Negro Leagues Baseball Museum in Kansas City. "They
didn't care what color you were, and they didn't care what
gender you were. Can you play? Do you have something to
offer? Can you bring something to the table? All right, let's do it."

What Clowns owner Syd Pollock saw in Stone was a gate
attraction. With the exodus of players like Robinson, Larry Doby,
Monte Irvin, and Don Newcombe to the American League and
National League, the Negro Leagues were failing. Signing a
woman Pollock had discovered barnstorming with the New

Orleans Creoles—a minor Negro Leagues team—would draw fans to the ballpark, even if only out of curiosity.

Stone, five-foot-seven, 135 pounds, grew up in St. Paul, Minnesota, where she was known as "Tomboy" and played everything, including basketball, track, and even football. But her first love was baseball. She'd been playing organized baseball since she was twelve and her parish priest helped her land a spot in the Catholic boys' baseball league.

In her early thirties at the time of signing (though Pollock thought she was in her early twenties), Toni Stone batted an estimated .243 in two seasons in the Negro Leagues, all while enduring the racism of Jim Crow and sexism from fans, opponents, and even some teammates.

Stone's story was chronicled in a biography entitled *Curveball, The Remarkable Story of Toni Stone*. Author Martha Ackmann uses the imagery of Stone "stepping into" her obstacles like a good hitter would step into a curveball:

> **Toni knew she was being used as a gate attraction. She was not deceived about that. She knew this was going to be her best chance to play baseball at a high level, and that's what she wanted more than anything else in life.... The thing with Toni was, fans would come see her play, but if she didn't play well, they'd come only once, so she played well. Even given that situation, given the jeers of some of the fans, given the way that other players treated her—some treated her well, not all of them—with all of those imperfect qualities of what she was hoping to do, she still stepped into it.**

Once during a shutout loss when Stone got her team's only hit, a resentful teammate fed her a double play ball late and low that left her vulnerable to being spiked. It was so obvious that manager Bunny Downs warned the team afterwards that sabotage against Stone could get them released. Another time, according to Ackmann, Downs left the policing up to Stone when she told him a teammate was sexually harassing her on the bus. Her choice for retaliation was hitting the player with a bat.

Stone spent many nights on the road in brothels—after boarding house owners ushered her in their direction, assuming the only woman getting off a bus full of men was a prostitute. Stone found a way to make it a positive, viewing them was as clean places to stay where she could wash clothes. She could also relate to the women there who felt like outsiders.

Stone's mental toughness served her well on the field too. She played fifty games for the Clowns in 1953, often being pulled for a male teammate in the middle innings. The highlight of her career—something Stone talked about until she died at age seventy-five in 1996—was getting a base hit off of Satchel Paige in an exhibition game. There is no box score to corroborate her story, but Negro League experts see no reason not to believe it.

"It was her favorite story; Toni told it a lot, and she never wavered in the way she told it," said Ackmann, who researched the book for three years. "I never caught Toni in a lie."

By the time Stone retired from the Monarchs in 1954, dismayed by a lack of playing time, she had earned begrudging respect from baseball writers, teammates, and opposing Negro Leaguers alike. Hall of Famer Ernie Banks described her as "smooth" to Ackmann.

"They knew that Pollock and [fellow Negro Leagues owner Abe] Saperstein loved to have gimmicks out on the field," said Adrian Burgos, a University of Illinois history professor who specializes in Negro League research. "But the gimmick was not just that she was a woman playing baseball. The gimmick was that she was a talented ballplayer who had earned a place to be there and kept it."

Stone's example opened the door for Mamie "Peanut" Johnson, a five-foot-three right-hander from Ridgeway, South Carolina, who grew up playing baseball with the boys on her grandparents' eighty-acre farm. She pitched with a swagger that served her well in parts of three seasons with the Clowns. She went 33-8 from 1953-55, according to reports.

Connie Morgan, perhaps the best pure athlete of the three, signed in 1954 out of Philadelphia and played for two seasons. She is the least known of the three women, preferring privacy and letting her play do her talking.

All three women were out of the game by 1956 and had faded back into obscurity when the Negro Leagues disbanded in 1960. It was more than thirty years later that the Baseball Hall of Fame invited seventy-five Negro Leaguers, including Stone, for a reunion in 1991 in its first ever salute to the Negro Leagues.

Johnson lived the longest of the three women, dying in 2017 at age eighty-two. She visited the White House, attended the unveiling of bronze busts of the three women at the Negro Leagues Museum, was ceremoniously drafted by the Washington Nationals, met with Little League sensation Moné Davis, and more.

But now, even among those who might recognize names like "Ng" and "Nakken," there are many unaware of Stone, Johnson, and Morgan. Ackmann said she gets that all the time from readers, who wonder why they never heard of Stone before reading Ackmann's book. The same goes for playwright Lydia Diamond, who learned about Stone when someone gave her a copy of *Curveball*. Diamond spent the next nine years writing a play about Stone, which debuted off Broadway in 2019. (Scheduled openings in San Francisco, Washington, DC, and Milwaukee were cancelled due to COVID-19.)

"There always has to be a woman who is banging on the door first, but very often that's not the person that gets to go through," Ackmann said. "I think Toni's life underscores that."

Last December's announcement that Major League Baseball was recognizing seven Negro Leagues as major leagues might help. Even though MLB will only incorporate Negro

League statistics up until 1948, historians hope it'll bring more recognition for Stone, Johnson, and Morgan.

Kendrick said the three are a big part of the "Negro Leagues 101" educational initiative the museum is introducing to celebrate the 101st anniversary of the Negro Leagues' founding. The National Baseball Hall of Fame and Museum also focuses an educational spotlight on the play of women in baseball.

"The inspirational value of the story of the Negro Leagues is just as important as its educational value," Kendrick said. "That comes across triumphantly when we see the look on young girls' faces when they come in and see that there were women who played professionally. It plants a little seed of hope."

Carroll Rogers Walton is a former sportswriter for the Atlanta Journal-Constitution *and freelance writer who coauthored* Ballplayer *with Chipper Jones. This essay originally appeared in* Memories & Dreams, *Issue 2, 2021.*

Dolly White: Dreaming of the Diamond

By Tim Wiles

Dolly White's life has been all about sports, team play, providing opportunities for others, and giving back to her community. Born Delores Brumfield in Prichard, Alabama, in 1932, "Dolly" was always interested in sports and played them whenever she could, particularly baseball. Since her life in baseball, White has taken steps to ensure her legacy will be preserved by including the Hall of Fame in her will.

"Women have always been interested in baseball—as players and fans," White said. But opportunities for girls' sports were few and far between in Alabama in the 1940s. White has worked diligently ever since to bring sports to girls and women. "We always wanted sports programs, but we didn't have any," she remembers.

In the 1940s, Mobile, Alabama, was a center for shipbuilding, producing the "Liberty Ships" which ferried supplies to the war effort in Europe. White was first noticed as a ballplayer by off-duty ship workers who watched her play on the schoolyard. They told her of a league they had heard about—the All-American Girls Professional Baseball League, founded in Chicago in 1943.

In 1946, the thirteen-year-old White asked her mother to drive her to a tryout in Pascagoula, Mississippi, where she impressed league president and future Hall of Famer Max Carey. Because of her age, Carey sent her home to join a team and gain experience.

The next spring, the league office assigned Margie Holgerson, a local girl who played for the Rockford Peaches, to keep an eye on her. After hearing about team chaperones, her parents gave their consent, and White was off to Spring Training in Havana, Cuba, in 1947 to follow her dream of becoming a professional ballplayer.

Her first couple of seasons saw White riding the bench like any young rookie—waiting for an opportunity. "It takes a break to get a break," said White, remembering how she cracked the lineup after teammate "Shoo Shoo" Wirth broke her leg sliding. On her fifteenth birthday, the seventh-inning stretch featured a recording of "You're A Big Girl Now."

White was on the South Bend Blue Sox in 1947, the Kenosha Comets from 1948 to 1951, and finished up with the Fort Wayne Daisies in 1952 and 1953. The Daisies won two straight pennants with White's help, playing third, second, first (her favorite position), and in the outfield. In 1952, the Daisies were managed by future Hall of Famer Jimmie Foxx.

"Jimmie Foxx was a nice guy, a real gentleman, nothing like the Tom Hanks character in the movie [A League of Their Own]," said White. One of her prize possessions is a home run ball she hit with Foxx's signature on it. In her final season, White hit .332. Then, at age twenty-one, she retired—for the first time.

Before graduating from high school in 1950, White had already played three seasons of professional ball. Like many of the other girls, White used her earnings to pay for college expenses. "My father used to say, 'You don't educate girls,' " said White. He loved her, of course, but that was the prevailing attitude in Alabama in the 1940s: no higher education for girls, and no sports either.

White graduated in 1954 from Alabama College, now called the University of Montevallo. She soon moved to neighboring Mississippi, where she put her physical education degree to work teaching and coaching. She earned master's and doctorate degrees from the University of Southern Mississippi. She taught and coached girls' basketball, swimming, and other sports along the way.

In 1963, she accepted a faculty appointment at Henderson State Teacher's College (now Henderson State University) in Arkadelphia, Arkansas, where she taught physical education and recreation courses and coached and coordinated the recreation degree program. She retired from Henderson State in 1994.

White was instrumental in the construction of a softball facility at Henderson State, which began a softball program in the 1990s, and also in the development of the parks and recreation system in Arkadelphia. She served on the state grants committee for parks and recreation for over a decade. She received a lifetime achievement award in 1993 from the Arkansas Recreation and Park Association and was named to the "Reddie Hall of Honor" for service to the university in 1998. In 2004, she was named a Distinguished Alumna by the University of Montevallo.

In 1977, she married Joe Herman White, who had retired after career military service, which included Pacific Theatre service in World War II, service in Korea, and two tours of duty in

Vietnam. After his retirement as a chief warrant officer, Joe and Dolly ran a farm for many years until Joe's death in 1991.

In the last decade, in addition to delivering Meals on Wheels, White has served as President of the AAGPBL Player's Association, a position she has held since 1998. In addition, she has served on the Hall of Fame's Education Advisory Council since 2002, appearing frequently at Hall of Fame events and taking part in the Electronic Field Trip program "Dirt on Their Skirts," televised live from Wrigley Field in 2002. A typical day for White includes fielding questions from students and reporters about the AAGPBL.

After a lifetime spent playing sports and creating opportunity for others, White began thinking about her legacy and that of her fellow players from the AAGPBL. Her long association with the Hall of Fame caused her to ensure that the Museum—with its *Women in Baseball* exhibit and other educational programs— would be remembered in her will. She has also donated photographs and team yearbooks from her playing career, as well as her 1953 championship trophy.

"I looked at the motto of the Hall and decided I wished to earmark my gift to preserve our history, to honor excellence within women's baseball, and, perhaps most importantly, to connect generations of women and girls who love this great game," White said. "Your mission and my mission are the same."

Tim Wiles was the Director of Research for the National Baseball Hall of Fame and Museum. He is currently the director of the Guilderland Public Library in Guilderland, NY. This essay originally appeared in Memories & Dreams, *Issue 1, 2006.*

Chapter 9

In Their Own Words

Rookie Recallings

**From your first year in the big leagues all the way
to being a Hall of Famer, you learn a lot**

By Johnny Bench

I was nineteen years old in August, 1967, when I first got the call-up to the big leagues. I drove from (Triple-A)

Buffalo to Cincinnati and was immediately put into the lineup by my manager, Dave Bristol, against Dick Ellsworth. I didn't have that much time to think, but I felt like I was supposed to be there. When Dick threw me a fastball in my wheelhouse, I popped it up, but I didn't feel overmatched.

The nucleus of the team was guys like Tony Pérez, Pete Rose, Vada Pinson, and Deron Johnson, who really welcomed me. My locker was next to Vada, a total class gentleman. He spoke in a quiet voice [and] sat there and polished his shoes. He loved to have his spikes shining. His locker was meticulous—everything was neat, everything was in its place—as was his preparation. The way Vada went about his business made an impression on me.

Around the batting cages, I knew to keep my mouth shut, but there was no hazing for us young kids. In the dugout, it was Deron Johnson giving me advice. He would say: "Hey kid, you ever see this pitcher before?

He's going to try to throw this little slider out there." And Tom Helms helped me get a place to live in a hotel that rented out rooms.

We had coaches who were just terrific, like Whitey Wietelmann and Hal Smith, who was our catching coach. Hal always had the gentlest manner, even with the younger players. He told me, "I don't have to work with you a lot, kid." I can never say enough about Hal.

Johnny Bench won the National League Rookie of the Year Award in 1968 as a twenty-year-old catcher with the Cincinnati Reds.

I wanted to take charge, even my first year in the majors. I remember Milt Pappas saying, "He chews me out just like a veteran would," and that's why they gave me the nickname The

Little General. I would say, "Hey, let's go, everybody on time, on the field. Let's go!" Looking back, I probably wasn't supposed to do all that in my first year.

Entering my last game of the 1967 season, I only needed two or three at-bats to disqualify myself as a rookie the next year. As fate would have it, before I could get those at-bats, I suffered a [lacerated] thumb on a foul tip against the Cubs. That's what left it open to me becoming Rookie of the Year in 1968.

With my thumb recovered the next spring, I expected to play, and play well. I wasn't thinking about winning awards, but here I am on the cover of *Sports Illustrated* in the spring of '68 with four other potential Rookies of the Year: Mike Torrez, Alan Foster, Don Pepper, and Cisco Carlos.

Don Pavletich was unbelievable in Spring Training that year and won the catching job. Don hurt his right arm in the fifth game in Chicago, and it was the last game he caught that year. I caught the next fifty-four games in a row without a day off—and caught 152 of the 158 games we had left in 1968.

Winning the 1968 Rookie of the Year Award was special, but the most special part of that season was the All-Star Game at the Astrodome. I'm a twenty-year-old All-Star, and I was scared to leave my locker. Then Willie Mays, who was sitting across from me, walked over and said, "*You* should have been the starting catcher." That made everything right.

I felt like a rookie again in 1989, when I was inducted into the Hall of Fame. Here I am in Cooperstown, looking at the Hall of Famers around me—guys who were my absolute heroes—and everyone shared their congratulations.

It's a busy weekend for the new Hall of Famers. Everyone's pulling at you, everyone needs a ticket, everyone needs a room. That's why, now, at Induction Weekend, I try to make every new guy feel like he's special, try to make his family feel important—because they are.

I started a tradition with the rookie Hall of Famers to sit them down in a rocking chair at the Otesaga Hotel, overlooking beautiful Otsego Lake. I tell them, "Everything's going a mile a minute. Stop and think about where you are and what you've accomplished." I want them to take the time to let it all sink in.

That's what really makes Hall of Fame Weekend so special—being able to welcome these guys the same way I was welcomed into the Hall of Fame fraternity when I was the rookie.

Johnny Bench was named National League Rookie of the Year in 1968, launching a career that culminated in his election to the Hall of Fame in 1989. This essay originally appeared in Memories & Dreams, *Issue 6, 2019.*

Family Service
A Hall of Fame hurler recalls his father's love of country and baseball
By Trevor Hoffman

My dad, Ed, was best known to baseball fans as the Singing Usher of Anaheim Stadium. He was a great singer, but he was also a great father and a man who served his country.

Dad had been singing professionally around the world and was about thirty years old when, in October 1942, he felt compelled to enlist in the Marine Corps to fight and protect his country during World War II. He went through MCRD (Marine Corps Recruit Depot) in San Diego and then was sent into the Pacific Theater. He made it back home three years later.

When I was a kid, it was clear how proud he was to be an American and a Marine. He was proud of his service. He fought for love of country, and he had a sense of duty to America. That part of him never wavered. From the earliest I can remember, he always flew an American flag at the house.

Dad didn't talk a ton about his service. He saw the ugliness of war. While it wasn't a long period of his life, I'm sure he was affected by some of his mates not returning home. He knew he was one of the lucky ones. He was older when I was born, and discussion of his service would only come out when he was asked to sing the national anthem. At first, he would sing it for our Opening Day games at Little League. His connection with being a singer and the national anthem would lend itself to a conversation about his service as a Marine.

At that time, he worked as a postal clerk, which was an early shift. He'd get home at about two o'clock in the afternoon and head to Anaheim Stadium, where he worked as an usher. He actually used to sing with Gene Autry, the owner of the Angels at the time, so that's probably how word got out that singing was in dad's background.

He gained notoriety as the Singing Usher at Angels games, but rarely was he on the docket to do it. He would come in a pinch if the scheduled singer got stuck in traffic coming to the ballpark. Just in case, he would always have his harmonica to tune up.

When I was eight or nine years old, he would occasionally take me to the ballpark with him. I'd sit in the locker room with him, and then he'd go off to his post and say to me, "Just don't get in any trouble." He really let me run around the ballpark as a kid.

My older brother, Glenn, gets the credit for Dad's first big league singing gig. He had the foresight to write into his contract with the Red Sox, as a high school senior, that if he ever made it to the big leagues, the team would fly Dad out to sing the national anthem.

Dad loved baseball, but even though Glenn and I both became big league ballplayers, it wasn't ever his agenda to get us to play. Neither of my parents were pushy, and there was never any pressure. Dad did teach us to give it our all and finish what we start. If we wanted to do something, we'd buckle down and grind at it.

Pops showed me what humility looks like; he exemplified that. You think of Marines being somewhat rigid with rules, but he was a pretty relaxed guy. He was a humble guy. The way he went about his business, he never complained and provided for his family. Those are some attributes that I've tried to emulate and pass on to my kids.

If my dad had been around for my Hall of Fame election, I think he would have been proud of me, not only for the recognition, but because I did things the right way—that I honored the game. And he would have been so smitten with being able to sit on a rocking chair and smoke a cigar on the back porch of the Otesaga Hotel, alongside the legends of the game.

Maybe it's coincidence that baseball brought me back to San Diego, but because Pops spent some time here as a recruit, this is where we would vacation as a family when I was a kid. Whenever we had the chance to hook up a camper to the back of the car, we'd drive down from Orange County to vacation on the beaches in San Diego. I feel lucky to have made this city my home and to have played so many years for the Padres, an organization that so often recognizes the military.

To me, the military represents freedom and sacrifice. I'm thankful for the service of my dad during World War II, and for everyone who has served, including some who have given the ultimate sacrifice for us to enjoy this great country.

Trevor Hoffman saved 601 games during his eighteen-year career as one of baseball's most feared closers. He was elected to the Hall of Fame in 2018. This essay originally appeared in Memories & Dreams, *Issue 5, 2020.*

Right at Home
For one Red Sox broadcaster, true love is a day at Fenway Park
By Joe Castiglione

Fenway Park has been my home away from home for nearly thirty years. Since 1983, I have broadcast more than 2,400 games from what writer John Updike dubbed that "Lyric Little Bandbox of a Ballpark." I have been blessed to witness these games from some of the best seats in the house, though my introduction to Fenway was entirely different.

That came in the most important summer in Red Sox history, the "Impossible Dream" season of 1967, when I visited Fenway for the first time with college friends. We purchased bleacher seats at game time (oh, how times have changed!) and sat on wooden benches for a late August game against the Washington Senators. Carl Yastrzemski, who was on his incredible run to the Triple Crown, homered, but the Sox lost on a late-inning double by the Senators' Hank Allen.

Twelve years later, on April 5, 1979, I called my first MLB game on Cleveland Indians television, a blowout win for the Red Sox and Dennis Eckersley. Four years after that, on Opening Day 1983, came my debut in the Red Sox radio booth—and again Eck was on the mound. My long and winding road through Red Sox history was off and running.

There have been so many memorable games…some when least expected. I can remember the cold misty night of April 29, 1986, when with Fenway more than half empty (and most of the local media focused across town on a Celtics playoff game), Roger Clemens became the first major leaguer to strike out 20 batters in a nine-inning game.

There was the "Morgan Magic" streak in 1988, when the Red Sox won 12 in a row and 24 straight at home; the electric atmosphere whenever Pedro Martínez pitched; and the 1999

All-Star Game, when baseball's greats gathered to salute Ted Williams on the pitcher's mound.

And then there've been the World Series championships, like that amazing run in 2004, fueled by the steal of second by Dave Roberts and the walk-off hits by David Ortiz in Games Four and Five of the ALCS, or how about Dustin Pedroia's indescribable defensive gems and key hits en route to the 2007 title, and Bill Buckner emerging from the left field wall to help raise the championship flag the following Opening Day.

But Fenway is special beyond the great moments. It's a place with its own character and personality…the Wall, the triangle in center, Pesky's Pole in right, and what the late Bart Giamatti called the "eccentric angularities of Fenway."

For me, though, it's even more than that. Most of my duties for the Jimmy Fund of the Dana-Farber Cancer Institute take place at Fenway. It's also a unique classroom for my students at Northeastern University. Each fall, I take my broadcasting class there to meet with Red Sox executives for seminars.

Fenway also has been a second home for my family. At the age of ten, my oldest son, Duke, worked as a gopher in the visiting clubhouse. Later he sold cokes and peanuts in the stands, and as a college student worked as a security guard. Another son, Tom, worked as a vendor and then as an emergency medical technician, where he literally saved the life of a Fenway usher who had suffered a heart attack. Daughter Kate was our official booth pitch counter from age six until she was old enough to sell ice cream at the home plate concession stand.

What a joy it's been to be part of such history. A century after its birth, Fenway Park remains baseball at its best.

Joe Castiglione has called Boston Red Sox games on the radio since 1983. This essay originally appeared in Memories & Dreams, *Issue 2, 2012.*

Sharing Words of Wisdom
**Frick award winner Bob Wolff recounts lessons learned
from a life spent in broadcasting**
By Bob Wolff

The impact of the early baseball radio broadcasters may
never be duplicated. They were the complete link between
the game and the listening public, and their solo calls had the
undivided attention of those who tuned in. They were known
for their voices, their descriptive ability, and wearing well with
their audience.

Very few added more to the menu. At that time, it wasn't
needed. The listener supplied the imagination. Being a major
league announcer became one of the most secure jobs in the
sports field. Broadcasters became part of the franchise—the
voice of the team—not just in baseball, but in other major sports
as well. But with the advent of television, in came analysts
and personalities. Voice and description were no longer as
important. The picture became the focal point.

When I broadcast World Series games, my name and those
of the other announcers were always listed in the TV-Radio logs.
When I broadcast the Rose Bowl, Sugar Bowl, or Gator Bowl,
it was listed there as well. Not anymore. Present listings don't
include announcers. People may like one broadcaster more
than others, but on most games, they no longer tune in to hear
their favorites. They tune in to watch the game and assume the
announcers will do the required job.

The broadcasters who get top assignments are all excellent
craftsmen, but video is now the main attraction. Today's play-by-
play announcers continue to identify the players, add notes, and
banter with the analyst or analysts, but their description of the
action is abbreviated to captions, not wordy statements. A TV
announcer on a home run can register his excitement with the
tone of his voice rising, but the words may be simple: "Wow—

what a shot! John does it again. His two-run blast gives the Yankees a 4-2 lead." No embellishment is needed.

Each broadcaster gets a mini-book of statistics and notes from the ball clubs before games to use if needed. Picking out the most newsworthy ones is helpful.

I cherished the "word art" of radio, but that's not a requirement for TV employment. The television experience is a mix of video action, player and game notes, replays, analysis, comments, banter, and peaks of excitement, designed to be informative and entertaining. I grew to appreciate the mixture, particularly working to hold an audience in a one-sided game or if the home team was losing.

Most of the early broadcasters preferred radio work. It's a format where they could control the pace and the content. On television, if you're talking about a subject and the camera suddenly shows the manager speaking heatedly to a player, you have to be nimble enough to weave that into your comments. That's a challenge I enjoyed.

When used at the appropriate time, adding some humor is a great plus for a long season. It was a great treat to do the play-by-play on NBC-TV's *Game of the Week* with Joe Garagiola as my partner. No announcer is wittier than Joe, who's also an outstanding analyst. I always felt that we provided a full package on the airwaves, appealing to various groups. Our director, Harry Coyle, gave us freedom to let that happen.

In the TV age, voice is no longer that important in selecting announcers. It's not the caliber of the voice that counts, it's the style. The voice should be pleasant or distinctive, the tone should have appeal, and, above all, the content should be newsworthy and reflect the excitement of the occasion. This enhances the picture.

How lucky I was to have the opportunity to demonstrate vocal excitement with my words when calling Don Larsen's perfect game in the 1956 World Series, punctuated by catcher Yogi Berra's gleeful leap into Larsen's arms after the final strike.

The sole sponsor then was the Gillette Safety Razor Company. (I continued with Gillette for two more World Series and their important bowl games.) Today, the "rights money" is so high that sponsors participate but no longer select the announcers. The network owning the rights makes that selection, and FOX uses the talented duo of Joe Buck and Tim McCarver, who have become part of the World Series tradition.

Radio still plays a part in television, though. Radio calls are more vivid, more specific, and delivered in a more excited voice. TV game highlights usually rely on radio calls for excitement.

I learned many years ago that when a game ends with a pulsating finish, the TV broadcaster—after giving the final score—will remain silent while the camera focuses on shots of the winners and losers, the crowd's roar, and fans' reactions. To enhance the game's climax, during the final out or play or game-winning hit, field goal, shot, or strikeout, I'd use a faster descriptive pace on the radio to accentuate the tension and emotion that was gripping both the viewers and myself.

I wanted to leave the broadcast booth knowing that I closed the telecast having given it my very best effort.

Bob Wolff, the 1995 Hall of Fame Ford Frick Award Winner, was officially recognized by Guinness World Records as having the longest career of any sportscaster of all time, a total of seventy-eight years. This essay originally appeared in Memories & Dreams, *Issue 2, 2011.*

Expressly Amazing

A Hall of Fame career got rolling when the Mets won the 1969 World Series

By Nolan Ryan

The 1969 baseball season was amazing, especially for the Mets. When I look back on that year, I think about all the different people who contributed to that winning effort.

Tom Seaver was by far the leader of that pitching staff. He was so consistent, and he had a career year in '69. Everybody marveled at the year he had.

I had met Tom in minor league Spring Training the year that he signed, which was 1966. Our paths didn't cross again until I was in the big leagues two years later. He had a big influence on me because he had a very professional and mature attitude, and it helped me start focusing on my career and what I had to do to be successful.

That year (1969) was truly a team effort, because when we would call somebody up from Triple-A, or when we traded for someone, they contributed to our winning ways. We had a great team. There was Cleon Jones having a solid year, and then the acquisition of (first baseman) Donn Clendenon in June.

That summer, I can remember watching the moon landing on television and marveling at the accomplishment—not only that they landed on the moon, but that those astronauts were able to leave the moon and come back home. The whole situation was phenomenal, and it was just hard to comprehend that we were capable of doing that. The fact that I grew up about twenty miles from the Space Center (in Houston) and was aware of the development of NASA made it even more interesting.

That season was also a year of adjustment for all pitchers because of the mound being lowered and having the feel that you were pitching from flat ground. They also shrunk the strike zone, so there was no high strike at all. Pitchers noticed it more than hitters.

I was twenty-two years old and was struggling with my control and consistency. That was a challenge for me at that point in my career. Adding to that challenge was that I was on a different schedule from the rest of the pitchers because I was in a top-priority Army Reserve unit in Houston. So every other weekend, I went back to Houston for military duty. Because of that, I never pitched on a regular basis while I was with the Mets.

Gil Hodges was a very fair manager, and he expected you to play the game right. His demeanor and the way he carried himself certainly influenced the team. He had a very positive effect on us players.

The 1969 New York Mets pitching staff featured Nolan Ryan (third from left) and fellow Hall of Famer Tom Seaver (first from left). Ryan served as a spot starter and reliever during the 1969 season, culminating in the Mets World Series triumph over the Baltimore Orioles.

So did Yogi Berra, who was our first base coach. From a pitcher's perspective, we didn't have as much one-on-one with Yogi as we did with pitching coach Rube Walker, but I think everybody was very at ease with him and enjoyed having him on the team. Yogi brought so much experience in so many postseasons and had so much success.

In the Playoffs, Gil gave me the opportunity to contribute. Those were great games in front of Mets fans. By that point in my career, even pitching at Shea Stadium in front of 50,000 people, I had a comfort level with it.

In Game Three of the Championship Series against the Braves, I was in the bullpen and Gil called on me in the third inning. I was really surprised that he made a pitching change that early, and also by the fact that he went to me—I didn't anticipate being in the game at that early stage.

To be in a World Series, that was a dream of all players, and it was a dream come true for me at my young age. I was thrilled to get that opportunity, and Gil put me in again in Game Three against the Orioles. By far, it was one of the most special moments of my career, to get that last out to put our team ahead 2-games-to-1 in the World Series.

When you experience things as I did in the Playoffs and the World Series and have a year like the Mets did, it helps you in your development. That season was an important foundation for the growth of my career.

In 1969, it all fell into place. The little things just seemed to go our way. When there was a break that year, it went our way. Sometimes the difference in whether a team wins or doesn't is whether a ball falls in your favor, and I really felt that's what happened with that ballclub.

Nolan Ryan won or saved two of the Mets' seven victories in the 1969 postseason. He was elected to the Hall of Fame in 1999. This essay originally appeared in Memories & Dreams, Issue 2, 2019.

Case Closed

What made Mariano Rivera the game's most feared relief pitcher? Desire and heart

By Joe Torre

The skill was always there with Mariano. But what made him special was his desire.

He could will himself to do great things.

There were times I wanted to give him a day off, but he'd go out to the bullpen anyway. I tried to keep him away, but he'd find his way down there. And then in the eighth or the ninth inning—when the game was on the line—he'd be ready.

He always seemed to be ready.

Batters knew what was coming. There was nothing tricky about it. It was going to be the cutter, and everyone knew it. But I think it was the lateness of his cutter that made the difference.

There are a bunch of pitchers who throw cutters. And there are early indications that it is a cutter, so the batter can figure it out. But Mariano's ball would cut so late, the hitter had to already commit by the time the pitch got to him. And by then, it was too late.

But it wasn't like he didn't work for everything he got. He grew into that role as closer. And being the closer is different from pitching the sixth, seventh, or the eighth inning.

In 1996, Mariano was our set-up man, which was a blessing for me because I only had to be smart for six innings. He came in for the seventh and eighth, then John Wetteland finished the game. And that was it.

Then John left as a free agent, and Mariano took the job. He had a great year as our closer the first year in 1997, but the first few times out, he stumbled around a bit. Like a true champ, though, he kept fighting through it. And eventually, he wound up the best that you've ever seen.

By the time he was at his peak, Mariano changed the game just by being in the ballpark. If you were in the other dugout as the manager or a player, you didn't want to see him in the game. So it really put the pressure on your team to have a lead to keep him out of the game. That was really necessary. And when you feel pressure as a hitter, you're not at your best.

When you talk about a stopper or a closer, Mariano is *it*. Very few times did he have to walk off the mound without people shaking his hand. It was that simple.

There's a lot to say about Mariano. But I sum it up like this: I think the key for Mariano is his heart.

Joe Torre managed Mariano Rivera with the Yankees from 1996 to 2007, a stretch that included four World Series titles and six American League pennants. Torre was inducted into the Hall of Fame in 2014. This essay originally appeared in Memories & Dreams, *Issue 1, 2019.*

Our Rite of Spring
Despite many changes, Spring Training remains baseball's proving ground
By Peter Gammons

There are condominiums where the Ramada Inn once stood in Winter Haven, Florida. There are some new fast-food restaurants, and a strip mall with a Chili's is across the street from where orange trees once stood in 1974.

In the back of that Ramada Inn was a single tennis court, where in March 1974, a good three dozen fans watched an unusual doubles match take place. On one team was Ted Williams; on the other, Carl Yastrzemski.

Ted was fifty-five and already a Hall of Famer for seven years. Yaz was thirty-four and still very much an active member of the Red Sox. Ted didn't move too well then. Yaz ran around every shot so that he could hit a backhand, never changing his bottom hand (baseball bat) swing. When Ted missed a shot, there was the expected expletive shouted out, while Yaz would grimace and mumble and look down.

"Ted can't take losing to Carl," said one spectator, Red Sox vice president Haywood Sullivan. "And you know Carl isn't going to let Ted beat him, not at this point in his career. What makes them Hall of Famers is what makes this so much fun."

Yastrzemski's team eventually prevailed. "Every (---) gets lucky sometime," explained Williams.

Spring Training was so simple back then, especially in a Tennessee Williams town like Winter Haven. They'd be lucky to get a thousand fans at a game. Players went to barbecues at locals' houses. During morning practices, players and fans mingled with one another. Word of phenoms—from Walter Bond for Houston in '64 to Mike Anderson of the '72 Phillies—spread by landline phones or word of mouth. So would home runs you thought you'd never see, like one Bobby Darwin hit in Orlando for the Twins or another Mark Corey belted for the Orioles in Fort Lauderdale.

Teams often had to bus to separate minor league fields for detail work, like the "back field" in Miami where Earl Weaver taught all his trick plays. Drills were simple, easy, and one time during batting practice, *Boston Globe* scribe Clif Keane noted Mike Torrez as not moving from one spot for forty-two minutes. Writers could hang out with players in the clubhouse during games.

Spring Training today is big business. The Cubs, Yankees, and Red Sox sell out most of their home games by New Year's Eve. Travel companies book elaborate Spring Training packages. Taxpayer dollars have funded lavish twenty-first century complexes. And Fort Lauderdale, West Palm Beach, Vero Beach ("Dodgertown"), and Miami have long since given way to complexes with dozens of fields for major and minor league players.

Fans' access to players is more limited, and the media gets but a few minutes in the morning and after games. When pitchers leave games, PR people announce, "Padilla will be available for ten minutes in ten minutes."

Still, for all its changes, Spring Training remains the break from many a winter back North, a joyride for people who love baseball. Last spring, fans in Central Florida fell in love with a twenty-year-old Braves rookie named Jason Heyward, whose first spring home run was pictured on ESPN.com less than an hour after he hit it. Marlins rookie Mike Stanton had a batting practice round of homers in Jupiter that was posted on YouTube thirty-five minutes after his session. Phenoms Stephen Strasburg and Aroldis Chapman sold out every Nationals and Reds game they were scheduled to pitch.

These fresh memories are now part of my Spring Training vault, like the Williams-Yaz tennis match, or the Yankees ten o'clock in the morning "B" game in Fort Lauderdale in which there were so few fans that I *heard* the "zzzzzzz" of Dave Righetti's curveball. Or the time I got chills watching a fifty-something Sandy Koufax throw batting practice in Dodgertown.

Then there's the time I was on the back field in Fort Lauderdale watching Yankees pitchers' fielding practice with manager Buck Showalter, noting how unathletic their phenom, Brien Taylor, appeared, then marveling at a kid I thought should play shortstop.

"Remember the name," Showalter told me. "It's Rivera, Mariano Rivera."

That was eighteen years ago, Spring Training then. Now Mariano is in a waiting room in Cooperstown. The road to The Hall still runs through Spring Training, as different as it may be.

The 2004 winner of the BBWAA's Career Excellence Award, Peter Gammons is an MLB.com columnist and MLB Network contributor. This essay originally appeared in Memories & Dreams, *Issue 1, 2011.*

Houston Strong
As Jeff Bagwell's induction approaches, an Astros teammate reflects on what it means to be a Hall of Famer
By Craig Biggio

The night before Jeff Bagwell was elected to the Hall of Fame, I went to his house and hung out for three or four hours. We have the same agent, so it was natural for us to get together. We got caught up on our lives and our families, and it made the night go quicker for everyone.

The next day, Jeff got the call. I know that feeling. He was truly happy and honored.

To have been able to be associated with Jeff—to play together as long as we did in Houston—is incredible. Now we share being Hall of Famers as well.

It was so much fun for me coming back to Hall of Fame Weekend last year. It was everything that every other Hall of Famer said it would be. The first year, it's great, you're happy—but you've got the stress of making a speech and making sure everything is right for your family and guests. But after your first year, you come back and you realize you're part of the greatest team you'll ever be part of.

We had so much fun hanging out in Cooperstown…we had a tremendous time just getting to know all the Hall of Famers. Getting to know these guys on a personal level is special. I really enjoy it.

Jeff's going to have that same experience. My advice to him—and to any new Hall of Famer—is to go and have fun and enjoy the people you're there with. Because you didn't get there on your own.

For Jeff and me, it was always about the game and trying to get to the World Series. We just loved playing the game, and the only thing we wanted to do at the end of the day was to reach the World Series. We got there once (in 2005), and it was hard just to get there. But to have that legacy with him—and to be able to share it with all the fans in Houston—is special.

The coolest thing for me is to be able to enjoy being a Hall of Famer with the fans. I live in Houston, I still work for the Astros, and I look at it as all of us—including the fans—did this together. That's the thing I enjoy the most.

I still can't believe I'm a Hall of Famer. You play the game because you love it, not to get to the Hall of Fame. But once you're there, you really appreciate what it means.

Craig Biggio was a teammate of Jeff Bagwell for fifteen seasons with the Houston Astros. He was elected to the Hall of Fame in 2015. This essay originally appeared in Memories & Dreams, *Issue 2, 2017.*

Old Elephant Ear
A Hall of Fame third baseman stayed loyal to the glove that he brought to "the show"
By Wade Boggs

Believe it or not, I used the same fielding glove for the first 15 years of my major league career, from 1982 to 1996.

I had a contract with Rawlings, and when I came up with the Red Sox in Spring Training of '82, they gave me a couple of gloves. I started breaking one of them in, started taking ground balls with it, and started liking it. It fit my hand really nicely. After a while, I turned it into my "gamer," where I only used it in games.

Wear and tear took the best of it after probably five years, so I had it rebuilt—I actually had a glove put inside of it. The webbing was changed out five or six times from other gloves over the years. And I would take it to a leather shop and they would sew in patches, like where the palm would split.

Parts of the leather became so worn that the glove was nicknamed Elephant Ear.

In 1990, it was stolen during Spring Training, but I got it back. We put together an ad in the paper in Winter Haven and acted like we were a collector. The ad said, "Buying memorabilia and used baseball equipment," and the phone number we used was the phone number of the police department.

Wade Boggs used "Old Elephant Ear" through the 1996 season, manning third base for the Boston Red Sox and New York Yankees, winning two Gold Glove Awards along the way. (Doug McWilliams)

The perpetrators actually called the police and offered a bunch of stolen equipment, so officers went to their house, arrested them and got all the equipment back, including my glove. Like a shiny penny, you may lose it, but it keeps coming back!

I went on using that glove another seven seasons. I used it for the two Gold Glove Awards I won in New York in '94 and '95. This glove was also in the World Series, and that was the last year I used it, in 1996.

It wasn't superstition—the glove was just so comfortable, it felt like an extension of my hand. If I put the glove down for a grounder, the ball found its webbing. It was perfectly molded. I had a lot of superstitions, but the glove wasn't one of them.

Over the years, I'd play catch with various other gloves, but then I'd discard them after a couple months because I knew they wouldn't break in the way I wanted them to. It really takes a long time to get it to the point where it feels that comfortable.

And I love that this glove is now at the Hall of Fame. It's a big part of my history. I have a lot of bats and some other pieces of equipment in Cooperstown, but I think this completes that full circle of my accomplishments.

The old Elephant Ear was with me a long time.

Wade Boggs played third base with the Red Sox, Yankees, and Devil Rays during his eighteen-year career. He was elected to the Hall of Fame in 2005. This essay originally appeared in Memories & Dreams, *Issue 6, 2017.*

Hitting the Mark
For this major leaguer, trips to Cooperstown renew a love of the game
By Ichiro Suzuki

Last November, I visited Cooperstown for the fifth time since coming to play baseball in America in 2001.

Even though it was a cold and drizzly day, my Cooperstown experience is never complete without walking to Doubleday Field and stepping on that sacred soil. I realize it's now widely accepted that Doubleday Field serves merely as the symbolic birthplace of baseball, but that doesn't diminish its aura for me. Its symbolism is powerful, and as a baseball player, it's still the Promised Land.

A visit to Cooperstown has a purifying effect. It inspires introspection and contemplation. Without a place like this, baseball might not have entered my life. And even if it did, it might not have brought me to America. It's not just me, but all my contemporaries should be thankful for the opportunity Cooperstown has created for them.

Living in this era where money is disproportionately emphasized, there's a real danger of losing the purity that originally attracted us to baseball. You'd expect our affection to grow as we live out our dreams on the field; instead, we're pushed to focus on the occupational aspects. Cooperstown, though, has a way of cleansing your heart, and that's what makes me want to return over and over.

On my first visit, I got to hold Shoeless Joe Jackson's legendary bat, Black Betsy (with my hands slipped inside white protective gloves, of course). I was overwhelmed by the high-pitched sound that resonated from that nearly hundred-year-old instrument. I was astonished a bat could even produce such a beautiful sound. It was as if it were made of solid gold or silver, not wood.

On my most recent visit, the staff emphasized their Yankees
collection by preparing several cherished items from the
franchise's rich history. I held Babe Ruth's jersey, bringing his
woolen pinstripes so close to my face that I felt I could actually
smell the Babe. I turned it over and saw something I'd never
seen before, the number '3' on a Yankees uniform. Then, I got
to hold the glove he used in the 1926 World Series against
the Cardinals.

Ichiro Suzuki poses with a bat from the Hall of Fame collection during a
tour of the archives on a visit to Cooperstown.
(Baseball Hall of Fame/Milo Stewart)

For me, this is one of the most enchanting aspects of
Cooperstown. Feeling the equipment of yesteryear's legends
brings to life a bygone era that, until that moment, I only knew
as hearsay. When I can actually grip Joe Jackson's bat or feel the
heaviness of Babe Ruth's jersey or handle his mitt, I feel a deep
and tangible connection that's indescribable.

When I first started going to Cooperstown, I probably was on a specific mission to learn or feel something. Now I just enjoy going for the pure pleasure of stepping into that sacred place.

I also like the fact that at about two hundred miles northwest of Manhattan and mostly accessible only by car, there's an effort required to get there. That effort ultimately makes the journey even more satisfying. If it was right there within reach, there would be no exhilaration in the journey. There's a beauty in that quality. It's like the cherry blossoms in Japan. They bloom for only a week or so a year, so there's an aura attached to them. Their impressiveness would be diminished if they stayed in bloom for the entire year.

By virtue of its location, Cooperstown has the same aura; just far enough away that you appreciate the trip, yet not too distant to be burdened by it. For me, that's an important part of its charm and something that makes visiting there so invigorating.

Ichiro Suzuki played nineteen seasons with the Mariners, Yankees, and Marlins, collecting 3,089 hits in his MLB career. His thoughts were translated by Brad Lefton for this story. This essay originally appeared in Memories & Dreams, *Issue 2, 2013.*

Index

Subjects in photos
listed in italics

Acknowledgements

Thank you to the staff of the National Baseball Hall of Fame and Museum, with special thanks to the following individuals for their help in researching, selecting and editing the essays, photos and artifacts featured in this book: Kelli Bogan, Sean Gahagan, John Horne, Cassidy Lent, Scot Mondore, Craig Muder, and John Shestakofsky.

In addition, we thank the staff of Mango Publishing who worked on this book; Elina Diaz, Brenda Knight, Lisa McGuinness, Chris McKenney, and Robin Miller, along with our agent, Valerie Tomaselli of MTM Publishing, for her support and guidance.

Finally, and certainly not least, we thank those who contributed essays for inclusion in this book; Johnny Bench, Craig Biggio, Hal Bodley, Wade Boggs, Larry Brunt, Steve Buckley, Adrian Burgos, Joe Castiglione, Alex Coffey, Wayne Coffey, Paul Dickson, John Erardi, Bill Francis, Tom Gage, Peter Gammons, Jim Gates, John Grisham, Trevor Hoffman, Jim Kaplan, Tyler Kepner, David Krell, Tim Kurkjian, Neil Lanctot, Jim Leeke, Steve Light, Luis Mayoral, Terence Moore, David Moriah, Craig Muder, John O'Dell, Scott Pitoniak, Phil Rogers, Carroll Rogers Walton, Nolan Ryan, Debra Shattuck Burton, Dan Shaughnessy, Tom Shieber, Claire Smith, Curt Smith, Larry Stone, Ichiro Suzuki, Joe Torre, Danny Torres, Larry Tye, George Vecsey, Tim Wiles, Chief Justice Frank L. Williams, Bob Wolff, and Steve Wulf. We are forever grateful to you for sharing your baseball experiences and vast knowledge of the game, as well as your continued support of the National Baseball Hall of Fame and Museum.

About the National Baseball Hall of Fame and Museum

The National Baseball Hall of Fame and Museum is an independent not-for-profit educational institution dedicated to fostering an appreciation of the historical development of baseball and its impact on our culture by collecting, preserving, exhibiting, and interpreting its collections for a global audience as well as honoring those who have made outstanding contributions to our National Pastime. Opening its doors for the first time on June 12, 1939, the Hall of Fame has stood as the definitive repository of the game's treasures and as a symbol of the most profound individual honor bestowed on an athlete. It is every fan's "Field of Dreams," with its stories, legends, and magic shared from generation to generation.

Visit baseballhall.org and follow us @BaseballHall on Twitter, Facebook, and Instagram for all the latest Hall of Fame news and fascinating stories from the National Pastime.

Mango Publishing, established in 2014, publishes an eclectic list of books by diverse authors—both new and established voices—on topics ranging from business, personal growth, women's empowerment, LGBTQ studies, health, and spirituality to history, popular culture, time management, decluttering, lifestyle, mental wellness, aging, and sustainable living. We were recently named 2019 *and* 2020's #1 fastest growing independent publisher by *Publishers Weekly*. Our success is driven by our main goal, which is to publish high quality books that will entertain readers as well as make a positive difference in their lives.

Our readers are our most important resource; we value your input, suggestions, and ideas. We'd love to hear from you—after all, we are publishing books for you!

Please stay in touch with us and follow us at:

Facebook: Mango Publishing
Twitter: @MangoPublishing
Instagram: @MangoPublishing
LinkedIn: Mango Publishing
Pinterest: Mango Publishing
Newsletter: mangopublishinggroup.com/newsletter

Join us on Mango's journey to reinvent publishing, one book at a time.